*Winifred Black/Annie Laurie and the Making of Modern Nonfiction*

# Winifred Black/Annie Laurie and the Making of Modern Nonfiction

KATHERINE H. ADAMS *and*
MICHAEL L. KEENE

McFarland & Company, Inc., Publishers
*Jefferson, North Carolina*

ALSO OF INTEREST

*Women of the American Circus, 1880–1940*, Katherine H. Adams
   *and* Michael L. Keene (2012)

*Seeing the American Woman, 1880–1920: The Social Impact of
   the Visual Media Explosion*, Katherine H. Adams, Michael L. Keene
   *and* Jennifer C. Koella (2012)

*After the Vote Was Won: The Later Achievements of Fifteen Suffragists*,
   Katherine H. Adams *and* Michael L. Keene (2010)


*Frontispiece:* **Winifred Black, 1912 (E. Blanche Reineke).**


LIBRARY OF CONGRESS CATALOGUING-IN-PUBLICATION DATA

Adams, Katherine H.
    Winifred Black/Annie Laurie and the making of modern nonfiction
/ Katherine H. Adams and Michael L. Keene.
        p.    cm.
    Includes bibliographical references and index.

    ISBN 978-1-4766-6296-1 (softcover : acid free paper) ∞
    ISBN 978-1-4766-2266-8 (ebook)

    1. Bonfils, Winifred Black, 1869–1936—Criticism and
interpretation.    2. Journalism—United States—History.
3. American literature—Women authors—History and criticism.
4. Reportage literature.    I. Keene, Michael L.    II. Title.

PN4874.B6233A33 2015
070.92—dc23                                                             2015023926

BRITISH LIBRARY CATALOGUING DATA ARE AVAILABLE

© 2015 Katherine H. Adams and Michael L. Keene. All rights reserved

*No part of this book may be reproduced or transmitted in any form
or by any means, electronic or mechanical, including photocopying
or recording, or by any information storage and retrieval system,
without permission in writing from the publisher.*

Front cover: Winifred Black in 1913 (Library of Congress)

Printed in the United States of America

*McFarland & Company, Inc., Publishers
   Box 611, Jefferson, North Carolina 28640
   www.mcfarlandpub.com*

KHA: To Chad and Jane
MLK: To Claire

# *Acknowledgments*

Kate would like to thank her dean, Maria Calzada, for a sabbatical taken during the spring of 2013. She is also grateful to her chair, John Biguenet, for his ongoing, wonderful support.

Mike would like to thank the Hodges faculty of the University for time to work.

And as always when we write, we thank the tremendous librarians of Loyola University. Pat Doran, Jim Hobbs, and Jessica Perry provide us with fantastic interlibrary loan service. The *San Francisco Examiner* came to us on microfilm along with many other sources, without which this book could not have been written.

We would also like to thank Willie Wax for his generous assistance with the photograph contained here and with research on the Sweet/Black/Bonfils family.

# Table of Contents

| | |
|---|---|
| *Acknowledgments* | vi |
| *Introduction* | 1 |
| 1. The War Hero/The War Criminal: Winifred Black's Father | 9 |
| 2. Ada Sweet—Role Model | 13 |
| 3. The Power of Black's Personal History in Building a Journalism Career | 20 |
| 4. Initiating a Career in Nonfiction: What a "Stunt Girl" Could Do | 29 |
| 5. Building a Reputation Among Newspaper Kings | 39 |
| 6. Black's View of the Writing World That She Entered | 50 |
| 7. A Complex Persona | 65 |
| 8. An Array of Nonfiction Techniques | 73 |
| 9. Black's Subject Matter: The Changing Definition of "Normal" | 92 |
| 10. Gender Distinctions | 99 |
| 11. Prejudice Against the Other: Concerning Race, Sexual Preference and the Women Who Aren't Like Us | 107 |
| 12. Independence and Dependence/Parents and Children | 117 |
| 13. Working Women | 121 |
| 14. The Power of Beauty | 132 |
| 15. Dating, Domestic Violence and Marriage | 144 |
| 16. Feminism and Suffrage: Women as Citizens | 162 |
| *Conclusion: In Short* | 173 |
| *Chapter Notes* | 175 |
| *Bibliography* | 191 |
| *Index* | 207 |

# *Introduction*

> Sometimes it seemed to *Examiner* readers that wherever they looked about the world there was the ubiquitous Annie, hot on the trail of sin, corruption and old-fashioned human interest.
> —John Tebbel, *The Life and Good Times of William Randolph Hearst*

Journalist Martha Winifred Sweet Black Bonfils died on Monday, May 25, 1936, having published a column on the Friday before in the *San Francisco Examiner*, where she had begun working in 1889. The coverage in the newspaper the next day led with the local name that she used for her byline: "Annie Laurie Is Taken by Death." Detailed accounts of her career and tributes to her took up four to five pages each day for a week, much more space than the newspaper gave during that decade to obituaries for any politician, scientist, gangster, or movie star, including President Howard Taft in 1930, Mabel Normand in 1930, Thomas Edison in 1931, John Dillinger in 1934, and Will Rogers in 1935. On May 26, one article offered the strong praise that so many others would develop, leading with the power of the name with which she had begun her career so long before: "'Annie Laurie' was not her name. It was a by-word. It was the nom de plume under which America's best known newspaper woman ended her long career. It was the name which headed every important crusade for the right—every campaign against injustice, and every widespread call for help for the needy in the Hearst newspapers."[1]

Long articles concerned a city memorial, attended by "thousands and thousands." Mayor Angelo J. Rossi had immediately assembled a group to plan the ceremony, where he was one of the many city and state officials who spoke, proclaiming, "Faithful, kindly, loving, and benevolent, she was justly looked upon as one of the most outstanding women ever to have graced the life of our great city."[2] Chief of Police William J. Quinn declared that "her loss is keenly felt by every member of the department." Municipal Judge Thomas M. Foley followed him, saying that "this great woman was characteristic of our city and the richness of experience, travel and intellect she brought to writings will always go down in the glory of her city she so loved."

Judge M. C. Sloss added, "Like every other old San Franciscan, I have read her writings for a great many years. I feel that Annie Laurie was one of our most effective writers, particularly on subjects of human interest."[3]

As further articles reported, at a Catholic church service following the civil ceremony, the sanctuary was completely full and crowds amassed outside.[4] The large group of pallbearers included Mayor Rossi, Chief of Police Quinn, the chief of the fire department, the directors of several veterans' groups, and administrators of hospitals and homes for juveniles as well as judges, admirals, rabbis, and priests.[5]

Beyond these two services, the *Examiner* also reported on other types of tributes paid to this reporter. When the news of her death circulated, the city's board of supervisors and city council adjourned their meetings out of respect to her memory, as did the office of the police commission, the board of education, and the courts. The board of supervisors created a resolution stating that "she hated vice, deceit and sham in social and public places, and scourged evil doers with unsparing lash. Annie Laurie was the heart of San Francisco, full of courage, fortitude, generosity and charity."[6] As the *Examiner* continued to quote such memorials and review her career, one of the many articles commented humorously on her unending desire to get the story: from death, Black probably wished that she could describe, as no one before her, "the land beyond the end."[7]

## Nationwide Notice

Though Black's death received the most coverage in the city where she primarily worked, it was also reported across the nation, in small-town and big-city newspapers where her articles had appeared and where they had not. At her death, long and glowing reports of her career appeared everywhere: in Butte, Montana; in Ogden, Utah; in Albuquerque, New Mexico; in Lincoln, Nebraska; in Racine, Wisconsin; in El Paso, Texas; in Danville, Virginia; in Washington, D.C.; in New York City; and in Winnipeg, Canada. In an obituary printed in a Fresno newspaper, film columnist Louella Parsons spoke of Black's death as a "great loss to all those who knew and loved her. Her indomitable spirit and never ceasing interest in all human subjects, including motion pictures, always amazed me.... She was a great woman and the ideal of those of us who followed her as newspaper writers."[8] Many papers featured articles on the first page, filled with superlatives, like "beloved newspaperwoman," as in the Bradford, Pennsylvania, paper.[9] On the front page, the New Orleans *Times-Picayune* commented that it was to her articles that "her tremendous public turned every morning for a thought with which to start the day."[10] The long obituary in the *New York Times,* which reviewed her entire career, commented that "the cause of the suffering and the helpless always elicited her sympathy and aid."¹¹

Accolades for Black had appeared long before her death: indeed, they had been forthcoming throughout her career. She was often recognized as the best of those journalists who were women, certainly a compliment if a somewhat belittling one. Newspapers that featured her writing in syndication sang her praises, as they hardly did for any other writers, providing part acknowledgment and part advertisement. An ad in the *Springfield Missouri Republican*, for example, in May 1921 described her as among the "foremost American women feature writers." *The Canandaigua* (New York) *Daily Messenger* in April 1922 advertised its "inspirational articles by Winifred Black, the greatest woman newspaper writer in America." Other descriptions relied on common terms for describing women journalists: the *Woodland Daily Democrat* in August of 1933, for example, referred to her as "ace of sob-sisters."¹²

Across the country, Black also secured coverage as not just the best of women writers but the best of all American journalists, these evaluations appearing in newspapers that featured her work as well as those commenting upon it. "The Real Annie Laurie," which appeared in the *San Francisco Examiner* in December 1892 when she had been working there for just three years, declared that "there is not a better all-around journalist in San Francisco than this lady and very few men in the profession who earn a better income."¹³ In 1905, the *Washington Post* reported that Black had been publishing remarkable columns. This review contains high praise for her work as uplifting, patriotic, and honest, the conclusion being that she ranked among the best writers in the country. The *Springfield Missouri Republican* in January of 1922 referred to her as "the world's most famous feature writer"; the *Daily Messenger* (Canandaigua, New York), in August of 1922, described her as "one of the world's most successful reporters."¹⁴

## A Cultural Icon

Other articles published throughout Black's career focused on her as a cultural figure, a known personality, a writer of great influence. The *San Bernardino County Sun* described her in 1921 as "loved by millions—everywhere."¹⁵ In announcing the addition of her column in March 1922, the *Coshocton Tribune* (Coshocton, Ohio) employed the headline "Most Widely Known Woman of American Journalistic Work Will Write for This Paper," and the text explained further that Black "has become a real personality in American life. She is the greatest inspirational writer of the day, and her articles are closely followed by hundreds of thousands in every part of the country. Her articles, cheery, wholesome, progressive and helpful, form a great force in American journalism."[16] Thus Black appears as a part of American life, someone to rely upon, a positive influence, gendered perhaps as cheery and wholesome, but also depicted as progressive and helpful, offering facts and advice about modern life.

Throughout the nation, in locations where she wrote for the local newspaper and even where she didn't, discussions of Black's writing often featured just her name or a part of it, with no identifying appositive at all. By 1911, she had developed such a reputation that an article from a Kansas paper typified the content of New York newspapers by declaring, "One has a popular humorist, or a celebrated cartoonist, another has a distinguished sporting editor, another a Winifred Black, and so on."[17] Even newspapers and articles that criticized her work referred to her as a writer that readers knew. When a paper in Kansas, in 1910, blasted Laura Jean Libby, of the *Chicago Tribune*, for writing "delightful tommyrot" and "flapdoodle," stories about love and sentiment, an ending comment was that "even Winifred Black is better than Laura Jean Libby."[18] In the *Woodland Daily Democrat* (California) in August of 1934, journalist Florence W. McGehee claimed that Black's harsh criticism of the wife of the late California governor was "about as rotten an example of bad taste, journalistically or otherwise, as has been seen in these parts in many a long day." Here her title includes just Black's first name—"Fie upon Winnie"—and the text takes up the sword against "Winifred the Great."[19]

## Name Recognition: Gained and Then Lost

Throughout the years, the credit given to Black's work could be seen in its spacial presence in papers across the nation. This authority generally involved large headlines featuring her name. At a time when very few newspaper articles even provided a byline, these columns often appeared with her large signature or with the headline "Winifred Black writes about…." In 1925, on the magazine page of many newspapers, her name began to appear in a large headline across the entire page, as the key element on the page, and her column on the right-hand side. As journalism historian Ishbel Ross, who had worked at the *New York World* and at *Harper's Bazaar*, commented in the first book-length study of women in journalism, *Ladies of the Press*, concerning how this presence functioned, "It was not the news that mattered as much as what Winifred Black had to say about the news."[20]

In papers across the country, Black's work appeared not only with many renditions of her name but with various drawings or photographs, her persona and appearance as a writer thus marketed along with her content. Beginning in 1912, her photograph, in a tintype border, a silhouette, accompanied her opinion pieces, with text wrapped around it. In January 1914, the columns featured a large line drawing of her, face forward, with lots of curly hair on her head. Various photographs and drawings followed, in which she looked sometimes younger and sometimes older, with different newspapers choosing different iterations. In July of 1925, a modern photograph appeared that featured her large eyes, and in January 1934 another one in which she wore a cloche hat, all very stylish.

Given these decades of fame and respect, given her long-term status as a nationally known writer, why did the career of Winifred Black receive very limited attention after her death, her achievements and certainly her writing generally erased from view?

Some recent histories have provided short accounts of Black's life and her work, but many variables have worked against extended study of her writing.[21] As a woman journalist, Black was less frequently allotted space on the front page, the presumed locale of "hard" or serious news, than male journalists. Anything appearing instead on the women's page, as some of her writing did, was assumed to be a fluff piece about the home. Her opinion columns on the editorial and magazine page also seemed less serious than front-page news, too focused on marriage and divorce, on women's work and daily life, on topics that really didn't matter. The investigative work that Black took on, assuming an undercover persona, received the derogatory label of "stunt girl" theatrics, as just a series of tricks employed to display women in a sexual manner. She also wrote in what has been labeled as another unserious, short-term genre, creating—as a "sob sister"—piteous stories of the women involved in murder trials, these articles judged as less than rational, separate from logical reporting of criminal evidence and verdicts.

Although Black's reputation suffered because she did not generally write "hard" news, in fact few journalists from the beginning of the century have received much critical attention. Those that worked on newspapers labeled as yellow journalism, with their large, scary headlines, detailed drawings, and sensational coverage of crime and love lives, did not always get taken seriously.[22] And even front-page reporters at more traditional newspapers did not sign their work and did not achieve the respect ceded to novelists, biographers, and historians. Some of the major writers at the beginning of the century, such as Theodore Dreiser, Frank Baum, Stephen Crane, and Upton Sinclair, got a start in daily newspaper writing, but their status did not stem from this work. Journalists such as Lincoln Steffens, Ida Tarbell, and Ray Stannard Baker—labeled as muckrakers not as "stunt girls" or the nonexisting term of "stunt boys"—secured a positive response for their magazine investigations, but their writing in newspapers received much less attention.[23]

Given multiple prejudices, against women in newspaper careers, against the writing that they would be allowed to do, and against any reporter as less consequential than the author of other genres, it is not surprising that even the best women journalists—the most prolific, respected, and influential—largely go unnoticed in histories of American writing. As Jessica Enoch and Jordyn Jack have claimed, "Public memory is often defined as a vernacular presentation of the past that significantly shapes understandings of the present as well as expectations for the future."[24] This presentation, reducing the work of women reporters from the first half of the twentieth century to stunts and sobbing, recipes and society news, has engendered what Gerda Lerner described as "collective forgetting" concerning the career of Winifred Black.[25]

## And the Development of Nonfiction

Although she has been given almost no credit for this effort, what Black did for almost fifty years was to develop the American genre of nonfiction. As historian Michael Robertson claimed, "Newspaper reporters and readers of the 1890s were much less concerned with distinguishing among fact-based reporting, opinion, and literature."[26] Taking advantage of the increasing freedom given to her by William Randolph Hearst and by a series of editors, by the column format, and by her own growing reputation, Black made a huge contribution to the development of nonfiction long before Joan Didion, Truman Capote, Tom Wolfe, David Foster Wallace, Malcolm Gladwell, and Chuck Klosterman. Tom Wolfe identified four main devices of what he labeled as New Journalism, echoing a term that had also been applied to some newspaper stories at the beginning of the twentieth century:

- telling the story using scenes (scene-by-scene construction) rather than historical summary as much as possible;
- providing dialogue in full (conversational speech rather than just a few quotations and statements);
- exploiting point-of-view (presenting every scene through the eyes of a particular character, frequently the carefully crafted narrator); and
- recording evocative details, such as behavior, possessions, friends, and family ("status life").[27]

In a career in which she wrote perhaps ten thousand short pieces and three books, Winifred Black created a nonfiction opus of themes and techniques, combining quasi-autobiographical details with characters and scenes to create cultural analysis that mattered, reaching a nationwide audience that learned from her and respected her work. Like the best writers of fiction over a productive career, she concentrated on human goals and foibles. And she applied the nonfiction techniques with which she experimented to the realities facing modern women: the work they did, their marriages and divorces, the violence they endured, their need for freedom. As she experimented with nonfiction, Black repeatedly registered the influence of family and the events of her life as well as the restrictions and opportunities of her chosen genre. Growing up in an era and family of robber-baron entrepreneurs, especially her father and sister, she became an actor and then a very active reporter, working for strong-willed newspaper owners, taking every opportunity that their publications offered. She lived independently and created, over fifty years, her own independent approach to writing and analysis, worthy of a place in public memory.

In a column from 1919, entitled "Winifred Black Writes about the Unafraid Girls," Black advises women to fake confidence when they don't feel it and move beyond fear and passivity. When they ventured onto trains, into new neighborhoods, and into offices, she writes, they will have the great experience of encountering much that is new: "Why, that's half the fun of life, the strangeness of it." And then she speaks of her own choices: "I couldn't live a day if I had to look at the same things and the same people and read the same news in the same newspapers day in and day out.... Here's to the next hour and the new face."[28] For generations of Americans living in small towns and large cities across the country, that strangeness of the next hour and of the next face came from the writing of Winifred Black.[29]

# 1

## *The War Hero/ The War Criminal: Winifred Black's Father*

It was within a culture of strong men and women that Winifred Black developed her nonfiction writing career and steadily advanced in it. She was surrounded by and learned from the type of bold propagandists and entrepreneurs that shaped American business, government, and social life in the late nineteenth and early twentieth centuries, manipulators expert at swaying public opinion in the tradition of the late nineteenth-century robber baron. She learned from her father, General Benjamin Sweet, who ran a Confederate prison in Chicago and invaded the city, and from her sister Ada Sweet, a federal pension agent who paid a bribe to get her job and defied a president to keep it. She learned especially from her yellow-journalism newspaper employers, William Randolph Hearst and Frederick Bonfils.

Winifred Black grew up with a father whose career crossed over the moral boundaries of power, patriotism, and persuasion, the line between fiction and nonfiction. Though Black was only eleven when he died, her sister Ada, born in 1852, was then twenty-two and had worked for him since she was twelve, his management of a prison camp and his subsequent federal employment leading to Ada's own long career in government, in which Black participated for short periods as her secretary. For both sisters, this father seems to have provided the ability to overcome and move forward, to maneuver in difficult circumstances—and to express persuasively a powerful view of reality.

Winifred Black's father, Benjamin Jeffrey Sweet, was an attorney and a Union Army officer in the Civil War who commanded Chicago's Camp Douglas as a military prison and used the power of this position to realize his desire for further advancement and the status of hero. He was born in 1832 in Kirkland, New York, and his family moved to a Chilton, Wisconsin, farm when he was sixteen. He attended Lawrence University in Appleton, Wisconsin; began practicing law; and became a member of the Wisconsin state senate in 1859. In July 1861, he entered the army, in a state division called the Iron Brigade, volunteering for service even though by that time he had a wife and three children. He sought continuous advancements: from lieutenant colonel to colonel and then commander. Wounded in Perryville, Kentucky, in October 1862, his right arm crippled, Sweet could not return to active duty. He went home to Chilton, where his daughter Martha Winifred, his fourth child, was born on October 14, 1863; she was called Mattie within the family.[1]

Although he couldn't return to the fighting, Sweet did not want his military career to end. And so, in September of 1863, he requested to re-enter active service, as a colonel in the Veteran Reserve Corps, charged with building a fort in Gallatin, Tennessee. From there he went to the prisoner-of-war facility at Camp Douglas in Chicago, in May 1864 assuming the position of supervising commandant. By the end of 1864, the camp housed 12,000 Confederate prisoners.[2]

Sweet came to Chicago accompanied by his eldest child Ada, then twelve, who attended the school at the Convent of the Sacred Heart in Chicago, then on Taylor Street. While going to school, Ada served as his secretary, in town at first and then on the base after the army forced Sweet to move there. During the fall of 1864, Sweet's wife and three other children came to the camp for a winter visit, Winifred then a year old.

As commandant, Sweet instilled a high level of discipline in order to gain control over the camp and eliminate protests and escape attempts. He built new barracks further from the fences, and thus from escape routes, availing himself of the prisoners' forced labor. Anyone attempting to escape was shot. Penalties for lesser infractions included solitary confinement, a torture rack, and beatings. "From this time forward," as one historian described his administration, "the darkest leaf in the legends of all tyranny could not possibly contain a greater number of punishments."[3]

Although Sweet had sought the position as his chance for continued leadership and advancement, simple maintenance of a camp during wartime would not impress his superiors, and Sweet sought greater funding for his building projects and greater notice for himself. He heard rumors that the camp prisoners, with help coming from Chicago and from Canada, planned some type of protest or rebellion during the Democratic National Convention, held in Chicago in July of 1864. Talk of insurrection indeed occurred in the camp and in living rooms in Chicago. But nothing happened in July and August, and most of the Confederate sympathizers left the area. Yet this rumor and possibility provided Sweet with the opportunity to act.

Even though there was scant evidence of an actual plan of rebellion afoot, Sweet took an unprecedented step in November: bringing his camp guards into Chicago to make arrests of citizens who may have been pro-

Confederate but had taken no action and instituting martial law across the city. He arrested lawyers and judges and their wives, describing these arrests to his superiors and to the press as just the beginning of his campaign against a huge nest of conspiring traitors. He then convinced the state's governor to place the Chicago militia under his command as well as 2,000 army troops stationed in Illinois. Until April 1865, with prisoners being removed from the city and tried elsewhere, Sweet held control: "He wielded more power over the city than any other person in its history."[4]

This domination of Chicago, involving regular raids until the war ended, led to two hundred arrests.[5] The supposed instigators of "rebellion" went to Cincinnati for military trials, an un-constitutional choice for these civilians against whom there was little actual evidence. These prisoners included Buckner Morris, a judge who had been a Chicago mayor and city alderman. He was held for nine months for participating in meetings before being exonerated by a military court. Richard T. Semmes, nephew of a Confederate admiral, received a sentence of three years in prison but was later pardoned. He had refused to fight for either army but had joined a Democratic club that was allegedly furthering the plot. George St. Leger Grenfel, an Englishman and former Confederate officer, received a sentence of death, reduced to life in prison at the isolated Fort Jefferson military prison located about seventy miles west of Key West, from which he escaped in a small boat in 1868 and died at sea. The *Cincinnati Enquirer* referred to him as the "last victim" of the trials held there.[6]

Though many contemporary accounts cited Sweet's fierceness and bravery, others noted the cost in human life caused by these raids and the subsequent trials. On November 12, 1864, the *Chicago Times* reported on what became a stirring series of finds: "The excitement in some parts of the city approached nearly fever heat by a report being current that another large capture of arms had been made in a barn." The *New York Times* reprinted this article on November 15 but commented further that "the men who have been examined are all fearfully ignorant."[7] The *Cincinnati Enquirer* found the testimony heard in trials there to be inconsequential.[8] The perhaps Confederate-biased New Orleans *Times Picayune* called the trials "interminable" and turned to sarcasm in describing them: Sweet had ferreted out a "band of loafers," and since he had no particular evidence of an attack, the case instead devolved into "ludicrous testimony" being "extracted from young ladies in their teens and old gentlemen in their—unmentionables."[9]

Was Benjamin Sweet a hero as he himself claimed or an ambitious and cruel scoundrel as he appears in many contemporary and later renditions of events? Did he save a city or arrest its citizens solely to bolster his own reputation? Most certainly, he made the most of a somewhat plausible attack plan and thus enhanced his own career: he was appointed U.S. pension agent in Chicago in 1869, dispersing funds to Union veterans, and then served as Deputy Commissioner of the Internal Revenue Service from 1872 until his death in January 1874 in Washington, D.C.[10]

Winifred was just a baby when her older sister went to Chicago to work for their father. But Ada was right there in Chicago and at the camp, from age twelve, the oldest of Benjamin Sweet's then four children, functioning as his assistant while attending school, involved in managing his military campaign, hearing his stories. His actions in Chicago became part of family lore, involving a vibrant entrepreneurial mixture of courage, tenacity, and self-promotion. His ambitious choices in war and peace led to a career for Ada and perhaps to Winifred's ability to maneuver in complex governmental and social spaces—and to her repeated consideration in nonfiction of various compelling and competing renditions of truth.

# 2

## Ada Sweet—Role Model

Winifred Black's father, Benjamin Sweet, the only wage earner in the family, died from pneumonia when Ada was twenty-two and Winifred eleven. Ada had worked for him at the prison camp and later at the pension office and for the internal revenue. The girls' mother, Lovisa Loveland Denslow Sweet, who was born in 1830 and married Benjamin Sweet in 1851, had grown up in Oneida County, New York, near her husband; she died four years after he did, in August 1878, hit and killed by a train in Lombard, Illinois.[1] As the supporter of the family after their father died and as a surrogate parent after the death of their mother, Ada provided Winifred with another role model who, like their father, seized the available opportunities, who combined a fierce dedication to family and country with an equally fierce ambition, and who recognized the power of public constructions of events, of persuasive nonfiction, in insuring widespread support for perhaps questionable choices.

After Winifred's father died, the family became destitute, without a wage earner and without land or family fortune. Ada Sweet, then twenty-six, had not married; she immediately began to support her mother, her younger brother, and her two sisters. By 1874, the year that their father died, their brother Lawrence Wheelock Sweet, born in 1855, had left home and headed West. He doesn't seem to have joined the military, no records list him, but he died in August of 1872 and was buried, according to government records, as a civilian, at the post cemetery at Fort Hays, Kansas, his age listed as seventeen.[2] In 1874, when Ada took over the support of the children still at home, Minnie was fourteen; Winifred was eleven; and Benjamin Jeffrey Sweet was three years old.

In recognition of the father's service and of the family's desperate situation, without regard for new civil service requirements, President Grant stepped in to offer help. Black later succinctly described what happened: "When my father died and the comfortable fortune he was supposed to leave his family melted in the mysterious way that fortunes have a tendency to do, President Grant appointed Ada United States Pension Agent at Chicago, a position which she held for something like eleven years."[3] Before this nomination, intended to honor a prominent soldier and help his family, the president had refused to appoint women to these disbursement positions, which were supposed to be reserved only for veterans.

## When Ada Served as Her Father's Assistant

Though Ada had gone to Chicago, as the oldest, to work for her father during the war, and though she later secured her pension job because of his service and friendships, she also sought to show her independence from him, and from his strict discipline, in the stories that she told to Winifred as well as to the press. When she toured the barracks with her father, she felt immediate sympathy for the men housed there, as she later remarked: "I often went into the prisoners' quarters with my father, and my heart ached for the homesick 'Johnnies,' as they were called." And at the camp, she overheard one escape plan without telling her father about it and actively aided in another. Their newly built barracks too far from the fence for tunneling, some prisoners sought to seal themselves into empty barrels being returned to local merchants. One soldier, as Ada told an interviewer thirty years later, had himself placed in a sugar barrel, and a friend "rolled him into the cart which had called to haul the empty barrels and boxes away." A half mile outside of the camp this prisoner broke free from his barrel and ran. Ada Sweet remembered "being glad for the poor fellow."[4] She even helped to hide another soldier who then escaped: "The man slipped away from the other prisoners, and hid in our basement. I just kept quiet and didn't say a word. About an hour later his absence was discovered. The alarm was given and a search was made, but it was too late. The man had run the guard and escaped. It was one of those things a child will do."[5] Ada often spoke not only of her joy in the rare escapes but of her sympathy for prisoners who died there, many the victims of her father's discipline: she said that she could not walk by their graves "without that swelling of the heart which even in childhood greets a tragic presence."[6]

Though Ada often voiced her early independence from her father, she also took advantage of what his position and influence could do for her and for the family. She became one of eighteen pension agents in the country, making the highest salary paid to a woman by the government.[7] She replaced David Blakely, who had secured the job when her father became Deputy Commissioner of the Internal Revenue Service. Some of the nation's newspapers reacted to Grant's appointment of her with less than a professional tone: a Dallas paper commented, "Oh, sugar!" and then went on to declare its amazement over this choice of a woman for the job.[8]

## Embroiled with David Blakely

With David Blakely, Ada would continue to have questionable connections. He was editor or publisher, between 1857 and 1880, of a series of small-town and city newspapers, such as the *Bancroft Pioneer* in Mower County, Minnesota; the *Chicago Evening Post;* and the *Minneapolis Morning Tribune.* Having developed friendships with a number of politicians, Blakely began participating in Minnesota politics, serving as the Secretary of State and the Superintendent of Public Instruction. This wheeler-dealer, with a career involving entertainment, publishing, and government, made secret arrangements with Ada Sweet that surfaced in the press in the spring of 1876, when Winifred was twelve, leading to a federal investigation into why Blakely had resigned and why he had recommended Ada to President Grant at the exact time that she needed the post. His act of ceding the job to her had seemed generous in 1874 when Ada took over, but in 1876 newspaper articles accused her of having bribed Blakely to resign and to support her candidacy.

Here was a story as confused as that of her father's supposed invasion of Chicago, involving a morass of opportunists. When the scandal broke in 1876, it appeared that Blakely had secured a loan, the size of which varied from report to report, from a United States marshal named Benjamin H. Campbell, a well-connected man whose son-in-law, Orville E. Babcock, President Grant's private secretary, had been accused of involvement in a tax evasion swindle dreamed up by whiskey distillers, a small group called the Whiskey Ring, by which they defrauded the government of millions of dollars.[9] Whether to secure the job or help a friend, Ada seems to have agreed to give Blakely $1,500 a year from her office's federal funds to pay his debt to Campbell.[10] In 1876, she denied various allegations at various times. When news that she might be making payments for her position first hit the papers, she denied it and said humorously in response that her job had cost her nothing "except for a shot gun and a bull dog to keep off Chicago widowers."[11] As the matter came out further during that spring, newspaper renditions varied on whether she was paying the debt, whether the money came from the federal budget or her own accounts, and whether she had to continue paying the money to keep the job. After investigators came to Chicago, Ada appeared in Washington at hearings on May 9. At this session, she admitted that she had made ongoing payments to Blakely from federal funds.

Throughout this investigation, Ada maintained public support not just because this nest of men was embroiled in other forms of bribery, but also because such corruption did not seem possibly to be the purview of women—such disbelief and sympathy would also be extended to Lizzie Borden when she was accused of murder in 1892. In a Louisville, Kentucky, newspaper, Blakely and Campbell appear as well-connected con men persecuting a "poor girl" who could not have been involved in such a swindle: "Marshal Campbell has kindly offered to refund to Miss Ada Sweet the money of which he robbed her, in conjunction with the merciless Blakely. These gallant gentlemen have seen so many Radical thieves escape justice that they do not think anything wrong in swindling a poor girl."[12]

## Accosted by Charles Guiteau

Ada Sweet kept her job and made no further payments, but two years later, in 1878, she found herself again embroiled in the spoils system, this time encountering the man who would become the most infamous opponent of civil service corruption, Charles J. Guiteau. This is the man who went on to kill President Garfield in 1881 because he felt betrayed by the government; Guiteau had expected a prime appointment, like an ambassadorship, for having supported Garfield for the presidency. Guiteau, certainly, suffered from delusions concerning his own influence but not concerning a president's power to confer appointments on his friends.

Before he appeared in Ada's office, Guiteau had suffered a series of reversals. He had been turned down by New York University when he failed the entrance examinations. He had then joined a utopian religious sect; attempted unsuccessfully to practice law; and began wandering from town to town lecturing to anyone who would listen to his religious ramblings. In 1878, Guiteau sent Ada a letter and then came into her office to see her, gesticulating wildly while claiming to be competent to fill any position involving pensions. "I did not pay much attention to what he said, as I saw he was insane," she told newspaper reporters concerning his claim that he had been unfairly ignored, but officers removed him from her office before he could use it.[13]

## Further Crises and Ambitions, Within Public Service

As her career continued, Ada participated further in the vagaries of civil service. In the fiscal year ending in June 1880, she dispensed five million dollars and earned a salary of $12,000. With this salary that year, she secured rooms in a large house in York Township, DuPage County, west of Chicago, with Minnie living there and not working (she married later that year); and Winifred and Benjamin away at boarding school, Winifred at the Burnham School for Girls in Northhampton, Massachusetts.[14] Ada continued in her job under President Hayes, who came into office in 1877, but in the fall of

1881, with Chester Arthur in the White House, veterans' organizations began asking for one of their own members to assume her position.[15] Editorials in the *Chicago Tribune* and other newspapers centered on her family, not her job performance or past corruptions: those against her appointment falsely claimed that her siblings were all grown, and those favoring her continuance spoke of the stellar career of her father. When Grover Cleveland became president, he asked Ada to resign so that he could give the job to one of his associates. She wrote back that she had a year left on her term, that she had done the job well, and that she refused to acquiesce. Then she released this letter to the newspapers to accuse the president, who had made campaign promises about ending patronage, of removing a good civil servant to please a friend who wanted the job. Seemingly as a result of her public construction of events, on April 23, 1885, newspapers reported that Cleveland had decided that Ada could keep her job to the next year, the end of her third term, unless there was a claim against her work performance, which there was not.[16]

This victory appeared in the press in gendered terms as had Ada's continuance in the job in 1876, but this time with the thesis not her vulnerability as a woman, which made her an easy target for con men, but her determination and her assertion of women's rights, taken more or less seriously by various newspapers and magazines. Author Eugene Field, best known for his children's poetry and humorous essays, wrote many verses to and about Ada in which he celebrated her resolve, in sing-song rhymes. In his column "Sharps and Flats," syndicated by many newspapers, one verse began, as Winifred Black later quoted it,

> Oh, Ada Sweet,
> It is a treat
> To see you stick so
> To your seat,
> Sweet Ada, bitter sweet.[17]

Striking a more respectful tone, the *Indiana Progress* claimed that most men who found themselves pressured by a president and his powerful cronies would have been intimidated and would have resigned: her victory was thus "a feather in the hat of the woman's rights cause."[18]

Ultimately, in September of 1885, Ada resigned and told the newspapers that, given all that she had endured, she "desired to become independent of the whims of political schemers": governmental officials had not defeated her but instead she had ultimately sought to free herself from them.[19] She said that she was glad to be away from "jealousies and petty persecutions" and onto something new, a job with a manufacturing firm, where Winifred would act as her secretary, as Ada had done for their father.[20] Ada's choice to leave the job she had fought for, like some of her earlier career choices, seemed to surprise and intrigue: as one newspaper commented, she "has the knack of making things hot."[21]

Ada did volunteer work toward the end of her career, moving from paid work to community activism, a different path than that taken by earlier generations of women and one by which she continued to emphasize the power of the individual woman as she fought in Chicago for better ambulance service, more street lights, and a sewage treatment plant. As she worked on a bill concerning compulsory education in November of 1892, the *Chicago Tribune* described her as a "leader in many of the public spirited movements in this city," as "everyone knows." "What Miss Ada Sweet Says" appeared as one of the sub-heads of this article.[22] On November 17, 1892, Sweet gave a talk on the influence of the press, before the Press League, in which she claimed that newspaper coverage often degraded women, something she had certainly experienced, but that they could cooperate with reporters to improve their cities and nation.

## Ada's Influence on Her Sister

In *Good Housekeeping* in 1936, in an autobiographical series published a few months before her death, during a hard spring in which she was very ill and may have felt a pressing need to record her life story, Winifred Black wrote at length about her sister, praising her for being so much more than beautiful: "Oh, she was a great girl, was sister Ada, and a fine, broad-minded, deep-hearted, generous, kindly woman; and that, you know, is a little strange for a beauty to be." Black recognized that her sister's help had launched her into a writing career. She further praised her sister by comparing her to other women leaders that she had known: "My sister Ada was the most interesting woman I ever knew. And I have known Sarah Bernhardt; Ellen Terry; Clara Barton, the founder of the American Red Cross; Evangeline Booth, commander of the Salvation Army; Adelina Patti, the greatest opera prima donna who ever lived." Black spoke with admiration of her sister's work as a pension agent and of her refusal to acquiesce to President Cleveland's demands: "But when the Administration tried to persuade sister Ada to resign, she wrote the President of the United States a respectful, courteous, charmingly worded letter in which she positively refused and absolutely declined to resign."[23] Black also had great respect for her sister's civic efforts and wrote, in the *Examiner*, about her clean-up efforts in Chicago in May of 1892. Her article begins, "The Chicago women have just done something. Something amazing. They have accomplished a result that has been the despair of men for years. They've cleaned the streets."[24] Black would initiate civic improvement efforts through the *Examiner* for San Francisco just as her sister did in Chicago.

For Winifred, Ada was the sister who helped to raise her and the other children, who supported them after their father died and was their sole caretaker after they also lost their mother, who fought established political powers to get and keep her job and then to reform her city. In her sister as in her father, Winifred had a model of strength and perseverance, of ambition, of quests occurring within and outside of societal expectations and even the law, of persuasive constructions of truth and moral rightness. The careers of both family members demonstrated the ultimate power of the individual, who might war with the government and succeed, with the press at times denigrating but also aiding in the effort. Winifred certainly emerged from a tradition of determination, of ambition, and of highly public and powerful constructions of truth.

# 3

# The Power of Black's Personal History in Building a Journalism Career

In Black's own discussion of her past, she stressed a tradition of leadership and strength—and of powerful discourse. She also wrote about the development of her own career in writing as involving her father's connections and her sister's influence. She thus isolated how they enabled her to succeed as a writer and then how she did so. Using her own past, she emphasized that her presence at the newspaper was not a fluke; she was not a short termer, not someone who would just spend a few years writing part-time for a women's page. Instead, she was a full-time, full-career journalist. Prepared and ready, grounded in the events of her past, as a woman without formal education beyond high school but with long-term training and much to contribute, she presented herself before the public as a career woman with the right and responsibility to inform and lead. She thus used her own autobiography as she stressed, in many articles, that especially with some encouragement and help, women could move forward on their own.

## A Determined Writer, with a Network of Family and Friends

Like a son entering the business world, Black relied on her father's contacts early in her career, using his name and authority to enter difficult spaces. She thus took advantage of the positive aura surrounding his service in the war, not the years in Chicago, to obtain the career boost that could be available to a daughter as well as a son, experiences which she often wrote about to stress women's abilities to employ advantages as they made their own way.

In 1892, for example, as Black often recalled, she attempted to board a campaign train and interview President Benjamin Harrison, who was not speaking to reporters. She was able to get aboard the train because of her own friendship with the governor of California, but she got in to see Harrison because of her father, thus becoming just the second woman to interview an American president, through determination and connections:

> And they explained to me that they had taken the matter up with the President and that he remembered my father and the Iron Brigade; he was sending for me to come back to his drawing room and would have a talk with me. I straightened my disheveled hair as best I could, set my hat at a fairly respectable angle, snatched my handbag, which contained my copy paper and two or three well-sharpened pencils, and went back to see the President of the United States.[1]

Similarly, as she described an exclusive interview that she gained with a man in hiding who might become the new governor of Kentucky, she discussed her use of her father's past, depicting herself, like a man in business, as employing her own skills as well as her family connections. Democratic Governor William Goebel had been killed by a sniper right after his election in February of 1900. The runner-up, William Taylor, who may have been involved in the assassination, had gone into hiding. More than 1,500 armed civilians were in possession of the Capitol, calling for his arrest. Black later wrote about the opportunity that she secured during a torrential rainstorm to meet this man. In this tense situation, when "the other newspaper correspondents were all at the big hotel," she made a special connection with one of Taylor's guards, by employing her father's service record:

> He was a mountaineer, of course, and most of the mountaineers are Republicans, even yet. My father was carried from the battlefield by one of those very mountaineers 'way back in the Civil War and was hidden in the log house of some men of the same blood and the same persuasion as this Captain of militia. Of course I told him about that, and before I had time to get even half-dry, we were confidential friends.

After Black established this connection, this confidential friendship, the guard quickly got her in to see the would-be governor.[2] In making the assertion "Of course I told him about that," Black indicates that her own persuasive use of her father's reputation—as a soldier in the war, wounded and saved, and not the invader of Chicago—ceded her a standing among soldiers and among politicians that was difficult for a woman to achieve.

Throughout her career, Black constructed herself as a daughter of a war hero, and like him in being tenacious and strong. She also wrote of admiring her sister's career—her civic responsibility, leadership, and persuasion. And she often spoke and wrote about Ada as having placed her within a community of writers (a difficult claim for a woman to make), as not an oddity who would invade the newsroom for just a few years, but as someone who had been moving into this career from childhood, someone who as an adult was fully capable and worthy to be a writer.

Ada made sure that her sister knew she could draw on powerful examples of professional women writers from her own family history, predecessors who created a lineage, such as men more commonly claimed. Emily Chubbuck, who wrote as Fanny Forrester, was a first cousin to Benjamin Sweet and grew up twenty miles away from him in New York state. She wrote her first novel, *Charles Linn*, in 1841. She published novels such as *The Great Secret, Allan Lucas, Kathayan Slave*, and *My Two Sisters*; short stories anthologized in her two-volume *Alderbrook*; verse collected in *An Olio of Domestic Verses*; and two autobiographies, *Trippings in Author Land* and *Memoir of Mrs. Sarah B. Judson*.

As a teenager and in her twenties, Black also met contemporary writers through Ada's group of friends, including highly successful women engaged in long careers, "literary lions," as Black often later recalled:

> My friend, or rather my sister's friend, was Mary Mapes Dodge, the editor of the *St. Nicholas* magazine. She gave Sunday evenings at home, and beautiful Ida Madeira of Baltimore and I were often asked to sit at the corner table and pour tea or chocolate or coffee for the literary lions of the hour. From our point of vantage, Ida Madeira and I saw Mark Twain, William Dean Howells, Mary Wilkins Freeman who sometimes stopped and looked at us through her tangle of red hair with her sharp blue eyes, and asked us rather searching questions as to what we liked and what we hated. And we were delighted to tell her whatever she wanted to know.[3]

Mary Mapes Dodge began her career in 1859 by helping her father to publish two magazines, the *Working Farmer* and the *United States Journal*; wrote a popular collection of short stories, *The Irvington Stories* (1864), and novel, *Hans Brinker, or the Silver Skates* (1865); served as associate editor of *Hearth and Home*, edited by Harriet Beecher Stowe; and then became editor of the *St. Nicholas Magazine*, a children's publication with a circulation of 70,000.[4] Mary Wilkins Freeman had begun writing stories and verse for children while she was still a teenager and ultimately produced twenty-seven novels and thirteen collections of short stories. She is best known for two collections, *A Humble Romance and Other Stories* (1887) and *A New England Nun and Other Stories* (1891). In the work of these women whom she met during her young adulthood, Winifred Black saw a place for women writers. Neither Dodge or Freeman chose the path of a full-time job in daily journalism, as Black would, and perhaps they would not have had such an option in an earlier generation, but they were women for whom writing provided long, independent careers such as Black would seek for herself, part of a community she had a right to join.

## Entering the World of Politics

As she recorded many moments of growing up within a writing community, made available to her through the connections of family, Black also had the chance along with her sister to move into the political world that she would investigate later as a reporter. When she was age seventeen in 1880, for example, Ada took her out of boarding school to attend a Republican Party convention:

> When I was a gangling girl with my hair in a braid and my dress down to my shoe tops, Colonel Robert Ingersoll took my sister, Ada, and me to a great political convention in Chicago. My sister had taken me out of boarding school to go with her, and I sat with Robert Ingersoll on one side of me and Manning Logan, the son of General John A. Logan, on the other side. On that great and exciting day at the first political convention I ever saw, I recognized one of the speakers. It was the handsome, broad-shouldered man who my father had said would one day be President.[5]

She thus entered a highly influential space, as a young man might be more likely to do, getting the preparation for a career that would involve her attendance at many such conventions and her own insightful analysis of the proceedings. The "handsome, broad-shouldered man," James A. Garfield, nominated Ulysses S. Grant, who sought an unprecedented third term, the delegates reacting with great excitement to Garfield's rhetoric if not to the nomination. Later, with the delegates deadlocked between General Grant and James G. Blaine, orator and lawyer Robert Ingersoll, Ada's friend, went to the podium and called for Garfield's nomination. In this exciting venue, among powerful participants, Black witnessed political wrangling and the impact of the individual persuader.

As Black frequently constructed her childhood years, they offered not just a general education but special preparation for becoming a writer, for participating in a tradition in her family and in Ada's circle of friends of women supporting themselves by conducting active research and evaluating American scenes. Black credited these writers, these active Americans, as well as her father and sister, with helping her to establish herself in the professional world.

## As the Romantic Actress

As Black constructed herself as writer, recognizing family background as important to women as well as men, she also sought to emphasize that she was, even as a young woman, someone who could move beyond family, propelled by her own courage and willpower. In her discussion of the career that she chose before journalism, she acknowledged all that Ada did for her and all that she did for herself.

With high school over, Black worked temporarily for Ada as her assistant, but she sought a movement out into a bigger, more exciting world as well as a means of support. Part of her story of herself, of the preparation that ultimately led to a career in journalism, included working on the road as an actor. As she described entering a troupe as an ambitious young woman, she concentrated on the type of risk and independence that would also be required at a newspaper.

Black began touring with an acting troupe in 1882, at age nineteen, a controversial choice at the time, the travel especially placing women "beyond the boundaries of propriety."[6] Ada had encouraged her sister to pursue this unconventional means of pursuing an income and success, as Black later wrote: "Sister Ada turned my restless, gay, irresponsible feet into the strange, winding roads, up hill and down dale." This profession could offer excitement along with regular and predictable pay, even if for brief intervals, more than most other careers obtainable for women without substantial education.[7]

Black joined the Egbert Comedy Company, led by F.G. Egbert, a group of nine, including four women. She acted not as Mattie Sweet or Martha Sweet but as the perhaps more dramatic Winifred Sweet. In March of 1885, for example, the troupe performed for a week in Alton, Illinois, at the Opera House, the program changing nightly. For ten days, at the Union Square Theatre in New York, their repertoire included *Led Astray*, a highly successful production in which Kate Glassford took the starring role and Black appeared in the crowd scenes. The troupe also played in small towns across the country, for just one night in each one, and Black found that she loved being on the road: "I rather enjoyed the idea of staying one day in a place."

Sometimes, the audiences and the lodgings were less than stellar, and she would describe these conditions critically but humorously, as what a woman worker could easily cope with and move on. In Smithville, Illinois, she had an uncomfortable, cold room, with just one bellboy taking hours to light a fire in the grate. People from the rural area came in to the lobby and made noise all that afternoon as she tried to sleep and then commented rudely as the actors left for the theatre, which featured cold dressing rooms and annoying theatregoers: "The people in the audience never laughed when they ought to, and they always laughed when they ought not. Anything at all approaching the nature of a love scene they seemed to think excruciatingly funny, but they never smiled during the comedy scenes."

In her depictions of this experience, Black recorded other, more serious moments of failure and success that a woman on the job might experience. She got the chance to move into a small speaking role as a last minute replacement—the moment she envisioned as proving her ability to become a star.

She came on stage during a crucial moment of the third act, employing an "exaggerated walk" and then a "tragic voice" for her one line: "My lord, the carriage waits."[8] Then in New Orleans, at the St. Charles Theatre, Black finally got the chance to appear in a starring role: for a week in October of 1888, she appeared in the title role of *Zozo, the Magic Queen*, before "a full house with packed upper galleries." An enlarged cast helped to create a spectacle of singing and dancing, in a fairy land, a review noting that Black performed the role very well and that the "mechanical and calcium effects," which created a magic lake, greatly increased the show's impact.[9] Black herself would describe the part in much less stirring tones, as a working woman realizing what her strengths and weaknesses were: "And I traveled through the south as the 'Magic Queen,' leading an Amazon march, fighting a broadsword combat, doing a song and dance, and otherwise comporting myself as magic queens were supposed to do. I wasn't a very bad actress, I think, but I wasn't a particularly good one, either."[10]

Such leading parts proved hard to come by. Black toured Canada with a small part in *The Wages of Sin*, which she labeled as a "roaring melodrama," with no chance at a larger part in this or other plays. She was not becoming a new Clara Morris, a famous actress then appearing in New York and on tour: "I didn't like the parts they were always trying to get me to play. I wanted to be a romantic heroine. I wanted to weep and denounce. I think I had Clara Morris as a vague model. But nobody seemed to care about my opinion as to my abilities." As Black later concluded, "I DIDN'T make much of a success on the stage," or at least not the type of success that she had envisioned.[11]

With Ada's help, Black decided to take on another challenge that would again lead her to the road and to persuasive characterizations: she made the initial movement towards a writing career, for which she had family history and connections. She frequently recalled the tremendous impact made by Ada in this instigation of a professional future when she read her sister's letters from the road before the editor of the Chicago *Tribune*:

> I was on the road playing Henrietie in "The Two Orphans," and I found some of the experiences in a Number Two Road Company rather amusing. I wrote to sister Ada about the drafty small-town theatres where we had to break the ice in the pitcher in the dressing room.... Sister Ada took my homesick letter with her when she went to a dinner. After dinner, by way of diversion, she took out my ridiculous letter and read it aloud to the company. Something in her way of reading or in her voice made the unimportant letter quite dramatic, and the editor asked if he might publish it in the Sunday paper and if I would please write one or two more letters about the experiences of a young girl on the road. The editor said something about these letters being a lesson to stage-struck girls.[12]

Her letters ultimately appeared in the *Chicago Tribune*, with the byline of Columbine, for the purple flower that a traveler might come upon in meadows and woodlands, as well as other Midwestern papers in January and February 1889, such as *The Marion Star* in Marion, Ohio; the *Decatur Daily Republican* in Decatur, Illinois; the *Springfield Leader* in Springfield, Illinois; the *Mitchell Daily Republican* in Mitchell, South Dakota; and the *Lima News* in Lima, Ohio; and even papers in other regions, such as the *Wilmington Messenger* in Wilmington, North Carolina, and the *Oil City Derrick,* in Oil City, Pennsylvania.[13]

Before she became a journalist in San Francisco and in New York, and by syndication across the country, as she often recalled the story, Black lived independently on the road as an actor, taking on different roles as she soon would as a newspaper investigator; and then she achieved success as writer of personal letters, acquainting readers with the oddities of life on the road and the hard work of the actor, starting her writing career by recording what she had experienced. Her later discussion of these first career moments stressed the ability of a young woman to take chances, find at least a first glimpse of a career, and keep moving forward, aided by encouragement from family. These facts would matter to Black, as her own biography certainly but also as an indicator of what young women could do, a nonfiction example of agency in adult life.

## A Daring Adventure

As Black's later constructions of her story stressed, she let go of a future in acting, but did not get married or return to her sister's home; instead she moved immediately to a greater level of adventure, taking a dangerous trip alone, in fact, that would lead to the career of a lifetime, a progression that again involved her in independence, risk, and the adoption of various personas.[14]

In October of 1880 in Chicago, her sister Minnie married C. Frank Weber, who had been born in Germany. Minnie died in September of 1887. After her death, Weber moved to San Francisco and then Winifred's youngest brother, Benjamin Jeffrey, left for Arizona, on his own, terrifying Winifred and Ada, who had raised him and who had already lost a brother, Lawrence, in Kansas in 1872, at about the same age, seventeen or eighteen. With the experience and ability needed to deal with difficult travel, Black set out to Arizona, as she later described this adventure to the wild West during which she relied on the sort of vague clues that she would follow later as an investigative journalist:

> Along about this time my sister Ada was beginning to worry about a younger brother who had suddenly taken it into his absurd youthful head to disappear. She wanted me to go West to look for him. He had last been seen on a train going to California or Arizona or somewhere; so, with a few rather distant clews, I packed my trunk, put my banjo in its leather case, and started West to find the prodigal brother. I got off the train at Holbrook, Arizona, and drove 125 miles across the desert in a buckboard with no top and no back and with a Mormon elder, who was also the mail carrier, for driver. It took us days to get to the cattle town where I was bound. But when I arrived there, I soon forgot the heat and the hunger and the rather unpleasant lack of companionship in the dreary desert. My lost brother was located on a ranch in the White Mountain Apache country. The trail there was marked by sunken graves, which, I was told, were the graves of white settlers murdered by the Apaches not enough years ago to make me comfortable. I had a wonderful time at the ranch.

As Black repeated this story of a "wonderful time," she featured her ability to take on a challenging quest as a woman on her own, already accustomed to travel, danger, and independent decision making. Her tale of this adventure would also focus on marriage opportunities that she encountered on the frontier and rebuffed automatically, as not what she was "cut out" for:

> I was no raving beauty and no marvel in any way, but those cowboys in that neighborhood were all young Americans, and not one of them had seen a girl of his own kind since he had left Chicago or Brooklyn or St. Louis or whatever it was he did leave to come West and be a cowboy and grow up to be a cattle king.
> During the three weeks of my stay in the White Mountain Apache country of Arizona I had fourteen proposals of marriage. I didn't think that I was cut out for a cattle king's bride or even for the wife of a gay and gallant cowboy, but I grew quite conceited about all this and began to look upon myself as a dangerous Circe (we didn't call them "vamps" in those days).

Securing a promise from her brother that he would write to Ada and report that "he hadn't fallen from a horse and hurt his back or anything like that," Black left and went on to California where she stayed with her brother-in-law, Frank Weber, "who was trying to forget the anguish of my sister Minnie's death by new surroundings and new investments in the glorious climate of California."[15]

While this story stressed her independence in her search for her brother, it also revealed that she was looking for more than marriage and a ranch. Her Arizona tale is hard to verify in historical records, and she never told it in specifics: it may or may not have occurred in just that way. But certainly she made rhetorical use of it, as something a sister would naturally do on her own—journeying across the nation, finding a brother in Indian territory through her own investigation, evading early marriage on the frontier. A woman would naturally voyage alone into the Wild West—and not find love with a rancher or cowboy there. Such a woman could certainly become a journalist, as so many other women could also.

This story of the lost brother involved the independence and trust in her own abilities with which Black would venture on from Arizona alone to San Francisco. Her next powerful autobiographical story concerned her voyage on to the choice of a hometown and a lifelong career.

From Arizona, as her story continued, Black went on to San Francisco to visit Weber. She was immediately attracted to this city: "I made up my mind that I was going to stay in San Francisco. By hook or crook, by fair means or foul, somehow or other, I was going to stay and follow every one of those steep streets up and down those steep hills and find out what was on the other side." Much later, in 1915, in an article about her campaign to save the Palace of Fine Arts after the Panama-Pacific International Exposition, she again spoke of her love of the city: "I love it so dearly that when I came back and rode up Market Street and I heard the conductor say 'Kearny' and I looked out and saw Grant avenue and Stockton and Powell, it was all I could do to keep from laughing and crying and singing all at once—just because the good old names were as woven into the very core of the memories of the heart that they were a part of my very life."[16] Though she may have gone to San Francisco initially to help her brother-in-law and sought to stay there because she loved it, the city's ultimate attraction would soon be a new career: "I suddenly found in California: the newspaper world, the most dramatic, the most incredible, the most fascinating world there is!"[17]

—⚘—

In Black's public discussion of her relationship with a heroic father and a determined sister, both able to forge their own way in politics and business in complex circumstances; in her construction of her family as bringing her into a strong community of writers; in her career as an actor on the road; in her lone trek West to find her brother; and in her subsequent trip to San Francisco, indeed in all these stories of her past, Black proved herself to possess the background, connections, support, and drive with which to launch a lifelong career in journalism. Though she always praised William Randolph Hearst, her first full-time newspaper employer, for the opportunities he offered her, she regularly maintained that her past prepared her—not just to write briefly for a women's page or to perform a few stunts but to instigate a full, active career as investigator and social critic. In this powerful rendition of an American past, Black depicted herself as a woman having the preparation to make choices and to make her own way.

# 4

## *Initiating a Career in Nonfiction: What a "Stunt Girl" Could Do*

From Chicago and then Arizona, her progress later constructed not as a fluke but an example of the family resources as well as the drive and independence that women possess, Winifred Black crossed the country to San Francisco. There she immediately became a key member of the inner circle of another late nineteenth-century entrepreneur, William Randolph Hearst, whose power, like her sister's and her father's, involved business, newspapers, and government. The nineteenth century proffered limited definitions of what women could accomplish at a newspaper; the assumption that they would not be appropriate writers of front-page news curtailed many careers but it enabled Black to develop her own approach to nonfiction. The freedom and creativity that her work manifested, throughout her career, began in her hiring as a stunt girl, a role that allowed her to abandon the restrictive formats of traditional news.

Hearst's need for a stunt girl that would enable him to beat out the other San Francisco newspapers provided Black with the opportunity to get a newspaper job. When Black sought a full-time job in journalism, in January of 1889, the odds were slight that she would still be working at a newspaper three or four years later, and certainly not forty-seven years later as one of the nation's best known writers. In 1890, of 3,014,571 women documented by the Census as working outside of the home, only 888 worked as journalists, 4 percent of the total of 21,849 reporters.[1] In a column from July of 1890 in the *Examiner*, Black labeled herself as "that singular anomaly, a lady journalist." When she continued by claiming that "there are a dozen men to one woman in journalism," the actual number was two dozen.[2] The conclusion Black stated about this era in her autobiography was accurate: "There weren't any newspaperwomen to speak of in those far-off and deluded days."[3]

## For Most Women: A Limited Role at the American Newspaper

At the end of the nineteenth and beginning of the twentieth century, women's lack of presence in the newsroom stemmed from society's presumption that they shouldn't be there at all. In 1897, female essayist Haryot Holt Cahoon described the quick and ultimately downward trajectory of even the few successful female journalists, who were there presumably on a lark and could not persevere:

> In the world of modern wild-cat journalism the woman reporter lasts about four years. She brings her education, her personal attractions, her youth, her illusions, her energy, her ambition, and her enthusiasm to the encounter, and the first year she rises rapidly. The second and third years she enjoys the zenith of her popularity; with the fourth year she begins the descent, lingers about the horizon for a time, and then she disappears from view. There is no vocation into which women have entered where disillusions materialize so rapidly as they do in journalism.[4]

How fortunate it was, Cahoon argued further, that a woman would soon weary of the hard work and would then marry and retire since daily journalism could cause a "blunting of her moral sensibilities, a surrender of her womanhood to the gutter."[5]

Other writers similarly argued that the rough space of the newsroom, the dangers of investigation, and daily analysis of current events were not appropriate for women. In 1903, Edwin L. Shuman, in his influential textbook *Practical Journalism*, described this inability to take risks and make judgments and concluded that, for women, "the work of news-gathering, as a rule, is too rude and exacting."[6] Another textbook writer, Charles Olin, went further in 1906, in his text *Journalism*, in discussing women's inadequacy for writing and editing hard news:

> Unlike teaching or almost any other calling, the labor of news getting and news editing is, from its exacting and severely practical nature, especially man's work. Editorial work, except within narrow limits, is also beyond the capacity of the ordinary woman because it usually concerns subjects of which she has little more than superficial knowledge and in which she has little interest—politics, finance and business. In the local field, too, the bulk of the reporting has to do with men and with men's affairs, which can be better treated by those of the masculine gender.[7]

In 1882, a Philadelphia reporter listed the prejudices awaiting women in the newsroom given these negative judgments: "Their abilities were questioned, their intentions suspected, their reputations bandied from sneering lip to careless tongue and on every hand they were met with discouragements."[8]

As Jean Marie Lutes argued in *Front-Page Girls: Women Journalists in American Culture and Fiction, 1880–1930*, women writers were often assumed "by virtue of their gender, to be incapable of deliberating rationally, transcending their personal interests, or making neutral judgments."[9]

Given their supposed liabilities, the few women working at newspapers in 1890 and 1900 gained access to only a limited role in a city newsroom, where part-time or freelance rarely led to full-time. Outside the space of hard news, women found some opportunity in society or fashion writing for the women's page, what journalist Mary Twombly referred to in 1889 as "the pitifully narrow groove to which women are generally confined on newspapers ... a necessary but illy-defined adjunct of the press."[10] Indeed, in 1974 when journalist Lindsy Van Gelder discussed the narrowly prescribed beginning of her own career, she judged that "the women's page was for frivolous, boring, puffy, irrelevant, 86-ways-to-make-tuna-casserole news."[11]

At the beginning of the twentieth century, at the newer style of newspapers given the derogatory label of yellow journalism, a few women did not women's-page articles but stunt-girl reporting, a personal form of risk-taking outside of the boundaries of "serious" analytical writing for which they assumed an undercover persona to write about powerful institutions, such as hospitals for the poor and mentally ill. Nellie Bly feigned insanity in October 1887 to investigate reports of brutality and neglect at the Women's Lunatic Asylum on Blackwell's Island. That fall she also went to matrimonial agencies supposedly in search of a husband and sought employment as a domestic servant. In February of 1889, she got arrested so that she could enter a woman's jail. In August of 1888, Nell Nelson at the *Chicago Daily Times* did a twenty-three part series posing as a worker in a box factory. Eva Gay, at the *St. Paul Globe*, took a job as a steam laundress and as a chorus girl. Though such stunt roles undoubtedly created opportunities for women, they also required an emotional approach, wrought with body imagery. Ishbel Ross commented in 1936 about this limited opportunity: "Newspaper women had to go in for dizzy self-exploitation before they could make themselves heard at all."[12]

## Enter William Randolph Hearst

In a bleak environment for women writers but with the stunt-girl role providing a possibility for creative work, Winifred Black had the good sense to apply at the *San Francisco Examiner*. In 1889, the Sunday feature section had two pages of women's content that featured "Toilet Talk" by Shirley Dare, author of *Art of Good Manners: Or Children's Etiquette*, as well as gossip columns and beauty articles. Hearst was not looking for a woman to fill that slot though Black's pieces would appear sometimes on those pages. What he sought as he attempted to create the San Franciscan answer to Joseph Pulitzer's *New York World* and its Nellie Bly was a stunt girl.

When Black came to the *Examiner*, William Randolph Hearst had been its editor for two years, fully backed by his father's vast fortune. In the winter of 1859, his father George Hearst had mined thirty-eight tons of high-grade silver ore, moved it across the Sierra Mountains on mules, brought it to San Francisco smelters, and thus reaped $91,000 (or roughly $3,550,000) in profit.[13] He then invested further in equipment and mining rights and made a huge fortune in gold, silver, and quartz mining. Though he bought a large home in San Francisco and moved his family there, he generally lived in his mining camps. His son William Randolph, born in the same year as Winifred Black, went to St. Paul's School in Concord, New Hampshire, where he was thoroughly unhappy, not part of the eastern social class, and then his mother insisted on Harvard. While there, he served as business manager of the *Harvard Lampoon*, expanding its advertising revenue by 300 percent and its circulation by 50 percent.[14] In the fall of what should have been his senior year, he went to New York City to study Joseph Pulitzer, who was creating exciting city journalism at the *New York World*, the sphere that the younger Hearst sought to enter.

When Hearst then came home to the West Coast, his father having been elected to the U.S. Senate in January 1887, he had the opportunity to take over the newspaper that his father had purchased in 1880 to strengthen his position within the Democratic Party. With a circulation of just 15,000, the *Examiner* significantly lagged behind the *San Francisco Call* and the *San Francisco Chronicle*, both tied to the Republican Party, but William Randolph Hearst planned to employ Pulitzer's methods at the *World* to immediately alter these numbers. Giving his paper a grand motto, "Monarch of the Dailies," he acquired the best equipment and the most talented writers, including Ambrose Bierce, Mark Twain, and Jack London. He installed large headlines and line drawings that crossed several columns, sensational crime tales, dramatic human-interest stories, extended sports coverage, serialized stories like a Jules Verne tale on the front page, and investigations of municipal and financial corruption, the younger Hearst as editor often attacking companies in which his father held an interest. His news articles, written for "excess and excitement" in imitation of Pulitzer's, aimed to take on "the pace and coloring of short stories" and provide the "heroes and heroines of a morality play."[15] This new *Examiner* soon dominated the San Francisco market.

When the *Examiner* was undergoing so much change and growth in circulation, Winifred Black came to its offices seeking work, drawing on her acting skills to exaggerate her work with Midwestern newspapers: "Her stage experiences," as the historical study *Great Women Reporters* commented, "had prepared her to act like an experienced reporter when she applied."[16] And she thus described this key start to her career: "So the first day I got a chance I went to the office of the *San Francisco Examiner* and gave the doubting Thomas of a City Editor to understand that I was a newspaperwoman of broad experience, and would cover not only myself but the paper with glory if he'd only give me a chance."[17]

## Learning from Sam Chamberlain

This doubting Thomas was Hearst's managing editor Sam Chamberlain, who had worked as writer and editor at the *New York World*, the *New York Herald*, the *New York Evening Telegram*, and *Le Matin* of Paris, Hearst's "most flamboyant and ostentatious employee ... known for his sartorial splendor as well as his drinking binges."[18] Chamberlain decided to send Black to cover a flower show, not a job but a tryout. She later described this exciting opportunity as well as her actual knowledge level about the mechanics of regular reporting as compared to letter writing:

> I took a small wad of yellow copy paper from the City Editor's room when he told me to go and get a story about the flower show. I knew so little about the newspaper game that I never dreamed I could go down to the newspaper office and write my story. So I just hunted up a stepladder leaning against the wall in a dark corner of the flower show, put my yellow copy paper on one of the steps, and wrote the story as if my very life depended on it.[19]

On the next day, she experienced the great joy of opening the paper and seeing her story, for which she had jotted down and included as many details as possible but had forgotten the basic who, what, and where, which the editor had to add, her claims about her experience thus appearing a bit less truthful: "I knew that that City Editor must realize by this time that I had somewhat misled him as to my brilliant and thorough training." However, she had collected some vivid details and presented them in story form, and so he kept her on the job.

## Becoming a Stunt Girl

Chamberlain gave her a lesson about the basic who, what, when, and where after her first outing; he also began teaching her more about the sort of gripping details needed for *Examiner* stories. Chamberlain had "unerring news perception and understood and carried out feature ideas that were distinct," as an historian of his work commented.[20]

Chamberlain continued Black's education, moving her into the stunt-girl role, by engaging her in the latest Nellie Bly story. In November 1889, the *New York World* announced that it was sending Bly around the world, in a bid to circle the world more quickly than Phileas Fogg in Jules Verne's *Around the World in Eighty Days*. Having learned about this plan to mesmerize readers, *Cosmopolitan* editor John Brisben Walker decided to dispatch Elizabeth Bisland, who had worked for the *New Orleans Times Democrat*, the *New York Sun*, and the *New York World*, on her own journey, a race around the world heading west while Bly headed east, a contest for the faster time. On November 14, 1889, Bisland departed westward from New York while Bly left New York on a boat to Europe.

When Bisland got to San Francisco, Chamberlain sent Black out to get the interview, her opportunity to do the basic who, what, and where, which most readers knew about this contest anyway, along with much more, an array of details and an innovative structuring of them that would make a connection with the reader. Black often repeated Chamberlain's verdict concerning her first draft, advice she cited as essential to her later work: "'This is a bad story,' he pointed out. 'Very bad, indeed. We don't want fine writing in a newspaper. Remember that. There's a gripman on the Powell Street line—he takes his car out at three o'clock in the morning, and while he's waiting for the signals he opens the morning paper. It's still wet from the press and by the light of his grip he reads it. Think of him when you are writing a story. Don't write a single word that he can't understand and wouldn't read.'"[21]

## Developing a Style and a Persona

Chamberlain didn't make the changes this time, as he did with the flower-show story, but instead expected Black do the work. And in this revision he helped her to begin to create the effective style that would define her career. Black started her revised article with a description, about Bisland's surprising strength: "She doesn't look like a very daring creature, this little woman with the gentle voice and appealing dark eyes. But she's going around the world for seventy-five days, and she's going alone." And Chamberlain also encouraged her to describe the contest in a clearly dramatic, unexpected, and ironic manner, which she did while also indicating Bly's actual name, cited in very few articles:

> *Dramatis personae.* Elizabeth Bisland, a black-eyed and comely young lady of enormous aspirations in the globe-trotting line. Bound around the world in seventy-five days, determined to outdo Phileas Fogg, the hero of "Around the World in Eighty Days."
> Miss Jane Elizabeth Pink Cochrane (alias "Nellie Bly"): Another black-eyed young and comely maiden of extreme peripatetic ambition. Also bound to

beat the mythical Fogg and make the circuit of the globe in seventy-five days.

Scene. This planet.

The action in this sensational drama is divided. One of the principals is heard of by telegraph as follows:

"Nellie Bly" on time.²²

Black had learned about recording the basic facts after writing her first *Examiner* story, but with this subsequent one she was embarking on an innovative form of nonfiction that she developed throughout her career, way beyond the who, what, and where, with various dramatic means of engaging readers in a world beyond their own.

To then become a competitor to Bly, Black also took on a fanciful name of a stunt girl, such a moniker helpful in creating a newspaper character. She chose "Annie Laurie," and her friends even began calling her Laurianna, her name having already changed from Martha or Mattie Sweet to Winifred Sweet to Columbine. She ultimately wrote approximately 16,000 articles as Annie Laurie for the *Examiner*.²³ Her mother, as Black often explained when asked about this choice, sang the popular parlor song whose lyrics came from a story of the 1680s concerning William Douglas, who had fought in Germany and Spain, before falling in love with Anne Laurie, the youngest daughter of Robert Laurie, a baronet. The version sung in 1889 contains a detailed portrait of the young woman for whom Douglas would "lay me down and die":

> Her brow is like the snowdrift
> Her throat is like the swan
> Her face it is the fairest
> That e'er the sun shone on.²⁴

Black used this name, describing a perfect but ultimately unattainable woman, for her west coast writing until the early 1930s, way beyond the era of the stunt girl. Perhaps Black had thought that "Winifred Sweet," her name from her acting career, might seem like a descriptor if it appeared as a byline, making her a bit more "sweet" than she would like to appear.

Armed with an appropriate nom de plume and the experience from her first pieces, Black appeared to Chamberlain to be ready to enter the world of stunt-girl nonfiction. Her initial idea for this particular sort of work, however, came not from Chamberlain or Hearst but from her sister Ada. In 1889, Ada was working to secure ambulance service for Chicagoans and better treatment especially for poor women within the health care system. In September, Ada began asking the mayor to initiate an ambulance corps. In early December, the *Chicago Tribune* supported her efforts by publishing several editorials concerning the desperate need for ambulances to replace the rough rides and treatment encountered in the police wagons then sent out on all emergencies.

Then, on December 13, 1889, the *Tribune* published a story purportedly by an eighteen-year-old employee and close relative of Ada Sweet, the reporter using the name Annie Myers when she was taken up by the police on the street and put into a patrol wagon for suddenly becoming ill and the name Nora Marks when she wrote the article. Marks (Myers), in fact, was actually Eleanor Stackhouse Atkinson, who wrote investigative pieces at the *Tribune* from 1888 through 1890.[25]

In this piece, Atkinson as Marks wrote that when she fell and seemed to faint on Halsted Street, several kindly passersby got her up and walked her to a drug store. Then police came and put her on a stretcher, a large picture of her upon it appearing on front page. These untrained men banged her around as they took her to the hospital; one pinched her nose to get her awake and then asked her about drinking and drugs. She told the policeman and the nurse about her connections to Ada Sweet, but they refused to contact anyone for her.[26]

On the front page on December 13, Atkinson's long exposé of the current system was followed by "How Miss Sweet Found Annie," written by Ada Sweet concerning the harsh treatment and ineptitude she encountered as she sought her young relative. Then following these two was another long piece by Sweet, presenting her arguments for an ambulance service, the dramatic scene thus followed by analysis, a presentation that ultimately led to ambulance service for the city.[27]

To prepare for a similar police wagon and emergency-room story, undertaken in January of 1890 as a service to her own city as well as an indication to Hearst and Chamberlain of her capabilities, Black made herself pitiful and in need of assistance, as had Atkinson. She dressed in old clothes and worn shoes; she used belladonna eye-drops that dilated the pupils to achieve a glassy stare. Engaging readers in this quest, she wrote in her front page article especially about the difficulty of putting on this act and then fainting in front of men: "I had already chosen a convenient pile of boxes to faint against, but when I saw the crowd of men in the cigar shop near where the boxes stood my heart failed me and I walked on. But I found it no easier to faint further on. The streets and sidewalks were so muddy that I could not bring myself to fall to them. At the corner I stopped long enough to let me heart regain its normal pace, took a long breath, and with my lips between my teeth, walked slowly back."

After she appeared to faint on the street, as her article continued, the police dragged her across the sidewalk ("Either man was strong enough to lift me with one arm but they preferred to drag me") to an old police van for a trip to the hospital: "It seemed impossible that a person with a fractured limb could live through the terrible pain that that tumbling, rumbling, jerking, jolting old rattle-trap would cause him." At the city receiving hospital, the staff decided that she had been poisoned and decided to force an emetic down her throat: "The young doctor in a matter-of-fact way grabbed my nose so that I had to open my mouth to breathe, the matron held my hands and the doctor with his other hand held the bowl of mustard water to my mouth." When she struggled, "they got my head against the chair and forced some of the nasty mixture down my throat." Then another doctor came in, frustrated by her desire to take no more of the emetic, and attacked her viciously:

> The doctor took two strides and was beside me. He gripped my neck with both hands, digging his thumbs into the hollows below my eyes. I screamed with pain and rage and managed to push him aside. This seemed to infuriate him. He grabbed me by the shoulder with so fierce a grip that my shoulder is lame yet. It took the skin right off. He threw me backward onto the bed with spiteful vehemency and snarled:
> "Let her lie there, and if she makes any fuss strap her down."[28]

Like Eleanor Atkinson and Ada Sweet, Black then moved from a first-person experience article to analytical pieces about the health crisis. She wrote about subsequent visits with the mayor and police department surgeon, of whom she requested that five emergency hospitals be erected in various parts of the city, each with an ambulance and a doctor that would go out on calls to administer aid.

This long first-page story, which led to better emergency service for her city's residents, as had Atkinson and Sweet's in Chicago, became the first of Black's stunt-girl stories. Soon afterwards she entered a local fruit cannery as a worker, the Grand Opera House as a chorus girl, a women's prison as a Salvation Army administrator, and offices of divorce lawyers as a desperate wife, in all these cases allowing readers, through characters and scene, to enter new worlds. She repeatedly, as in the city receiving hospital piece, engaged readers in the costumes and make-up required, in the entrance into a new space and the conditions there, in her conversation with the divorce lawyers or chorus girls or prisoners, and ultimately with her analytical responses to all that she encountered. As Ishbel Ross described this part of Black's career, "She set the pace, just as Nellie Bly had done a few years earlier. She became a personality as well as a reporter.... She was one of the first Hearst stars."[29] In Black, as historians Maurine H. Beasley and Sheila J. Gibbons have claimed, the *Examiner* "found a woman reporter whose style and dramatic flair personified Hearst's brand of flamboyant journalism."[30]

---

In "Bigger Eyes, Fuller Lips, Broader Minds?" in *New York* magazine for July/August 2014, with the subtitle "the contentious past, present, and sci-fi future of 'ethnic plastic surgery,'" Maureen O'Connor begins with her own visit to a plastic surgery office, posing as a prospective customer:

"You've got some nice Caucasian features," Dr. Edmund Kwan says, inspecting my face in his Upper East Side plastic-surgery practice, where the waiting room includes an ottoman larger than my kitchen table. "You're half–Asian mixed with what?" Chinese mom and white dad, I reply. "You inherited a Caucasian nose. Your nose is nice. Your eyes have a little bit of Asian mixed in." He proposes Asian blepharoplasty, a surgical procedure to create or enlarge the palpebral fold, the eyelid crease a few millimeters above the lash-line that many Asians lack.[31]

As in O'Connor's essay, and certainly Barbara Ehrenreich's *Nickel and Dimed: On (Not) Getting By in America* and Ted Conover's *Newjack: Guarding Sing Sing*, Black found that the undercover persona gave her a chance to investigate, to get a story as she could not have done otherwise. Jean Marie Lutes argued in *Front-Page Girls* that stunt-girl work "intertwined the bodies of news writers with the news itself": the more recent use of undercover personas has done so also.[32] In her first years at the *Examiner*, Black learned through stunt-girl work about entering difficult situations to conduct research, not backing away from the realities of the prison or factory; she also developed the ability to create the innovative structure, narrator, characters, and scene of creative nonfiction, engaging readers through the particular to foster cultural analysis.

# 5

# *Building a Reputation Among Newspaper Kings*

Across the country, the stunt girl journalist had a short life span. Indeed the trend was beginning to wane by 1900. In 1895 Nellie Bly married millionaire manufacturer Robert Seaman, forty years her senior. She retired from journalism and became president of the Iron Clad Manufacturing Co. After Bly left the *World*, the paper decided on a catch-all designation, Meg Merrilies, for writers of stunt stories, taking away the personal authority of even the individual stunt name and substituting a gypsy name from a John Keats' poem that ends with "God rest her aged bones somewhere—She died full long agone!"[1]

While Bly's career would be limited to the stunt-girl era, Black "possessed an elasticity that Nellie Bly lacked" and "was able to adjust to the times," as John Jakes claimed in *Great Women Reporters*.[2] As she built a full career, she never abandoned the lessons she learned through her first undercover pieces; instead she would bring them to an array of nonfiction in an amazingly varied career that revealed the opportunities possible beyond the limitations of traditional front-page news.

## An Array of Newspapers and Techniques

From these first days as a stunt girl, Black built a strong relationship with William Randolph Hearst that helped her to gain the freedom to experiment with technique and subject matter. In an autobiographical essay, she thus described her career-long association with this controversial man: "William Randolph Hearst has been the strongest influence in my life. He has also been the best boss, the kindest friend, and the simplest-hearted, wisest, most understanding, most forgiving, most encouraging human being it has ever been my luck to know. And if you don't believe this estimate to be true and accurate, you just ask the first man you meet who has ever been in close professional touch with this man who is so loved and so hated and so feared and so envied."[3] Black's success with him, as his first female hire beyond the small staff of the women's page, led to opportunities for other women. Recognizing the importance of women readers, he brought them to the *Examiner* and later to the *New York Journal* and other papers through the promotion of women writers. Ishbel Ross, in fact, argued that he had the best record in that era of furthering the careers of women:

> Mr. Hearst, more than any other publisher, has helped to put newspaper women on the map. Hundreds of them have passed through his doorways, some to lose their jobs with swaggering swiftness; others to build up syndicate names and draw down the highest salaries in the profession. From the moment he entered newspaper work, he dramatized them; got them to make news. They became the most spectacular, the most highly paid, the most dashing newspaper women in the country, if not necessarily the finest news writers. Wherever a woman has shown particular promise elsewhere an effort has been made to lure her into his service.[4]

And his first and most trusted woman writer was Winifred Black; indeed she became "the one woman on his staff with access to his inner councils."[5]

Black worked for Hearst throughout her life, taking on the roles of feature writer, advice column writer, travel writer, and political investigator, her pieces appearing in his *San Francisco Examiner* (from 1887 to 1895 and from 1913 to 1936) and in his *New York Journal* (from 1895 to 1897 and from 1907 to 1913). Her writing also appeared across the country in syndication, made available through the Hearst feature service. She also worked for other powerful newspaper owners, Frederick Bonfils and Harry Heye Tammen, at the *Denver Post* and *Kansas City Post*, from 1907 to 1913. As one journalism historian described this varied career, "She never really had a permanent address. She transferred back and forth from the *San Francisco Examiner* to the *New York Journal* a half-dozen times and, for a period, left both for the *Denver Post*. She was hardly ever in the city where her paper was edited, anyway. She was always on the go, flitting around the country or, on occasion, overseas, to wherever the big stories were."[6]

From this beginning, outside of the regular boundaries of news writing and certainly way beyond the first lessons in who, what, and where, Black obtained more and more creative freedom, developing many types of nonfiction in an unprecedentedly long and varied career. At the beginning of the twentieth century, when very few journalists wrote with bylines and very few had reputations beyond their city room, Black was one of the best known newspaper writers, her columns that considered the roles of women and men, recent news developments, and many other subjects appearing in syndication across the country. From this beginning as an undercover persona, Black moved into a varied career, with an array of techniques analyzing the lives of women and men in modern America.

As she continued voyaging out as Annie Laurie for the *Examiner*, she conducted interviews with vivid characters whose stories might not fit on the first page but certainly could draw in readers as she depicted them in story form, a variety that she recalled:

> I remember that in one day I "covered," as the phrase goes, a ministers' meeting from ten to twelve; interviewed Lottie Collins, the famous ta-ra-ra-boom-de-ay dancer; went to see a Russian Bishop of the Greek Church and asked him if it were true that he burned an orphan asylum full of children to get rid of some incriminating papers; and went down to the morgue to try to help identify a poor girl who had found the sweet delirium of youth suddenly turning into somber tragedy. Quite a busy day for a little redhead.

Beyond the work of any individual day, the *Examiner* afforded her a broad range of the often sensational topics that enabled the paper to thrive, as she further recalled: "We had love nests and triangles and suicides and murders and great generosities and noble dreams, and nobody ever had much time for anything but life and lots of it in that strange, romantic, warmhearted, scatterbrain city."[7] Along with many lesser known Californians with stories worth telling, she interviewed the mayor and governor, acquainting readers especially with the odd characters who visited these offices seeking an immediate remedy to all their problems.

Black also joined with Hearst in initiating many civic campaigns, using the specific details of nonfiction to involve readers in local needs. Her article describing one invalid child, Little Jim, as well as the kind doctor whose hospital would not admit him, appeared in the *Examiner*, her details accompanied by a picture of the boy sitting in his dark room in a dark alley, his crutches leaning against a small table, and under the picture the legend, "Nobody wants us."[8] After the article appeared, with backing from the Hearst fortune and other local philanthropists, a special hospital ward opened to treat the most seriously ill. Along with Hearst, she involved herself in many other civic campaigns, such as saving the Palace of Fine Arts after the Panama-Pacific International Exposition in 1915 and curbing the city's trade in opium, cocaine, and heroin in 1921.[9] In 1928, she wrote a book called *Dope: The Story of the Living Dead*, her research and activism in San Francisco leading to her description of people across the country whose lives had been ruined by drug use.

## "The Children's Page" and Then Suddenly a New City

As Black moved beyond her stunt-girl beginnings into so many forms of nonfiction beyond the space of traditional news, she also began "the children's page," also called "the boys' and girls' page," in the Sunday feature section of the *Examiner* in June 1895, for which she wrote a short essay each week where she could experiment with various dialects, characters, and forms of humor. She also sought to engage children with contests: for the best drawing made without taking the pencil off the page; the best answers to puzzles; the best short essays about a particular topic, like an outdoor vacation or kite or a favorite fairy tale. In 1895, she also wrote a children's book called *The Little Boy Who Lived on the Hill: A Story for Wee Bits of Tykes*, with short tales concerning exotic adventures within a small neighborhood, stories that she told to her own son, Jeffrey, born in February of 1892 and named for her father. She had married fellow *Examiner* journalist Orlow Black, on June 20, 1891.

On October 13, 1895, reporter Robert Howe Fletcher began editing the *Examiner's* children's page; he started his first column with "'Annie Laurie has gone away! Isn't it too bad?' That is what all the boys and girls, from the primary to the ninth grade, have been saying this week."[10] The reason for the change was that Hearst wanted Black to come to New York, and she was willing to leave her husband and son Jeffrey, then three years old, to help launch a newspaper there. A new city would afford Black with new subject matter and an opportunity for cultural comparisons.

Early in his career at the *San Francisco Examiner*, William Randolph Hearst had envisioned running a large newspaper chain, and "always knew that his dream of a nation-spanning, multi-paper news operation was impossible without a triumph in New York."[11] In 1895, at age thirty-two, with the financial support of his mother, who had inherited her husband's fortune when he died in 1891, Hearst bought the failing *New York Morning Journal* to enter into a head-to-head circulation war with Joseph Pulitzer. His plan was to keep his newspaper at a penny but to offer as much "news, entertainment, sports, and spectacle" as Pulitzer provided at the *World*, with his mother's money enabling him to forego concern about revenue until he could build circulation, which grew quickly even after the *World* went down to a penny to compete.[12] The *Journal's* daily circulation climbed above the one million mark after the sinking of the *Maine* and the United States' entry into the Spanish-American War, a war that some dubbed "The *Journal's* War" due to the paper's immense influence in provoking American outrage against Spain.[13]

Winifred Black was among the trusted journalists that Hearst sent for to work at his new acquisition, the woman that his biographer David Nasaw called at that point "his most famous reporter."[14] As Black later wrote, she immediately stepped on a train accompanied by other writers and editors when Hearst asked them to join him: "They were going to New York, too, and they had no more idea why they were going than I did. We spent the first two days on the train speculating about it. It all seems so simple now. But at that time we had no more idea of a Hearst newspaper in New York than we had of one established at the top of the mountains of the moon."[15] She boarded the train along with baseball writer Charles Dryden, editorialist Arthur McEwan, caricaturist Homer Davenport, and Sunday editor Frank Noble— "the dependable nucleus he had carefully assembled."[16] Even though these journalists had no plan to work in New York, they would do so after the Big Chief got them on the train, their loyalty to Hearst trumping their lives in California: "We would have gone to the Fiji Islands or to Greenland's icy mountains if the Big Chief had wanted to send us to either of those probably delightful but rather remote places."[17]

Black's first articles from New York appeared in the *Examiner*, presumably pleasing San Franciscan readers with the clear preference for her own chosen hometown, her cultural contrasts pointing out the difficulties of life in the East. In "Annie Laurie in New York," she writes about class divisions there as well as the women seen on Fifth Avenue: "They walked about beautiful automatons, these sleek, well-groomed women. They did not talk to each other; they did not smile; they did not look at any one. They walked with the English stride, and swung their stiff arms, and they gazed straight ahead of them." In "House Hunting in New York," she describes ridiculously expensive neighborhoods and the difficulty of finding a place to live, using detailed descriptions to acquaint readers with hideous lodgings that she could barely afford.[18]

With her writing for the *New York Journal*, she switched to the name Winifred Black, which she used for the rest of her career though she continued to write as Annie Laurie at the *Examiner*. Always going "somewhere in a great hurry" in New York as she recalled, Black chased stories that involved "police stations, hospitals, soup kitchens, tenement houses, evictions, sordid murders: a terrific panorama of misery and human patience and human endurance under the bitter cross of grinding poverty."[19] The especially sensational articles that Black wrote, such as "Why Young Girls Kill Themselves" and "Strange Things Women Do for Love," helped Hearst raise circulation quickly through their detailed scenes.[20] As a *Journal* reporter, Black also traveled to get the sensational story, about a prize fight held in Mexico, for example, in February 1896, published with the title "A Woman among the Fighters."[21]

As a devoted San Franciscan, Black found New York not to her liking. She thus did not quite want this marvelous opportunity with which she had been presented: "The Big Chief was giving me a chance that most women in my profession would have fought to the death to get. But I didn't want a chance."[22] And so, just as she did in acting, heading West, and seeking a journalism career, Black continued to shape her own career and life.

## To the *Denver Post* and Charley Bonfils

Though she left New York, Black didn't return to San Francisco; instead she went to the *Denver Post*. Having divorced Orlow Black in December of 1897, she married Charles Alden (Charley) Bonfils in February of 1901, eight years younger, the newspaper owner's "personable and mild-mannered younger brother," who had obtained an engineering degree from the University of Missouri and worked as a surveyor of the river delta near New Orleans before joining his brother at the *Post* and becoming its assistant publisher.[23] Journalism historians have offered various views of this marriage since Black continued traveling for Hearst and later worked primarily from San Francisco while Bonfils remained in Colorado. Some writers have claimed, with distance as the evidence cited, that they were unhappy and estranged.[24] However, in *Great Women Reporters*, again without evidence, John Jakes asserts that Black's "second marriage was a happy one, although except for its early days, when she worked on her husband's paper for a time, they saw each other only periodically because of Winifred's extensive travels.... He was a merry fun-loving man who often burst into song in the editorial offices, and Winifred was quite devoted to him."[25] With Bonfils, she had a daughter, Winifred Mary, and an invalid son, Eugene Napoleon, who died at age nine.[26]

A failing paper, the *Denver Post* had new owners in 1895, the same year that Hearst bought the *Journal*. As similar purveyors of yellow journalism, they expected the creative work from Winifred Black that would rivet readers' attention. One was "cheerful, amoral" Harry Heye Tammen, operator of a curio and souvenir shop in the Windsor Hotel in Denver, a highly lucrative business, featuring Moon-Eye the petrified Indian on a stand. Tammen also owned a small circus, begun with his own dog that could turn somersaults.[27] With "an instinct as sure as Barnum's," he moved into a new career, in journalism, keeping a stuffed baby elephant in the city room: "The *Post*," an historian of the paper claimed, "was a lulu."[28]

The other new owner, Frederick Bonfils, could also be described as a wheeler dealer. He advertised lots for sale in Oklahoma City that were not actually located there. In Kansas City, he sold fake lottery tickets, calling his game the Little Louisiana Lottery to associate it with a well-known, high-stakes game of chance. After Buffalo Bill, local legends asserted, Bonfils "was the handsomest man who ever walked the Denver streets." He had no more knowledge of newspapering than did Tammen: "Some of his early signed editorials, in fact, indicate that Bonfils was barely literate."[29]

Neither of these entrepreneurs knew how to edit a newspaper but they knew how to sell one. In one of the first staff conferences, as the story of the paper is told, Tammen outlined the philosophy of sensational, local news that would guide the paper and Black's work there:

> "You've seen a vaudeville show, haven't you?" he asked the city editor. "It's got every sort of act–laughs, tears, wonder, thrills, melodrama, tragedy, comedy, love, and hate. That's what I want you to give our readers.... If a thing is horrible, explain why it is horrible and leave nothing to the reader's imagination. Nothing is too trivial to interest some reader, and never forget this: that more people are interested in a man's falling and breaking his arm on Curtis Street than are interested in a disaster in Egypt or China."

Without experience, they created "a brash, astonishingly uninhibited type of journalism that shocked and often outraged the traditionalists."[30] To promote the paper, Tammen and Bonfils sponsored a cross-country roller-skating contest, invited local women to wrestle a troupe of professionals, hired Harry Houdini to escape from a straitjacket while suspended upside down from the newspaper's balcony, and had a tightrope walker perform the slide for life, hanging by her teeth, over the street to the front of the *Post* office. Like Hearst, Tammen and Bonfils sought civic reform as well as the sensational. A regular feature called "So the People May Know" took on local issues, including the power of local trusts, corporations, and railroads; child labor; and corruption in Colorado politics.

By 1909, with this paper prospering far beyond the dreams of the owners, Tammen and Bonfils decided to buy the *Kansas City Post*, a Democratic evening newspaper. They sent Charles Bonfils there as managing editor along with Winifred Black and cartoonist Doc Bird Finch, who "headed a list of staff stars who would shuttle between Denver and Kansas City."[31] Like Tammen and Frederick Bonfils in Denver, Charles Bonfils insisted on large headlines and lurid stories, all so different from his paper's staid competitor, the *Kansas City Star*.

On these newspapers, Black continued creating scenes and characters, frequently deploying them to analyze local and state politics. At the *Denver Post*, she dealt with prescriptive attempts to teach morals in the public schools, a campaign led by judgmental citizens that she described with damning specifics. During the debate occurring in 1897, when Coloradans were attempting to eliminate the death penalty, she created hypothetical examples of women placed on death row. For the *Kansas City Post*, she did a series on Alma Vaughn, indicted for poisoning her husband, who had accused her of adultery and planned to leave her. Her coverage of this woman, who had been involved with a series of men, was not piteous or sympathetic but highly evaluative of her character: Vaughn had an affair with a married doctor "not because she was in love with him, or any other man, but because it gave her a chance to laugh secretly at another woman."[32]

## Across the Country and Around the World, for a Long Career

Black worked for both of these *Post* papers through 1913 while also doing special reports for Hearst, sent by him to cover the most dangerous of crises, like the hurricane in Galveston in 1900 and the earthquake and fire in San Francisco in 1906. In 1907, she went to New York for William Randolph Hearst to cover the Harry Thaw murder trial, the reporting that led to the sobriquet of sob sister. She wrote about many other trials during her career, interviewing victims' families, murderers on death row, and spectators who seemed addicted to the drama.

Throughout her career, Black frequently took extensive voyages for important stories, such as a change of administration at a colony for people with leprosy, or Hansen's disease, in Hawaii in 1890, the dedication and risks of suffrage campaigners in England in 1910, and the effects of war in France in 1918. At age sixty-eight, in 1931, she covered the International Narcotics Convention, in Geneva, pressing for international treaties of cooperation in fighting and controlling narcotics traffic.

Besides writing articles that appeared exclusively in the *San Francisco Examiner*, *New York Journal*, *Denver Post*, and *Kansas City Post*, from the beginning of the century Black wrote three or four columns a week that appeared in syndication in newspapers across the country, marketed through Hearst's feature service. She published this considerable part of her work under the name Winifred Black and never Winifred Bonfils, indeed with her chosen literary name often in the title of the piece: "Winifred Black writes about…." In these columns, using characters and scenes, she provided analysis of cultural expectations placed on women and men, considering an array of issues of modern life: conditions that women and men experienced on the job, dating and engagements, domestic violence, marriage and divorce, independence, the rights of parents over their children, suffrage, and many other topics. Through these columns, she became a national authority, often addressing readers directly as she engaged them in specific situations as well as larger issues. In 1974, journalist Lindzy Van Gelder claimed that only a few papers such as the *Washington Post* and the *New York Times* had recently begun covering job discrimination, domestic violence, and other "feminist issues," but Winifred Black had written about them repeatedly long before.[33]

Beginning in 1914, Black also took on a regular question-and-answer advice column, written under the name Annie Laurie, which appeared throughout the country but not in the *Examiner*. The column appeared with slightly different titles: "Advice to Girls," "Helpful Advice to Girls," "Pertinent Advice to Girls," and "Advice." Black produced this advice column until June

1930, often critiquing marriage, engagements, and women's lack for independence, creating her own approach to this genre. By the time that Black launched her syndicated advice column, Beatrice Fairfax, Dorothy Dix, and others were writing advice for young girls and women in a generally conservative tone.[34] Marie Manning as Beatrice Fairfax had produced the first advice column in a newspaper, for Hearst's *New York Journal* in 1898 and in syndication by 1900. Manning didn't deal with divorce in her columns until the 1940s; she advised young women to get married and to forgive an adulterous husband; she made no mention of domestic abuse. Elizabeth Meriweather Gilmer, writing as Dorothy Dix, began the Sunday Salad column at the New Orleans *Picayune* in 1895, which became Dorothy Dix Talks, for Hearst's *New York Journal* and in syndication. A "Victorian voice," she advocated for the sanctity of marriage and often criticized women for their hysterics, weakness, and lack of judgment skills.[35] Unlike these other writers of advice columns, Black began immediately to write about the independence of young women, about education, divorce, domestic violence, and work, not the usual topics for a women's page or an advice column, her answers often employing the same principles that her other columns and articles developed.

Increasingly after World War I, as she published two or three opinion columns and an equal quantity of advice columns each week in syndication, Black also wrote articles that appeared just in the *Examiner*, focusing on local issues and values. In these pieces, written under the name Annie Laurie until the 1930s and as Winifred Black in her final years, she created another voice and honed a local persona, more sentimental, enamored of her city and state and highly supportive of everything being done for Californians. These sweeter pieces perhaps reflect a more conservative, older writer though she crafted them at the same time that she was taking on difficult issues in other *Examiner* pieces and in syndication, and so perhaps they indicate not a change in the writer but an addition to her persona, a calm, reassuring voice both before and especially during the Depression. Her local pieces include highly positive travel articles, called "Side Trips from San Francisco," featuring little known destinations like La Honda and the Belvedere hills. She also recorded the help given to veterans by local organizations and the hard work of school teachers and nurses; she profiled members of the fire and police departments who participated in volunteer efforts. One column concerned the police's participation in a blood drive to help a seriously ill child: it was titled "Arise, Me Lads, and Take Salute, You Who Gave Blood to Aid Boy," and it began with a list of the officers' names. Through specific descriptions, she publicized local campaigns, like one to secure greater penalties for drunk and reckless drivers, and wrote about civic improvements, like taking billboards off of some streets. She also reminded readers of earlier times in the city, adopting a nostalgic tone, her readers for these pieces presumably older citizens. In several articles, for example "Old Song Stirs Tender Memories" and "Is 'Puppy Love' Just Like the Toothache," she recreated courting scenes of earlier eras. By the 1930s, as the memorials after her death certainly attested, she seems to have become a symbol of the city and the best of its citizenry and history.[36]

At the end of her career, Black still seemed to have been fully engaged in research and writing. In 1932, in an article concerning the speed of travel around the world, so much faster than when she voyaged to Molokai in 1890, as she recalled, she commented on the potential for learning through increased travel: "Italy, Spain, the Himalayas—why they're as close as the next neighbor's back yard. Aren't you glad you've lived in this strange age? A little confusing, a trifle perplexing—oh yes, that's true, but anyhow I'm glad of it all, aren't you?"[37] In 1934, after forty-five years on the job, Black still seemed to be fully engaged in it: "The newspaper game, why it's the only game in the world, that's all. You're either in it, heart and soul, head and boots, or you're dead and don't know it."[38] When Black was seventy-two, she flew over Mount Shasta in a plane at 10,000 feet, headline news in 1935. In October of 1935, as *Time* magazine commented in an article about her work and her service to her profession and to California and the nation, she was writing an average of nine articles a week, six for syndication and three or more for the *Examiner*.[39]

Winifred Black continued to produce her various forms of nonfiction until her death in May of 1936. She died on San Francisco on May 25, 1936, at seventy-three, in the company of her daughter Winifred and Annie Beavers, her assistant for thirty-five years, who in Black's last decade began to take dictation because her eyesight was failing. At her death, she was living at 3320 Baker Street, a five-bedroom home built in 1927, in the Marina District near to the Palace of Fine Arts, which she had fought to save after the end of the Panama-Pacific International Exposition in 1915 and again in 1926. Her funeral record lists her death as caused by "apoplexy from arteriosclerosis," hardening of the arteries, a condition with which she had been suffering since that February and that finally caused a cerebral hemorrhage.[40]

Black was survived by her daughter Winifred Mary and by her son-in-law, Charles O. Barker. As she said in her autobiography, "And so am I glad about my life. I have been twice married. I have twice stood at the grave of my own children, bone of my bone and flesh of my flesh. And I have had a young daughter marry and go far away from me to live a life of her own, choosing a quiet life of quiet contentment; and for this I am very thankful."[41] Her son Jeffrey Black, born on February 5, 1892, seven and a half months after her marriage to Orlow Black, had served for a few months in a Missouri militia in 1917, and listed himself as a writer on military enrollment documents.[42] His wife Emmaline came from Pennsylvania, and they worked as farmers in both Sonoma and Monterey. Jeffrey drowned off Carmel on Sat-

## 5. Building a Reputation Among Newspaper Kings 49

urday, June 19, 1926, at age thirty-two, after being caught up in the undertow. He had been staying there with his mother and with his aunt Ada Sweet, visiting with them at a cottage that his mother owned.[43] Black's invalid son Eugene Napoleon Bonfils, given his grandfather's name, had died at age nine, Black's major goal "to bring him happiness and surcease from pain."[44] Her daughter Winifred Mary Bonfils had married Charles O. Barker when she was seventeen and he was forty-two, his second wife. They lived in Los Angeles where he was a fruit farmer. She lived until 1991.[45]

—⚭—

In a full career as a writer, through which she raised her three children on her own, Winifred Black found work with newspaper entrepreneurs setting up new domains, Hearst and Bonfils and Tammen, and then reached a national audience both through their newspapers and through syndication. Amid changing definitions of the newspaper and the newspaper article, she experimented with not just the basics of older forms of writing, the front-page news that had been and largely remained the purview of male journalists, but newer styles of nonfiction. From her beginning as a stunt girl, and as she went on to interviews, travel writing, opinion columns, advice columns, and reform campaigns, she honed the stunt-girl concern with the particular, with the individual case and place, and with the active narrator who could bring readers into realities that they had not before examined.

# 6

# *Black's View of the Writing World That She Entered*

In the employ of powerful newspaper owners as the new century began, Winifred Black was that rarity—the woman writer who worked for much longer than four years and moved far beyond the society and home features of the women's page and the quickly fading gimmick of the stunt. Throughout her career, as she wrote many different forms of nonfiction, she analyzed them thoroughly and commented upon the opportunities for women within them. She frequently described stereotypical constructions of women as readers and as writers, which she often countered as she stated her own point of view. As she crafted nonfiction, she repeatedly deconstructed the limits of the traditional newspaper, and women's roles within it, while also asserting her right and ability to make such judgments.

## Involving Women with the News: A Special Edition

From the beginning of her career, Black advocated for both women readers and women writers of newspapers. As a fund-raiser for the Little Jim children's hospital ward, in San Francisco in December 1894, she chose an event with no connection to the charity but with a connection to her own interests: she asked women philanthropists in San Francisco to take over the editorial tasks of the newspaper for a special Christmas edition, with William Randolph Hearst having agreed to donate the proceeds from newspaper purchases and from specially solicited ads. This charity event gave her a chance to quite publicly, indeed for an entire month, enact her thinking about women and newspapers.

When Black wrote about the *Examiner*'s sponsorship of this edition, she spoke of the good that the money would do for invalid children but also of the good it could do for women readers. In 1886, Joseph Pulitzer's *New York World* had begun carrying special columns, at first in the Sunday magazine, devoted to women in the home, leading in 1894 to a daily page titled "For and about Women." During its publication period, from 1891 to 1894, the *New York Recorder* claimed 100,000 women readers, who supposedly chose the paper because of its "The Only Woman's Page," featuring content that would become standard fare: home economy and innovations, fashion, food, society news, gossip, and child training.[1] What Black believed that her special *Examiner* issue could do, beyond raising funds for the children's hospital, would be to ask women, for the first time, what they would actually like to see in a women's section and indeed in the entire newspaper:

> The second good it will do is the jostling it would give a whole lot of old ideas. Every newspaper man in the round world lives in a state of puzzled inquiry as to what sort of "copy" is interesting to women. Every newspaper that was ever published or will be published has a woman's page.
> The Christmas paper offers the enterprising journalist a brilliant opportunity to find out what women would put on that page if they had their way....
> If it be really true that the average newspaper is not at all the sort of thing the average woman likes, the Christmas Examiner will tell the story.[2]

Throughout the month of December 1894, Black made clear that women involved in charity work would and could write an entire paper: "The society women of San Francisco are going to edit the Christmas edition of the Examiner. They're going to write it—every line of it; they're going to manage the business department; they are going to get out the local news; they are going to attend to the telegraphic department; in fact, they're going to edit it from the 'corner' at the very top of the left-hand side of the first page to the last line of the last bit of local news on the last page." And here she writes again about women, as consumers of news, finally having control over that news: "This is the first time that women have ever had their say about the way a daily newspaper ought to be published. They have been looking on a good many years and they've been fairly bursting with advice that nobody paid any attention to. Now their chance has come to show what they can do, and they're going to use that chance to such an advantage that the cynics will be dumfounded."[3]

On Christmas Day, the special edition did not contain the limited "women's" content that many locals expected. The front-page center featured a large cartoon, of women running the paper and a small man leaving the office, with the heading "deposed." The pieces on the front page, stories about hostilities in China and Tammany corruption, revealed women's interest in international and national politics. The first section continued with articles about sports, price hikes by the gas company and the railroads, police corruption, and the new governor and mayor. The editorial page contained articles on racial prejudice and poverty.

This newspaper also contained content more narrowly described as focusing on women, but in a more serious vein than what was generally marketed to them. The front page included an article about the difficulties that heiress Hetty Green, of New York, had in attempting to control money left to her by her father. Other articles within this edition concerned women in the theatre, the conditions of their employment and the prospects there for ingénues; a woman earning a living by reading to older people; women on bicycles; and a woman golfer. Then spread over two pages appeared a group of pieces on the beauty of American women by region, featuring Gertrude Atherton on California: Julia Magruder on the South; Harriett Prescott Spofford on New England; and Octave Thanet on the West: all four concentrated not on physical appearance but on the beauty of perseverance, dedication, hard work, morality, and ideals. The paper continued with other articles by women: "A Christmas among Polar Bears," a children's story by Josephine D. Peary; "A Woman Who Dared," from the autobiography of Elizabeth Cady Stanton; and "In a Country Practice" by Sarah Orne Jewett. The edition also featured a long article thanking Hearst and Black for furthering this project and for thus demonstrating their support for women readers as well as children in need of hospital care. This edition also contained long lists of people that donated to the hospital, pages of special ads, and an article about the particular women doing the work, thus constructing the Hearst papers and Black herself as making a charitable difference in the community while furthering the priorities of half of its citizens.

After the issue came out, Black continued to discuss women as readers and writers. In the next days, she published several pieces about women's ability to say what they wanted to read and do the hard work of creating that content, their efforts contradicting so many stereotypes about women: "They didn't go into hysterics in print, as some observers doubtless hoped they would. They didn't crowd out news matter for fashion gossip, and they showed in every line of that great paper that they were intelligent, well-informed human beings who read the papers and understand them." Here she speaks of modern women, in comparison with those of other eras, as being fully able to take on a task and move forward with it: "How many 'old' women would have dreamed of publishing, writing and editing a big daily paper? Why, the woman of twenty or even ten years ago would have swooned at the very idea."[4]

## Beyond the Special Edition: Women as Readers and Writers

Beginning with these articles from 1894, Black frequently wrote about women as newspaper readers. For a column in May 1910, she begins by discussing a man who says that his wife won't have newspapers in the house because she finds them too distressing, here the stereotypical woman who works within the home and doesn't see any need to learn about the world, a straw (wo)man that Black depicts as not typical and not laudatory. Here Black argues that especially women who work in the home need newspapers, more than men and women out seeing the problems of the nation firsthand: "Women need newspapers as no man in the world ever needed them." Women have to face life with courage and fortitude, she continues, and to teach harsh realities to their daughters as well as to their sons. It is not noble or unselfish to be ignorant in the home, like a heroine in a fairy tale or the Lady of Shalotte, Black maintains further: it's just so limiting not to know. And next she discusses the proper place of women as engaged in the world, as readers and as citizens, aware of the "real truth" of other women, explored not just in nice features that might appear on traditional women's pages but in all types of news:

> The newspaper is the mirror wherein the average woman sees the world going about its business outside the quiet tower room of her home. And I am one who believes that tragedies and sorrows, and bitter griefs and terrible betrayals, should be reflected in the mirror too, as well as all the sweet and lovely things of life. We are part of the world, we women. We are no better and no worse than the rest. If we are to bear our share of the sorrows of existence with courage and noble fortitude, we must know the real truth about what other women have to bear.[5]

While she spoke of women as active readers of newspapers, interested in the entire content, she also commented on the opportunities they had as reporters, not to totally determine the newspaper's content, as in a few special editions, but to work within and to expand existing structures.

Indeed, though she certainly recognized the difficulties for women, she often maintained that they brought special attributes to the job through which they could expand their own careers and the purview of nonfiction. Like Judith Butler, she believed that both men and women, in journalism as in other spheres, might demonstrate traits that were traditionally gender typed—and she also believed that women could take advantage of the courtesy that men sometimes felt obliged to extend to them to find the information that they sought: "The ideal newspaper woman has the keen zest for life of a child, the cool courage of a man and the subtlety of a woman. A woman has a distinct advantage over a man in reporting, if she has sense enough to balance her qualities. Men always are good to women. At least I have found them so, and I've been in some of the toughest places."[6]

Black would not consider limitations on what women might read and what women might write, and she further attempted to reconstruct the few opportunities that they did find, as not lesser or constricting, but as the means to a full career, perhaps better than many men's because the alternate paths that they sometimes trod could lead to more creativity than could be found in front-page news.

## The Women's Page as Just a Beginning

Though Black never sought to be a fashion or society writer, she wrote about the women's page as not necessarily a negative place to begin: if such a job was all that a woman could get at a newspaper, she should do it as well as possible and learn from it all she could—and then move on to a fuller career.

Black frequently argued that just because a woman might want to write, she wasn't necessarily suited to or interested in society content. In a column describing a new hire, she certainly recognized that a woman could find the work repetitive and dull, the social leaders not all that fascinating: "At first she thought it was fun but then it bored her, the people were stupid, and none of the women were really clever about their clothes, in spite of the money they spent on them. They were so supercilious.... She got so tired of talking about the beautiful Miss This and the charming Miss That, when they were neither of them even passable to look at nor interesting to meet."[7] In 1890, in a full-page piece, writing as one of several "Successful Women of the West" asked, as a subtitle indicated, to "Unbosom Themselves for the Benefit of Struggling Sisters," Black claimed that society reporting, for the unconnected young writer, who found the "best" families hard to approach and easy to irritate, could be more complicated than was generally realized: "Not very difficult? Try it and see."[8] But, this limited journalistic opportunity, Black claimed further, provided good training in investigation and writing style, in skills that could be applied to other assignments. Although some historians like Rebecca Abrams have dismissed the impact of early women's pages because they often did not reflect the personal lives or political conviction of the women who wrote them, other recent critics, like Linda Steiner, have noted, as Black did, that these newspaper sections did provide some opportunity to discuss women's issues—and for young women to secure a foothold at the newspaper.[9]

## Un-stunting the Stunt

Just as Black sought to carefully consider the opportunity provided by the women's page, she also created her own analysis of what was being both promoted and denigrated as stunt-girl journalism.

## 6. Black's View of the Writing World That She Entered

When she discussed her first investigative pieces, she constructed herself as using an undercover persona to improve conditions in her city and the nation. In 1912, when Winifred Black spoke to a press club at the University of Missouri, the first meeting of a state-wide organization of newspaper women, her theme was "making their lives count for something worthwhile through the mastery of the newspaper profession." She used as examples the reform sparked through her investigations of child labor and of health care. Small stories and big, she argued to the press club, could demonstrate a "social vision and a genuine desire for service," and an assumed persona could be the most efficacious means of conducting the investigation. About entering the city receiving hospital as a supposedly ill and friendless patient, for example, she commented that "those in authority on the paper began to hear rumors of queer doings at the City Receiving Hospital. Young girls wandered in with ugly stories; poor women who had been overtaken with illness on the streets, or hurt in accidents, sent their friends to tell the editors that all was not as it should be at the City Receiving Hospital. We could not publish these stories, of course, without positive corroboration. So one day I thought I'd go see what I could do about it." Her declared impetus was to improve conditions, not just create sensational work for herself.[10]

Even at the beginning of her career, she didn't always choose the most titillating of roles when she could get the story through a less hazardous disguise: her stated goal was to spark reform. When she investigated life in a jail, she wrote about the reasons that a reporter would not want to go in with her name and job known: "There was no use in visiting the jail in an ordinary way—like a Committee on Public Institutions. I had no mind for the studied demeanor and remarkable order which always edify such visitors. No, I must go in some way so that I could see the prisoners when they were not, as it were, on dress parade." But she did not see the need to take on the risky role of prisoner. Instead, she posed as a Salvation Army volunteer; she sought information not just titillation or danger.[11]

Sometimes Black found that a disguise that totally removed her from the action, that thus involved no bodily risk, provided her with a unique viewpoint. At a prize fight in San Francisco, held in a room full of men, she snuck in and sat in a dark and separate area, cordoned off from the crowd. As she noted in her article concerning this fight, she thus had the opportunity to see what men do by themselves in violent spaces: "Since I saw them, I know that women never see men as they are. Women do not know anything about men.... I had not been at the prize-fight five minutes before I saw that I was looking on a race of beings I had never seen before. I saw men in the crowd whom I have known for years. I hardly recognized them.... One gave a guttural snarl like the cry of an angry panther, and the other struck a blow for every blow given upon the stage."[12]

But certainly the use of any type of disguise or any hiding place was not always the most efficacious choice: as Black wanted readers to understand, she also entered new spaces clearly identified as a determined reporter. When Black wrote about the California Home for the Care and Training of Feeble Minded Children, the first of its kind west of the Mississippi, she started her piece with the worst of prejudices: "Fifty years ago people chained an idiot child in a dungeon and fed him as one feeds a savage dog."[13] To gain access to this new type of institution and get the specifics about the care of these children, she entered as a journalist, with a long list of questions for the administrators and with visits scheduled with the children. In this situation, as Black made clear to the hospital's administrator and recorded through the use of dialogue, she expected full disclosure and would certainly write about the lack of it:

> "Now, what do you want to see?" said Dr. Osborne, the Superintendent.
> "Everything," I said.

For Black, as she wrote her articles and depicted herself as reporter, the real "stunt" was to have the experience, shrewdness, and courage to get through doors and get the story.

## Not a Sobbing Sister

While Black constructed herself as an investigative reporter, certainly not a stunt girl, she dealt more directly with another derogatory label for women that began with the Harry Thaw trial, which she covered, at Hearst's request, for the *Journal* and for the *Examiner*, in 1907.

Thaw was a railroad magnate accused of murdering his wife's supposed seducer and rapist, architect and well-known New Yorker Stanford White. At the time that Nesbit's husband, Harry Thaw, murdered her former lover, in June of 1906, she was already well known to readers of the daily press through her photographs and Broadway appearances: she was a celebrity, a character of beauty and allure, perhaps the first supermodel. The sexual exploits of men with whom she associated, and especially of Stanford White, were also a matter of legend. At the trial, to absolve her husband of responsibility and guilt for this murder, lawyers and a willing press cast her not as supermodel celebrity and well-known partyer but as a mistreated innocent: the vulnerable, sexual child wife, forced into carnality by powerful men.[14]

For this trial from January to April 1907, four journalists sat at a special table in the courtroom—Winifred Black for the *New York Journal*, Dorothy Dix and Ada Patterson for the *New York Evening Journal*, and Nixola Greeley-Smith for the *New York Evening World*—three of the four thus working for

Hearst and one for Pulitzer. In their feature articles, they all purportedly constructed themselves as older, more worldly women undergoing this crisis along with the frail and frightened Evelyn, forced in court to reveal the hideous facts of violation by a vicious roué, thus constructing Thaw's violence as the result of a "brainstorm" resulting from intense love and White's unbelievable cruelty.[15] In discussing this daily coverage, Irvin S. Cobb of the *New York Evening World* labeled these reporters as "sob sisters," a name that became synonymous with a first-person, melodramatic style of writing, and he labeled this trial, as these women reported on it each day, a "carnival of mayhem." In his autobiography in 1941, *Exit Laughing*, Cobb wrote that "'sob sister' became the aptly alliterative title for any over-heated young female who mistook flowing hysteria for a true reportorial viewpoint. It is still in use and deservedly so."[16] These writers found their work powerfully denigrated by Cobb's descriptor, as Jean Lutes has commented: "In the space of three syllables, 'sob sister' recast trailblazing professionals as gullible amateurs."[17]

Cobb's depiction of Winifred Black, as an irrational writer portraying Evelyn Nesbit as a piteous, abused innocent, her suffering necessitating her husband's action, doesn't match her coverage of the case. Indeed, in her book *Sob Sister Journalism*, featuring many quotations from the coverage of this trial, Phyllis Leslie Abramson rarely quoted Black. Concerning the trial that merited daily coverage from January 23, 1907, until there was a hung jury, and thus a mistrial, on April 13, Black seems to have written only eleven articles. And within this small total, certainly not every article concerned Nesbit. At the beginning of the voir dire, for example, Black judged Thaw's lawyer as less than competent: John B. Gleason "took the floor with all the pompous delight of a little man who loves to get on a platform that will make him look tall."[18] Her articles also focused on other participants, such as a shy potential juror who suddenly found himself the center of attention. She wrote another long piece about District Attorney William Traver Jerome's careful questioning of the jurors, with only a bit of commentary about the wife of the accused: "His wife cowered down in her little straight-backed chair, frailer, whiter, bigger-eyed and more like a frightened child than ever."[19] One of her other articles describes Harry Thaw, not sympathetically as the devoted husband, but as a "big, overgrown, clumsy, broad-faced, slow-witted, big-eyed boy, a fellow brought up to nothing but the most selfish egotism and blind self-indulgence."[20]

The only time that Black describes Nesbit at some length, she does so to speak about her mother's lack of responsibility in not being in the court room and not raising her daughter well:

> Pale little Mrs. Harry Thaw grows paler every day until you cannot look at here without wondering where she finds the strength to sit through the long, long weary day in court.

> I wonder where Evelyn Nesbit's mother is, and what she is doing these days, while her little, foolish, light-hearted girl is wading deeper and deeper out into the dark waters of grief.
> Where was she when he daughter went into the life that meant shame and misery—comfortably at home in her easy chair?[21]

Given her scant treatment of Nesbit and the lack of sympathy and sentiment in these depictions, Black certainly doesn't deserve the appellation of sob sister. And Cobb, in fact, created piteous descriptions of Nesbit, as did William Hoster, who provided daily front-page coverage of the trial for both the *New York Journal* and the *San Francisco Examiner*. Hoster created many piteous descriptions of Nesbit, like the following:

> Throwing aside all modesty and pride, sinking every feeling to woman dear, bearing her bleeding heart to the world—Evelyn Nesbit Thaw flung wide open the book of her tragic life, that all might read.
> A tremendous sacrifice, and a soul-crushing story.
> But in the hour of deepest woe the girl wife of Harry Kendall Thaw has the consolation, which will be all sufficient to her broken heart,—she has probably saved the life of her husband.[22]

As one of the four at this famous trial that resulted in labeling women reporters as irrational and sloppy, Black spoke out against this label. Indeed, she declared, "I am not a 'Sob-Sister' or a special writer. I'm just a plain, practical all-around newspaper woman. That is my profession and that is my pride."[23] Her distaste for such a label was also noted in one of the long eulogies printed after her death in the *Examiner*: "Annie Laurie earned her standing and fame by rising through the ranks 'the hard way.' She earned the title of reporter by an impressive series of 'beats' where men reporters had failed, and she cherished that title as much as she detested being called, in the slang of the trade a 'sob sister.'"[24]

Other women journalists reiterated Black's judgment of the sob-sister label. Mary Margaret McBride, at the New York *Evening Mail* in the 1920s, said about the sob sister that she "loathed the title and fumed inwardly every time one of the men use it, which they did, far too often." When she came to the *Mail*, as she recalled, "it was nearly a year before I broke out of my sob sister ghetto to get a real assignment."[25] Agness Underwood, who worked as a reporter for newspapers in Los Angeles from 1928 to 1968, maintained in her autobiography that "I've never sobbed a story in my life. I'm a reporter." Indeed, when someone thought that Underwood might be weeping about a female murderer's guilty verdict, she maintained that "as for weeping, I was too busy to think about hydraulics. I wanted to get to the phone with the verdict and the quotes, and I did."[26]

Long before the Thaw trial, and repeatedly afterwards, Black warned about a tendency of men and women to get too emotionally involved with crime and criminals, avoiding the facts to choose an attractive hero: she certainly did not depict herself as involved in this sobbing trend. In an 1894 article entitled "'Annie Laurie' on Murdermania," using the specific case of a man who had killed a cashier during a bank robbery, she speaks about women who become enthralled with murderers, writing to them, sympathizing with them or feeling a sexual attraction, women with the leisure to do so and thus, Black claims, not working women. These people are "silly creatures ... repulsive to sensible people ... utterly lacking in common sense and common decency." "When a woman begins to sentimentalize about a thief," she continues, "when she sends flowers to a criminal and calls a murderer 'poor boy,' it is time for someone to ring up the patrol wagon."[27]

In an article from 1912 about women's ability to serve on juries, she considered the frequently repeated claim that the majority of women were too illogical and hysterical, like sob sisters reporting on a trial, to take on that key legal role: "Unreasonable, unfair, emotional, the sweetest, dearest, loveliest, most charming little things in the world, but oh! So swayed by trifles." Such accusations being unworthy of her attention, she turns to all-male juries and their illogical verdicts, discussing a case in which a woman swayed a jury into acquitting her even though she was clearly guilty of shooting her invalid husband in the back. This woman sent flowers to the jury foreman, Black claims in this piece about men entitled "The Illogical Sex," and the jury members fell for her campaign of flirtation and beauty, proving themselves emotional and "swayed by trifles."[28] Women jurors might have proven more logical.

Again in 1918, reviewing a case that involved piteous moments as had the Thaw trial, Black speaks against jurors and reporters who sympathized with a woman who got mad at her boyfriend and killed him, the verdict having been not guilty. Black recognizes that this woman had employed emotion on the stand as a manipulative form of defense: "She was young and rather pretty and her eyes were large and soulful, and she wore a modest and becoming little frock and a discreet hat during the trial, and whenever it was time to cry, she cried, with telling effect." Here Black claims that if women had been on the jury, the verdict would have been different. But men had a very difficult time voting guilty for women, she continues, especially those who were young and beautiful or older and maternal. Concerning the young woman employing the soulful eyes, she comments here that women pay a price in self-respect and the respect of others by availing themselves of such an opportunity. And then she turns to "we" to state how the majority of women seek to be viewed: "We don't want to be judged as if we belonged to another race. We're human beings first, and after that we're women, and after that we are either wives or mothers or sisters or daughters." But she recognizes that though the "we" of women know that they are human beings first, that many men don't recognize this equal status, in part because of the type of behavior that this woman employed to avoid a guilty verdict.[29]

In her writing further, Black critiqued piteous responses to crimes, simplistic sympathetic reactions especially to the women involved. In "No Double Standard of Justice," from April of 1915, she critiques sentimental, irrational support for women who may be guilty, on the part of journalists as well as women's clubs. Here, at the article's beginning, she indicates that she is siding with Helen Ring Robinson, a state senator from Colorado and "a woman of sense." The case being discussed here involves a woman in New York who poisoned her two children, angry that their father, married to someone else, would not leave his new wife. "Half of New York went into sentimental hysterics," Black claims, in support of a woman that she labels sarcastically as a "poor, persecuted martyr." In not extending such mindless sympathy, Robinson, Black maintains, was creating a warning needed "every time the public is nauseated by the story of some woman, old in crime and skilled in ill-doing, who murders her 'betrayer' and then escapes the punishment that is justly hers because the women's clubs rally around her and demand mercy for the poor, trembling victim of 'man's perfidy.'" The women supporting this criminal, who call themselves feminists, Black continues, think that they are thus advocating for the advancement of women, but they certainly are not: "Honest women do not need sentimental sympathy to keep them out of jail." Robinson will do more good in the Senate, Black goes further by declaring, than "any half dozen sentimental feminists who ever deluged a continent with tears over the fate of a self-confessed murderer."[30]

In this article as in many others, Black is clearly opposing "sob sister" sympathy, an irrational presentation in opposition to the facts, of which she was accused of in the Thaw case. Her use of a persona, characters, or scene in covering a trial or any other story, she repeatedly claimed, did not make her naïve or hysterical. The writer of the best nonfiction attempted to describe and analyze various forms of persuasion and weakness and perversion, not to be taken in by them.

## The Real Job of the Writer

While Black often wrote about what women as journalist was not, about the often prejudiced depictions of stunts or sobbing or recipes that denied the more pertinent aspects of their work and their contribution to the community, she also frequently depicted the career in a much more positive tone. She did not view herself as less for being a woman, or for being a daily journalist instead of a novelist, did not think of herself as a stunt girl or a sob sister or as just an advice column writer but as a writer of nonfiction, making a difference in her nation. Indeed, as her career advanced, she also viewed herself as a teacher or mentor, explicating the realities of her occupation and helping others to make a success at it.

Frequently in her columns, she depicted writing not as a distant choice, as a surprise or oddity, but as what some women and men, like those she met in Ada's circle of friends when she was a teenager and like her relative Emily Chubbuck (Fanny Forrester), were doing to support themselves and their families. In 1912, addressing women and men practically, she asserted that "writers are no different than anyone else. They write to make money, most of them. Why shouldn't they?" These artists, like musicians and painters, generally had themes that they wanted to pursue—and they could make a living doing so.[31] Black also frequently wrote about the opportunities especially for women to enter this profession and spoke directly to them: "It's one of the greatest professions in the world, so why wouldn't you be in it, if you like it and have ability for it? How are you going to find out about it? It's very simple. Put on your hat and coat and walk down to the nearest newspaper office and ask to see the City Editor. When you do see him tell him you're looking for a job, and if he has a job, and likes your looks, and finds you promising, he'll give you a chance. And then all you have to do is take orders—and obey them."[32]

As she guides women who might be entering the career, Black recognizes that they might feel that they were supposed to gush, concentrating on flowers and sunshine, even in writing not destined for the women's page. One article speaks to women as writers, offering specific advice on avoiding such silliness: "Don't say anything about the daisies that grew in the grass near the cesspool—we've talked too much about the daisies as it is. Don't mention the blue sky that rolls a glorious arch—even above the cesspool." Instead a writer must delve into realities and crises, what she calls the horrors of daily living: "Keep to the horrors—they're much more interesting than anything so commonplace as flowers and grass, and sunshine and floating clouds." She speaks of the delight contained in frank, unsentimental talk about life and the abandonment of the propriety and modesty that might especially restrict women writers: "Away with propriety! Down with reserve! To the woods with modesty! To the winds with dignity! Let's all be as frank as monkeys. Romance, poetry, beauty? Pooh! What do they amount to, anyhow?"[33]

In many columns, Black turns her attention from what nonfiction should not be to the best possibilities for it, not a sentimental or naïve approach to the realities of life but a detailed look at who Americans really are. "Why do I write of the ever-recurring storm of life, in ancient ballad or modern newspaper story?" she asks as she describes American soldiers in Europe, and her answer concerns the eternal draw of stories, the call to enter other lives. She claims that tales of individuals at the current moment, not just the basic facts of battles or treaties, are as compelling as those of any other era: "All around us men and women are living stories as full of interest as the tales of troubadours."³⁴

As she constructed herself as an authority on nonfiction, Black continually depicted the skilled writer as looking at everything closely—and only then moving to larger judgments. In one of her many articles about writing, she contrasts writing grounded in specifics with writing that delivers generalities or philosophical truths without reference to what is really going on. Here she claims that a young male reporter touring with the Salvation Army misses what is actually happening because he doesn't see the details. All he comes back with is what he wanted to think, based on generalities about his own prejudices concerning this group—and he went on to a career as a pharmacist, not as a writer. Indeed, she comments further, the editors who tried to work with him began to use their response to his article to describe other vague essays turned in to them: "He left out the bass drum."³⁵

In her articles about writing, Black also spoke about the specific details that form the best nonfiction, often in advice that she gave to young writers: "Have you been to the hospital for an operation? Begin at the beginning and tell all about it from the minute you felt that 'kind of sinking feeling' to the instant you came out of the ether. Describe the surgeon's knife, tell how the ether smells and minutely detail everything the nurse did for you and what you wanted her to do and she wouldn't and what she wanted to do and you wouldn't let her. All these things are fascinating in the extreme and they are so frank and honest and real—don't forget that." In her instruction for completing vacation essays for the children's page, she taught even the youngest writers to move from details to larger issues: "how big the trout was you caught—of course you'll measure him with great care before you send in his dimensions—and then whether you really like camping out and fishing better than living in a house with a comfortable bed."³⁶

In the confusing world of "facts," Black thought that writers of any age needed to be open to whatever they found, and she constructed herself as not naïve or sentimental but as determined to look closely and fairly at what she found. In 1915, concerning an evangelical group that other reporters made fun of, she claims that she tried to examine what they believed and what they did. She thus creates a space for herself as less jaded or cruel or close-minded, though as fully capable of analytical judgment as any other reporter.³⁷

Given the contradictions involved in what might be happening at any particular site, Black also wrote about the power of the writer in interpreting facts, in figuring out some part of modern reality and stating a thesis about it. In "A Woman among the Fighters," an article concerning a prize fight held in Mexico in February of 1896, Black describes the changing nature of truth, asserting that the writer must negotiate within an uncertain space to discern what is actually going on, a fact of nonfiction at its most basic and powerful. She begins to consider this particular subject matter in her subtitle: "The Trip 'Over the River' to Kill Time—Contradictory Rumors." To discuss the journalist's making of truth, Black begins the piece simply, in the first person: "Yesterday I went over the river. It's the thing to do in El Paso now." In this area unknown to her, she describes all the rumors that "they" hear and "you" hear, involving whether the governor of Chihuahua plans to ignore local statutes, let this fight go on, and "send his men on the wrong scent" or whether he will have "every spectator shot on sight." As far as she can discover in a short time, the fight manager is either a "hoodoo" or "as straight as a die." When Black gets back to El Paso, she hears rumors that the fight is going to occur at midnight in Juarez—or not. And she recognizes that the writer ultimately has to decide among all of these choices and that her rendition may well be accepted as fact.

## Nonfiction versus Fiction

In her columns, Black often contrasted what nonfiction could deliver to readers with what could be gained from fiction. In an article in 1919, she writes about a man in Los Angeles, Harry New, accused of murdering his girlfriend, Freda Lesser; he excused his crime by citing an amazing array of difficulties that he had overcome, and he falsely accused a senator from Indiana, who coincidentally had the same last name, of being the father who had abandoned him. In this piece, Black compared fiction with the great oddities of life itself, the jarring combinations of place and act: "We smile sometimes in our superior, worldly knowledge at the melodramas we see upon the screen and at the stories we read. No melodrama ever played and no story ever written is stranger than the strange tale which has come to light right here in the placid beauty of Los Angeles—a setting fit for nothing but contentment, peace and happy life."[38]

As she compared various genres and developed many individual profiles through interviews and other research, Black wrote about fiction as less complex and honest than accounts of real lives. She noted in 1922, for example, that in many modern novels the women characters seem independent, living apart from their dull parents and making their own way, but in the end they all get married to rich men and get fancy accessories. She writes that she wants to read real novels about real heroines, but she also claims that nonfiction can tell a more complicated story than does most fiction.[39]

In 1922 also, Black claimed that so many plays concerned women with a past, always slinking in and out, sexual beings involved with men they should have stayed away from. Instead, she claims, the actual woman works within the present, with a future that she is always planning for and that she will achieve. Black advocates here for women not to dwell on imaginary worlds but to carefully examine their own changing situations, aided by knowledge of an array of lives examined through nonfiction.[40]

Throughout her work, Black repeatedly claims that women need to study various realities, accessed through travel and experience perhaps, but also through writing and reading nonfiction. Only with such wide knowledge could they make the best decisions. "It is a rather complicated business, this being a woman," she claims in a newspaper column in 1915, "and it takes up a good deal of time and energy, just seeing to that."[41] "It's all on yourself—this business of living," she wrote in 1923. Here she cites the restricted definitions of women found in most tragedy, comedy, and farce and asks readers about the fuller sort of life that they might seek for themselves: this fuller life might begin in considering nonfiction renditions of the real choices made by real women.[42]

From the beginning of her career, Winifred Black took women seriously as readers and as writers. They needed a voice concerning the content of the entire newspaper as well as a separate women's page. As she wrote about women's abilities to record the details and make the judgments that might appear in all parts of the newspaper, she considered the women's page as a site from which to learn investigation and creative style. Similarly, the stunt-girl pose could enable a woman to conduct investigations that might provide a service to community and to the nation. In no format, including writing about criminals and trials, should women writers rely solely on sentiment; in any situation, they needed to record what occurred and evaluate all participants. As she constructed herself as a "plain, practical all-around newspaper woman," she assumed the right and responsibility to create a metadiscourse about the work itself, to help readers understand the value of creative nonfiction that addressed an array of topics, through techniques moving far beyond who, what, and where. Readers and writers of both genders needed to be fully aware of the importance of specific details, skillfully delivered, in examining the full picture of what people could be and do.

# 7

# A Complex Persona

Winifred Black assumed the right to define her own career, critique American writing, and forge her own style in years in which newspaper writing was becoming more formulaic. As the yellow journalism era came to an end, as the work of stunt girls or sob sisters began to look like silly excess, women who found jobs at newspapers, and they did so in larger numbers, were mostly relegated to the women's page with a few securing the training to join the male reporters of highly structured front-page news. But Black, at Hearst papers as well as so many others across the country reached by syndication, had a unique form of access to the front page, the editorial page, the magazine section, the feature section, and the women's page, where she developed a nonfiction voice with ever increasing authority. Throughout her career, Black continued not just to discuss what the writer did but to develop the techniques that would suddenly be re-invented by New Journalists in the 1960s. After receiving her first lessons from at the *Examiner*, on engaging the "gripman on the Powell Street line," Black excelled at an array of creative choices, the first among them her creation of a sympathetic, determined, professional—and changing—narrative persona.

## Engaging Readers with the Progress of the Investigator

As one of her key techniques, from her days as a presumed stunt girl and all through her career, Black involved readers in the process of investigation, taking them along with her as researcher. Black thus makes clear the power of determined action for reader and writer, involving moments and places that they would otherwise not understand, the result being a much fuller picture of life. Like Truman Capote in *In Cold Blood* and Barbara Ehrenreich in *Nickel and Dimed: On (Not) Getting By in America*, Black brings readers to the scene along with herself as investigator, a narrator as character leading and accompanying the reader.

In many of her pieces, Black writes about the work that the articles involved, speaking of herself as writer and for the process of nonfiction discovery. In "Preparing for Work" from March of 1890, Black discusses the life of Sister Rose Gertrude, the "English martyr" with "the most unquestioning faith I ever heard of," who had secured medical training in England before dedicating herself to a leper colony in Hawaii. Black writes about their difficult trip to Hawaii and the ordeal involved in getting the Board of Health to let them go to Molokai, an island surrounded by the highest sea cliffs in the world that housed this colony. When Rose Gertrude asks Black to go first and help set up a new clinic, she seeks to go alone, without the official group, knowing that harsh winds will make landing difficult. To involve readers, she includes dialogue with officials trying to discourage her from planning to hire guides and cross the difficult terrain if the ship indeed can land:

> "They will have to climb eight or nine miles over the mountain. It is too steep to go on horseback. When you get to the top of the range there is a long and difficult ride after that."
> "There isn't any other way to get there now, is there?" I asked.
> "No," was the reply.
> "Then I'll have to go that way, I suppose," I remarked calmly.
> "But—," he began.
> "May I go?"
> "Yes, but—"
> I stayed to hear no more objections, thanked him for his warnings and departed. To-morrow I start on my journey.[1]

As Black starts out the next day, the reader accompanies her, and then in subsequent articles learns about the arrival of Sister Rose Gertrude, the subject changing from the determination that it took to get there to what living among people with leprosy would require, Black's voyage, accompanied by the reader, providing the impetus for all that follows.

The determination of the reporter could enable the reader not just to enter the inaccessible place but also to meet people who otherwise would remain misunderstood or unknown. In 1894, Black writes about going to a ranch in San Diego County, where an author had sequestered herself from the press. Beatrice Harraden, British writer and suffragist, had published a debut novel in 1893, the best-seller *Ships That Pass in the Night*, and then had withdrawn from public life, with rumors circulating about why she had gone into hiding. In this piece, Black stresses the effort that this different sort of voyage required: "It's a good long way to go and everyone said I wouldn't see her when I got there, but I went. They told me down in San Diego that Miss Harraden was very reserved, and that she would not listen to the idea of being interviewed for one moment. I found out where the ranch was and where the railroad station nearest to the ranch was, and I started out."[2] Through the effort exerted to get there, Black engages readers in secrets to be discovered, in the real story of this writer that they will soon learn.

In bringing readers into natural crises, like cyclones and earthquakes, Black often began with what she had to do to get there and get the story. She started her first article on the hurricane at Galveston in September of 1900, for example, by describing her determination to be the first reporter on the scene: "I begged, cajoled and cried my way through the lines of soldiers with drawn swords who guard the wharf at Texas City and sailed across the bay on a little boat which is making irregular trips to meet the relief trains from Houston."[3] As she further describes the scene that would necessitate her tenacity and guile, she writes that "I found it almost as easy to get into Galveston just then as to Mars. Galveston was under martial law. No one was allowed to enter but the marshal and his men. Houston was packed with sensation seekers and sightseers, and those wild birds that follow every sort of storm like a kind of human stormy petrel, the newspapermen. All trying every kind of expedient to get into Galveston. The tracks were under water. There were no boats running from the mainland, and the police were on the job." Ultimately, as she reports, she got on the train by dressing as a male construction worker: "I wore a long linen duster, a boy's cap, and a pair of boy's shoes, and carried a pick on my somewhat inadequate shoulder. I did the best I could to imitate a manly swagger."[4]

As she investigated and transported her readers, she often engaged them further by expressing her own shock over what she found, her own surprise and interest thus engaging theirs. Concerning a clearinghouse in San Francisco where bank representatives met each day, she begins with her own amazement over what she observed in a secluded space inhabited by powerful money men:

I have seen over three million dollars change hands.
Not read about it on a bulletin-board of the races, or heard betting men talk of it—seen it, actually seen it. It was stupefying.
Three million dollars! Three million—why, when I was a little girl they used to tell me that it would take me just one month to make a million dots on a sheet of paper.
It all happened in the Clearinghouse.[5]

In writing about crime and criminals, instead of relying on emotional sobbing, Black often employed this technique of bringing readers into a new or frightening scene by involving them in the work of the researcher. In 1919, in an article concerning the trial of Harry New for killing Freda Lesser, she speaks to her readers about the murderers that she has interviewed and the traits that they all shared: "egotism, self will, unrestrained passions, willful self-indulgence." And she backs up her analysis of these killers as sociopaths, a term not yet in use but matching her list, by describing what she learned by entering prisons and interviewing these men:

> I have in the course of my experience sat up all night with fourteen different people the night before each one was executed, and always, and always, I have been stunned by the indifference and the trivialities of the hour.
>
> In one cell's strange creature they called the "wolf," because of a sneering habit that raised his upper lip and made his teeth gleam white, as gleam the teeth of wolves—he sat all night and played the accordion and smiled to himself. In another cell was rather a distinguished looking middle-aged American—he played pinochle all night with his jailors.[6]

Through the years, concerning crime and many other subjects, with her byline and picture presenting her as an individual known to readers, Black constructed herself as a determined writer, not just crafting a few wild stunts, but repeatedly taking readers where they otherwise could not go. Her courage and her hard work often on display, she appeared as a writer worthy of trust, who could get the full story, the risks she took not for entertainment but for the public's knowledge.

## A Changing Biography and Perspective

Throughout her career, Black depicted herself as a character, out getting the news and reacting to it. In constructing a persona, like David Foster Wallace, Maxine Hong Kingston, Maya Angelou, and many other writers of later generations, she employed not only the basic facts of her career as an investigator but other biographical facts, at various levels of truth and lie, creating a quasi-autobiographical narrator who could serve as a guide to many realities, a key element also in Tom Wolfe's New Journalism. She gave herself a set of strong and changing traits: given the needs of any individual story, she might appear as brave or frightened, as old-fashioned or modern, as right or wrong in her judgments, all carefully chosen attributes intended to enable readers to examine their own prejudices and preferences as they encountered new information.

In some columns, for various rhetorical purposes, her personal details certainly violated the facts of her life. In a column entitled "The Joy of Children" from 1913, on children as so much more than a duty, for example, she comments on her own mother's ongoing dedication—as though her mother were still alive. And in an advice column on October 14, 1918, concerning the importance of doing war work, she talks about having two brothers in France with wives both working for the government when neither of her brothers was actually there.[7]

In her columns, besides creating autobiographical facts, she often presented a nostalgic and simple version of herself, perhaps a sweeter Winifred Black. As one of a group of writers asked to choose the greatest women in the world, for example, she nominates not the famous but her own country school teacher: an invalid minister's wife who opened a school to support her husband and children. As she writes nostalgically and a bit facetiously, "We all went to it—all the queer, little, half-formed, half-savage creatures we called children in those days and there in that little village."[8] In another column, she writes about her memory of playing kissing games, focusing on the little embarrassments of such moments throughout childhood.[9] In such renditions in which she speaks for family life while examining the sillinesses of youth, she creates for herself an old-fashioned, secure childhood, without reference to being born during the Civil War, with her father in Chicago, her mother struggling with a large family and insufficient means.

While she could create a sweeter, simpler childhood for herself, she could also bring readers into the raw pains of her own adult life. One of her columns in 1917 concerns a woman whose husband had kept her from friends and family while he viewed himself as quite free to do whatever he liked. When she finally left, he wanted her back and she wouldn't have him: she was "no longer sorry, no longer melancholy, no longer bitter, no longer even cynical"—and no longer rendered helpless by the madness of love. And here Black comments about herself, perhaps alluding to her first marriage to Orlow Black or her second marriage to Charles Bonfils: "The ancients were right when they called love a madness. If I could have only realized it in time, if I could have only known, how much suffering I could have saved myself."[10]

Black also very rarely wrote about the death of a child, her son Eugene Napoleon, ill all of his life, having died at age nine. In *Roses and Rain*, in 1920, she writes about birds in the garden that come and go, beautiful and for a short time, like the little boy who had gone away:

> The little boy who lived with us in our little home is gone, too, and it is very lonely in our hearts without him.
> How selfish it is to wish to bring him back and lock up the eager brightness of his joyous soul in that restricted cage we call the human body.
> Fly on, free spirit. Do not linger here to share with us our sorrows and our grief, our little earthly hopes and fears and anxieties and disappointments.[11]

While Black used her biography to engage readers in an earlier or simpler life and in the pain and struggles of the now, she also involved them in varying elements of her own personality, used persuasively to engage readers. In many columns, she portrayed herself as quite able to make strong judgments that she expected readers to consider and respect. She often described a situation in detail and then stepped back to evaluate quite harshly and boldly, as in several pieces about coping with in-laws. In an article about a mother-in-law who is using up a young couple's money and causing dissention by expressing her distaste for the wife every day, Black employs this technique as she analyzes the situation: "I would not live under the same roof with any human being who disliked me so bitterly—not if that human being were a hundred times my wife's mother. Dislike and anger are as deadly a poison as cyanide of potassium, and I'd just as soon drink carbolic acid for breakfast and be done with it as to take the coffee which had been made for me by one who hates me and wants to make me unhappy."[12] In another column about living with an angry sister-in-law, Black again speaks frankly: "I'd move to a shed and live on bread and water before I'd live in the house with anyone I really disliked, even if I had the use of a motor and a butler thrown in for my pains."[13]

In this frank mode, as in these in-law columns, Black generally stresses that she would stand up for herself and that other women should do so. When in one column she dealt with the question of whether a woman should tell a friend that her husband was cheating on her, she replies that it depended on the answers to key questions: Did the woman have pride and self-respect or was she just someone who was dying to be married? What kind of man was the husband? Could the wife support her children and would the friend help her? Then she speaks strongly about her own preferences and character: "What would I want you to do for me in such a case as that? I would want you to tell me and to tell me quick. I don't want to waste my life 'pretending.' I'd rather live alone on a desert island with the buzzards for company than to pour my heart out to one who deceived me—I'd rather scrub floors for a living than to take one penny from a man who couldn't tell me the truth, the whole truth, and nothing but the truth."[14] Here she strongly argues that her readers, also, should want to know the truth about their spouses and to take action if necessary.

## Needing the Reader's Help

In considering and evaluating various behavioral choices, Black also indicates that she is capable of making the wrong choices, that she needs the readers' help to correct her thinking, and thus the readers and writer should unite in analysis and change. Indeed, she often uses an exaggerated, humorous tone to include herself with those who might make a too critical judgment of other people, and especially of the young. In a column from February 1914, her thesis is that the new activities of the young, like dancing the tango, do not necessarily indicate anything negative about them: "It isn't the tango, but the girl who dances it." And then she turns to herself forcefully, at age fifty-one, as someone hoping to avoid the judgmental tendencies that can occur with age: "When I get too old to love the lilt of a laughing tune, when I get too wicked to enjoy the sight of a room full of gay people dancing gaily—I hope someone will be kind enough to take me out and chloroform me."[15]

Black often did not just admit that she might make wrong-headed choices but created situations in which she dramatized herself doing so. In a column from 1915, about a sister-in-law, she encourages readers to look at their own weaknesses as she dramatizes a lack of awareness of her own:

> What an extravagant girl sister-in-law is! That dress she wore must have cost a fortune—and hats! I never see her in the same hat more than four times. I'm going to make two hats do me for the season, and I simply won't wear one of these barrel effects that are coming in now.
> I've invited the Twinkies to tea at the smart tea room that's just opened and, afterward, we're going to the theatre, and then we'll have a bite—something simple, mushrooms under glass, and a bird perhaps. Extravagant? I?[16]

She here thus involves readers in considering the harsh judgments in which we choose not to include ourselves.

Black's own doubts and fears could also be her means of drawing readers into a threatening scene, like the aftermath of a hurricane or cyclone. As she describes her first entrance into the housing for people with leprosy on Molokai, she admits to being frightened: "I confess I played the coward. I tried my best to screw up my courage, but do what I would I felt strangely faint-hearted." In the dormitories, what she encounters is "hopeless misery." In comparison to the nun she accompanied, these isolated people "are not upheld by the ecstasy of martyrdom." After admitting to being afraid and refusing to depict the experience of ill people or visits with them as simplistically uplifting, she quotes the families there, discussing marriages, children, food, and activities, her readers thus facing their own fears as they enter other lives.[17]

Along with admitting her own insecurities and thus involving readers in the danger and uncertainty of a new situation, Black also reveals her own serious errors in judgment, those shared perhaps by a majority of her readers, her recognition of her own mistakes intended to encourage them to reevaluate. When she writes about going to England, in 1910, to meet with radical suffragists, she admits that she had been critical of their attacks on property, labeling their militancy as both unseemly and unnecessary. In England, where women had no right of divorce unless a man was both physically violent and adulterous, where they could not assert legal control over their own children, as Black realizes during her visit, suffragists in five years had brought the vote for women from a impossibility to a impending reality, and they had done so to insure the basic rights of women and of children. "They are the most seriously, desperately in earnest human beings I ever saw or ever expect to see," she realizes, and, like revolutionary war soldiers, they are ready to die for their cause. And the more she learned about their struggles with police and their treatment in jail, beyond the radical stereotypes played upon in the American news, the more she "remembered all the cheap wit I had laughed over at the expense of these women with the shining faces and the proud lift of the head, and I hung my head and felt ashamed."[18] Like Black, her readers might also reevaluate why these English suffragists took risks and what they sought to achieve.

In her creation of a nonfiction opus, Black took advantage of many possibilities inherent in the narrator as character, as Tom Wolfe would also emphasize in his discussion of New Journalism. She always insisted on being judged as an experienced and skilled writer but she could also rely on various sorts of autobiographical details outside of her work as a journalist, describing a nostalgic childhood, for example, or the loss of a child, to affect her readers. She also donned a variety of personal traits, assuming an authoritative tone but also bringing readers into her own fears, uncertainties, and mistaken judgments, to involve them and seek change.

# 8

# *An Array of Nonfiction Techniques*

In her articles written for publication in San Francisco and across the country, Winifred Black constructed herself as an authoritative writer whose work appropriately appeared throughout the newspaper. In every section for which she wrote with increasing freedom, she constructed her job as involving readers in the specifics of a situation; thus they join her in the thrill and difficulty—and the importance—of conducting research and using it to evaluate modern life. Along with a complex persona, which Black could deploy to achieve various goals, she developed an array of techniques that moved readers beyond the plain facts of who, what, and where as they learned about new spaces and people, her work involving vivid forms of nonfiction that many writers employ today.

## Startling Leads

In opinion columns and more traditional news pieces, instead of opening with the basic facts of the case, Black often chose a shocking opener. Kathryn Harrison begins *The Kiss,* her story of a sexual relationship with her father, with "We meet in airports. We meet in cities where we've never been before. We meet where no one will recognize us."[1] Here she uses sentences with similar beginnings to increase the readers' interest and their confusion, to thus bring them into a perplexing situation. Winifred Black used a variety of untraditional leads to similarly encourage readers to keep reading and to consider the new and complex.

Black often chose the shocking short sentence that would bring readers into the piece but also make them think about cultural values. With "The perfect bride is dead," for example, she begins an article concerning a woman who committed suicide when her supposedly perfect marriage, what she envisioned as an happily-ever-after dream, metamorphosed into an intolerably dull reality. This beginning leads to ruminations on the unrealistic expectations that many women bring into marriage and on the facts of actual adult life.[2]

Black's quick beginnings could also involve a change to a well-known stereotype. In a column about May/December romances and her judgment that such relationships generally do not work, she provides no special commentary concerning the fact that the woman in the story is the older spouse.[3] "She's sixty, and he's twenty-eight," the piece begins, and moves on to differences of interests, the probability that the younger spouse will be lured away by younger friends, and the fact that if money or security or ego caused the decision to say yes, both parties have made a mistake. The gender switch, from the more common situation, points to the inappropriateness of all such choices.

Black also often used a thought-provoking numerical lead to bring readers into her research:

> There are 1,356 convicts in San Quentin. Out of this 1,356, fourteen are women.
> I wonder what that means.
> I went across the bay one bright, bright morning last week on purpose to see those fourteen women and to find out something behind the great stone walls of the penitentiary.[4]

In this essay, she then goes surprisingly into the beautiful environs—the green hills, yellow wild flowers, sunshine, and singing breeze outside of the prison—to move readers from the male convict to the female and then from a natural world that they would recognize to an unnatural one that they won't. In an article about juvenile courts overwhelmed by offenders, Black opened with statistics to acquaint readers with a recently worsening trend and then moved from numbers to the faces of these young girls:

> Twenty per cent of the thieves and burglars of Chicago are under eighteen years of age. Twenty-five per cent of the criminals of Denver, Colorado, are children. In St. Louis it is twelve per cent and in Kansas City ten per cent, of the criminal population who are boys and girls.
> Ten years ago it was an exceptional experience to see a girl much under eighteen years old earning her living in the cruel street. It is no longer anything out of the ordinary to find girls of eight, nine, and even seven years of age whose pitiful little faces are seared as with a burning iron, with shameful wisdom.[5]

A surprising lead could also bring readers not just to a place they had never been but into a situation occurring right in front of them, which they may have avoided actually seeing, as when she goes out to investigate the use of opium, cocaine, and morphine on San Francisco streets:

> The Street of the Living Dead—it sounds as if it were a good ways off—doesn't it?
>
> It isn't.
>
> It begins not one block from Market st., just half a block from Lotta's Fountain—to be exact. Yesterday I went down there, and what I saw in the open street in two short, hideous hours will haunt me, waking or sleeping, as long as my heart can beat and my brain remember.[6]

Here beginning with the question indicates that readers will learn about a reality much closer by than "a good ways off."

Besides beginning with the riveting fact or question, Black uses phrases that readers will know to engage them in the surprising content that will follow. She uses a line from "Little Bo Peep," for example, to open a column about the time missing from a man who nearly drowned: "Arthur George Goddard lost twelve hours out of his life last week and he doesn't know where to find them." At the end, after focusing on resuscitation and the mysteries of the brain, she repeats her opening line: "And that is how Arthur George Goddard lost twelve hours of his life and does not know where to find them."[7]

Beyond clever or shocking individual sentences, Black often begins with a specific instance to draw readers into a larger situation. Her 1910 article in Hearst's *Cosmopolitan* about the suffrage campaign in England, for example, starts with one woman's desperate plight:

> John Smith, of East Cheapside, London, went home one Saturday night a few weeks ago, and beat his wife. Also he beat his children. John Smith's wife didn't mind a regular beating—she was used to that. Except once, she had never missed a good beating on a Saturday night since the time her husband found out, about three weeks after they were married, what a lot of fun it was to see a woman crouch on the floor and cry and beg for mercy.[8]

During the most recent beating, Black continues, this woman fainted and couldn't beg for mercy because she had given birth five days earlier; facing no opposition, the husband kept on beating her and the baby too. The district visitor, a suffragette, called the police and caused the case to go to court, where the husband received a sentence of just ten days and went right home afterwards. Black develops the essay further by explaining that on the next day, for walking in a suffrage procession, this home visitor was cruelly treated by the police, laughed at by the crowd, and sentenced to three months in jail where she stayed in a dirty room, not allowed to see anyone, and was force fed. Black thus opens the piece by depicting the real plight of an individual woman without rights before moving to the sacrifice many women were making to alter this reality.

Black used many varieties of startling leads to encourage readers to come along with her into a new territory and thus gain a new and different appreciation of people and places. Instead of opening with basic facts, as in the traditional news format, she often began by drawing readers in.

## Challenges to Experts

Another technique that Black often employed may have originated in her stunt-girl beginnings. Concerning Nellie Bly's depiction of doctors who declared her insane on the streets of New York and on Blackwell Island, Jean-Marie Lutes claims in *Front-Page Girls* that Bly "countered an expert discourse that often disempowered women." By the late nineteenth century, Lutes explains further, "legitimate authority now resided in special spaces, like the courtroom, the classroom, and the hospital; and it resided in special words shared only by experts." Bly felt that such judgments, on women's health, labor, and civil rights, should be tested, and the journalist had the public responsibility to provide that test.[9] Throughout her career, not just in her first *Examiner* articles, Winifred Black exploited experts, generally male, to get her readers to reevaluate accepted judgments of both women and men. Certainly many later writers of nonfiction, in books as different as Ralph Ellison's *Shadow and Act*, Nora Ephron's *Crazy Salad: Some Things About Women*, and Malcolm Gladwell's *David and Goliath: Underdogs, Misfits, and the Art of Battling Giants,* structured their arguments by countering authorities or "giants," like those that curtail the freedom of African Americans, women, and Gladwell's grouping of "misfits."

Black often presents the judgments of experts at the beginning of her articles, using them as straw men against whom to place herself and her readers, her group portrayed as sensible, as not swayed by the latest of crazy theories or the oldest of prejudices. Black often directly disparages male experts who assume that they know more than generations of women and men about child rearing, education, and marriage. In article after article, she especially employs humor to expose such pomposity and miscalculation. She quotes experts quickly, not always with full citation, and even speaks to them directly, as to the idiot, before sharing her common-sense approach with the reader. One of her articles, about prescribing a family size, speaks the line that many others develop: "Do you gentlemen of the great theory never take time to stop reading and look around you at the people you know, or ought to know?"[10]

In her writing, Black was even willing to take on the best known of American experts. One of these, in 1917, was Dr. Harvey W. Wiley, an American chemist and doctor widely admired for urging passage of the landmark Pure Food and Drug Act of 1906, for serving as the first commissioner of the Food and Drug Administration, and for administering the Good Housekeeping Institute laboratories. Black begins one article by saying that Wiley had claimed in *Good Housekeeping*, in the article "The Housewife and the Eight-Hour Day," that a young woman could get and keep a husband by cooking well: she thus should not turn away from this basic, home-creating task of wives to take on any other responsibility.[11] Regardless of his reputation, Wiley becomes one of Black's ridiculous male experts to be disregarded or overruled, here through direct address: "Tell me truly, Dr. Wiley, do you and the rest of men really mean half of the astonishing things you say about yourselves? I hope not. I really do hope not." Wiley, Black claims, is depicting men as the lowest of animals, only concerned with eating, not with child raising, meaningful work, or love.[12] Wiley thus deserves criticism for his view of men as well as women—and Black and her readers have the right to admonish him.

In other articles, Black accepts some part of an expert's statements, but expects readers to be able to judge a situation more thoughtfully than this man. With the ironic subheading of "Women 'Way Behind!' Just Fancy That!" she states in 1928 that Professor Cody Marsh of George Washington University maintained that women had made no contribution to business, politics, and literature, Sappho being the one "possible exception." Black begins her own argument with a slightly angry reply, indicating that a particular woman must have hurt him and engendered this misogynous disgust for the entire gender: "Well, well, doctor, you surprise me, how sad you are about us! Whisper, I'd like to know who the woman is—but let's not be personal." Here Black readily agrees with the expert that women are not making as much money as men or securing the same level of public reputation. But, for Black, it isn't because of a lack of ability: the woman in business "has to swim against the tide every minute." And then Black continues to address Marsh as she further describes the American work culture that makes it difficult for women to succeed:

> Most of the men combine against her, not consciously perhaps, but listen, doctor, did you ever watch the expression on a man's face when a woman begins to talk about big money in a big way and it dawns upon him that she knows what she's saying. Tut, tut! You must have noticed it. I have—a hundred times. Men do not like women who are too successful in business—why should they? An independent woman is hard to manage.

Black ends here on a somewhat different note, claiming that women have many means of controlling men and that many men don't realize that they are being controlled—that perhaps the doctor has not quite comprehended modern realities.[13]

With her focus on moving quickly from the unacceptable as presented by experts to a more thoughtful viewpoint, Black often doesn't fully identify the experts whose claims she denies. In one article from 1923, for example, she writes that the president of a "great western university" had argued that there were too many women in college, with no clear reason for attending. She turns immediately from this vague attribution to all that college can do for women, who will be entering various professions with or without a thorough education. With woman suffrage as law across the country, Black claims further, states will not be able to deny women this basic right. Here the university president presents an older viewpoint, not worthy of much attention, one she immediately moves beyond.[14]

In many other articles, as Black moves assuredly forward, beyond a ridiculous claim, she assumes that the reader will naturally side with her, making the only sensible choice. In one column from 1912, she states an opinion quickly, that a reverend, a Dr. Brunner of Chicago, thinks people need to be taught courtship in high school. She immediately chides: "You don't say so, dear doctor; you don't say so in serious earnest and expect us to agree with you, honestly and truly now, doctor?" After discussing courtship as a natural occurrence between women and men, as a continuing part of families and communities, she ends with more ironic, critical questioning of the doctor, and a joke for the reader to enjoy: "Why don't you open a school and teach the frogs how to swim, professor?"[15]

Sometimes Black disparages the distant expert not just by critiquing his argument but by acquainting readers with personal details about him. She uses this format, for example, to oppose the eugenics movement. Early proponents of eugenics believed that, through selective breeding, the human species could direct its own evolution. Many of these scientists and the government officials influenced by them, who tended to believe in the genetic superiority of Nordic, Germanic and Anglo-Saxon peoples, supported strict immigration and anti-miscegenation laws and advocated for the forcible sterilization of the poor, disabled, and "immoral."[16] Black's article in July 1913 with the argumentative title "Some 'Unfit' Better for Humanity than the 'Fit,' Declares Writer" moves from "medical men" to one particular medical man, an unnamed speaker at an unnamed eugenics conference. She tells readers that she grew up with him and knows details that other eugenists might use to claim that he should have not been born: as a child, he had taken clocks apart and not put them back together correctly so perhaps he was not intelligent enough; his mother had tuberculosis so maybe he would become ill and not be sufficiently productive. In moving from the expert's words to his life, she points to the absurdity of this "scientific" means of separating the fit from the unfit.[17]

Sometimes Black goes from one false judgment of one male expert to men's general tendency to repeat and believe false judgments. In one article, she begins by considering a "gentleman who is called by his friends, and who loves to call himself, 'one who understands women.'" That is her takeoff place to write about all the old saws about women, like the old maid's plainness, oddity, and weird love of cats. In this article as in others, she ultimately responds sarcastically to all the expert's negative judgments, denouncing him as a misinformed, ironically described "wizard of a woman's heart," an apt target for the reader's derision.[18]

Another technique that Black often employed was to speak of experts not as being wrong but as laboring on and on to prove what every sensible person already knew. In one article about working women continually having to prove themselves on the job and then go home to all the housework, she begins with what "scientists" are proving about hours of work:

> Women's work is harder than men's—that's what the scientists are beginning to tell us.
>
> They weigh and measure and add and subtract and analyze and discuss—the scientists, and tell us something as a great piece of news—something that Grandma told Grandpa fifty or seventy-five years ago.
>
> And Grandpa never even thought of denying it.

Here the expert is right, but in Black's construction of history, generations of Americans have known these truths about women and men and families.

Though almost all of Black's rhetorically employed experts are men, and certainly they exercised institutional power in the nation, she also exploited the mistakes of a few women speakers, thus perhaps extending her reputation for fairness and common sense. Indeed, she sometimes labeled the nation's feminist leaders as experts going too far though she also signaled her agreement with much of what they argued. Charlotte Perkins Gilman, Black wrote in 1925, had asserted that men resemble little boys, a claim with which Black agrees: "Men do act like boys a lot of the time. They don't seem to grow up as women do." Here part of her evidence, like Gilman's, is that girls get past playing with paper dolls but grown men remain devoted to sports like baseball that they began playing as boys. Though she has gone this far with Gilman, Black then turns the piece to indicate that perhaps men have an approach to adulthood that women should consider. Perhaps women should also get away from their home and work duties and imitate men by finding a way to relax, returning to some of the joys of childhood. And she ends by indicating that the hysterics attributed to women, their supposed nervousness and unhappiness, might be relieved if they embraced what Gilman criticizes as men's lesser traits.[19] In this argument, she thus turns from the responsibility or seriousness that men may lack to the cost for women of taking on so much of it.

By constructing herself as a writer with the ability to counter the arguments of influential men and women, Black makes herself into a thoughtful interrogator, her writing the place to turn for an independent assessment of the authorities telling Americans that they should value one thing and not another, condemn one person and not another, such cultural and institutional decrees necessitating evaluation and not immediate acquiescence.

## Lists

Beyond the startling opener and the persuasive use of experts, Black often developed the nonfiction list, which Joan Didion would also make into a feature of her own writing, as in "On Going Home" from *Slouching towards Bethlehem*, in which she examines the contents of a drawer:

> A bathing suit I wore the summer I was seventeen. A letter of rejection from *The Nation,* an aerial photograph from the site of a shopping center that my father did not build in 1954. Three teacups handpainted with cabbage roses and signed "E.M," my grandmother's initials. There is no final solution for letters of rejection from *The Nation* and teacups handpainted in 1900. Nor is there any answer to snapshots of one's grandfather as a young man on skis, surveying around Donner Pass in the year 1910. I smooth out the snapshot and look into his face, and do and do not see my own. I close the drawer, and have another cup of coffee with my mother. We get along very well, veterans of a guerrilla war we never understood.[20]

The list allows Didion to review the unresolved memories encountered at her parents' home, her specifics revealing the complications of family. Such groupings, of noun phrases, verbs, or adjectives, helped Winifred Black to acquaint readers, through quickly stated specifics, with people and places that were new to them.

Black often relied on the quick list to provide descriptions of new places. In a *Cosmopolitan* article concerning tiny towns in Death Valley where men mined for gold, for example, she wrote that "three sounds assail the ear of the stranger in the rainbow country from the first gray of the start led dawn to the pink of the morning after—the wild wind calling from the smitten desert, the rattle of the roulette-wheel and the high-pitched voices of excited men talking."[21] With these noun phrases describing sounds, she introduces a barren landscape as well as the dramatic action of money made and lost.

Black also used groupings of noun phrases to depict not just places but people that the reader would not otherwise encounter. In a piece concerning a day spent at the San Francisco mayor's office, she relies on a list, in tight parallel structure, of those that come to see him:

> "They" are people with grievances, people with woes, people who want to go away from here and expect the Mayor to help them, people who want permits, people who have plans for ruling a city much superior to any ever thought of before, people who have yards of valuable advice to unreel, people who are friendless and want to get into the Almshouse, people who have hosts of friends and want to get positions for them.[22]

In another piece, for which she went to work at a California cannery as a supposed stunt girl, her focus is not on herself but on the women working around her, their labor conditions and their health. She uses descriptors to introduce these working women: "The girls who know no girlhood. The women who have forgotten their youth. Bond slaves of labor. The workingman is never without a champion, but the working woman has no vote to conciliate." And she also provides a dramatic list of participial adjectives to describe the work they do: "Heart breaking, back aching, health destroying work, be the canner never so young and ever so strong." Similarly in a column concerning a mother who sticks by her son, a murderer, spending all her money on lawyers and providing excuses for him even when she really knows the truth, Black again moves to a grouping of participles: "Fearing, praying, hoping, trying, watching, wondering—remembering, trying to forget—all the time knowing—knowing—knowing, too well—too well."[23]

While Black employed the list to portray a particular person or situation, she also chose it to move readers from an individual case to the larger problem. In her book about narcotic use, *Dope: The Story of the Living Dead*, Black employs data to discuss the use of opium, heroin, and cocaine in the United States, a much larger amount than in many other countries. She also discusses the history of these drugs and then employs a list of adjectives to describe their effect on addicts: "A narcotic addict is a poor, pitiful, suffering, aching, shivering, freezing, burning slave to the cruelest master the world has ever dreamed of permitting to exist." As this exposé continues, Black turns to a grouping of nouns to detail the intertwined impact of these drugs on the individual and the community: "Disgrace, humiliation, shame, hatred, robbery, murder, cruelty beyond belief, treachery beyond imagination—that's the crop that springs from the poppy fields."[24]

While Black's lists can delineate the darkest of situations, she also employed them, and especially groupings of hyphenated adjectives, to create critical but humorous depictions. Often they concern the excesses of what women do—and what American culture expects of them. In a piece about the fashion models seen in magazines, for example, she refers to them as "the self-conscious, posing, look-at-me girls, you-may-never-see-me again creatures."[25] In another piece, as she berates a high-school girl for being all flirt and no substance, she presents a thorough list of the traits too often encouraged in teenagers: "Poor little thing. Poor silly little vulgar, ill-dressed, flaunting, rustling, ruffling, mincing, affecting, languishing, head-tossing, eye-making, pouting, self-conscious, empty-headed little thing."[26] And in another column, she uses one of her extreme lists to discuss the daily obsession that weight loss can become for women: "Haggling, fussing, picking, and choosing, weighing and balancing, looking and calculating—all sensible, practical, much-to-be-praised methods. I wish from the bottom of my heart I knew how to use them, or could ever learn. I can't, and what's the use of pretending?"[27]

## The Longer Description

In many articles, Black employs the list to provide a quick sketch of a person or place. And, like the best writers of fiction and nonfiction, she also moved to longer descriptions to more fully engage readers. John McPhee, relying on a wonderful title for nonfiction, *Coming into the Country*, brings readers into the remoteness of the bush, involving them with placer mining, barren-ground grizzlies, a young Athapaskan chief, stalwart settlers. Tracy Kidder employs such description in *House* to delineate the more local realities of home construction. Black often similarly dwelled on details to bring readers "into the country" of new ideas.

When Black wrote about the hurricane and fire in Galveston in 1900, her prose stressed specific details. Describing her arrival on the island, she asserts that "the terrible, sickening odor almost overcame us," and she depicts "the hideous, hideous sand, stained and streaked in the starlight with dark and cruel blotches" of the blood of the wounded and dead. Black further tells of a man who had floated through the night on a bit of his roof, along with his wife who finally slipped into the water and drowned as he was sleeping; of men who ventured to the island on the first ferries to find what they could of their children and wives; of dead people burned in vast fires because so many bodies released into the water had begun floating back onto shore; of a mass of older wooden slabs with names and dates, floating, coming out of the cemetery. She also describes small, piteous details of loss, like a baby's shoes left by the shore after the child had fallen from his father's arms and drowned.

The country into which Black's readers would be coming could be far away or close by. In her *Examiner* articles about drug use on the streets of San Francisco, as an initial shock, she begins by describing high school boys, "well dressed, well shod," with "the strange and ghastly pallor" caused by drug use. Then she moves further into the specifics of the desperation to be seen, in town, right there:

> I looked and there out on the sidewalk, for every passerby to see, was a haunted creature, straight from the lowest depths of torment.
> 
> He glared at us with unseeing eyes, blazing eyes, the eye of a fiend. His fingers clutched around an imaginary throat and every muscle in his body twitched so that it was hideous to see.
> 
> No one molested him, no one even looked at him. Why should they, with the street full of such as he?
> 
> Scores of them we passed in the next three blocks. You don't believe it? I don't blame you. I wouldn't have believed it either, but there they were, in the open daylight. Men and women, and, worst of all, boys and girls.
> 
> Bedraggled, filthy beyond description, hag ridden, hideous—some slunk along with downcast eyes, muttering to themselves.

Some leaned against the walls, and from every alley and from half a dozen low windows peered white faces, drawn with terror, when they saw the Federal officers.[28]

## Character and Dialogue

In Black's writing, readers learned about an array of sites through lists and longer descriptions. They also entered the lives of particular characters through dialogue, a key part of creative nonfiction, providing the means of entering other realities, as in Susan Orlean's portrait of the priorities and fears of the child in "The American Man, Age Ten" and in so many pieces by Winifred Black.

Frequently as Black presented herself as a writer in pursuit of the story, she recorded her conversations with those affected by crisis events. When she wrote about entering hurricane-struck Galveston by nightfall in September of 1900, on the day following the storm, her articles relied on dialogue.[29] Like Dave Eggers did in *Zeitoun*, concerning the aftermath of Hurricane Katrina in New Orleans, Black recorded conversations with individuals affected, as when she saw a column of fire and smoke from the boat in which she traveled across the bay:

> "What a terrible fire!" I said. "Some of the large buildings must be burning." A man was passing the deck behind my chair heard me. He stopped, put his hand on the bulwark and turned down and looked into my face, his face like the face of a dead man, but he laughed.
> 
> "Buildings?" he said. "Don't you know what is burning over there? It is my wife and children, such little children; why, the tallest was not as high as this"—he laid his hand on the bulwark—"and the little one was just learning to talk."[30]

With 8,000 dead, the larger picture becomes real in the plight of one man's family.

When William Randolph Hearst brought Black from Denver to write about the earthquake and fire in San Francisco in April of 1906, she concentrated not on the number of blocks or buildings affected or on her own efforts to get there. Instead she relied on dialogue to create specific examples of survivors:

> I met a woman out in Jefferson square to-day who ought to sit for a picture of the Incarnation of the Spirit of San Francisco. She was standing in a funny little square tent made partly of boards and partly of ragged bits of cloth. She wore a dress that had been through the fire with her, but her bright hair was brushed neatly back from her rosy face. She was washing dishes, petting a dog, talking baby talk to a baby, and bossing some half-dozen of boys, all at

the same time. "Run down to the edge of the pavement with these beans," she said to one boy, "and see if you can't find somebody's fire to warm 'em a little by. Hike over to the commissary wagon; they're giving out eggs there. The baby can't eat these beans. Where are those blankets? Didn't I tell those rascals to put them out to air? Oh, yes; I've got thirteen boarders. Yes; we all sleep in this tent. No; they don't pay me a cent. Burnt out? Who isn't? What's the use of being blue about it though?"

As Black continues to describe "that woman out there at Jefferson square, homeless, without a dollar, cold and not overly well fed," she moves from specifics to general: this survivor is "a California woman, for all that," a symbol of a city that will survive.[31]

Dialogue could reveal individuals with whom readers should sympathize—and individuals with whom they should not. When Black began campaigning for the Little Jim hospitals for invalid children and planning for a women's newspaper edition that would raise funds, she employed a character, name not given, who comes into the newspaper office, making hideous statements that would drive readers toward her values and her campaign. This man says, as she reports this encounter, "The really charitable thing to do is to chloroform all people who are doomed to a life of hopeless suffering. That's what we're going to do when we get more civilized ... you are keeping real civilization back with all these sentimental efforts." She goes from this visitor to people who want to be paid to join in the effort, who claim that women can't edit a paper or that their efforts won't matter, encounters involving many types of negativity and judgment, all unacceptable forms of prejudice revealed through the ugly words with which they are expressed.[32]

Besides acquainting readers with types of people that they would otherwise not learn about, dialogue could change their judgments of people that they may have condemned unfairly on the basis of the bare, unexplained facts in front-page news articles. In one piece, for example, Black reports President Wilson's decision to allow controversial English suffragist Emmeline Pankhurst to enter the country for a lecture tour. In April 1913, in London, Pankhurst had been convicted of "counseling" unknown persons in the setting of a suspicious fire and sentenced to three years in jail. She had been released, however, after suffering the ill effects of fasting and forced feeding. When she arrived in the United States in October, she had at first been subject to laws forbidding entrance into the country to those guilty of crimes involving "moral turpitude," and many Americans indeed questioned whether she should be tolerated within this country. After meeting with Pankhurst as she entered Ellis Island, Black used dialogue to alter this common, negative image. Here she presents Pankhurst's polite and reasonable answers to her questions:

> "My stay in quarantine? Perfectly pleasant I assure you; everybody was most kind and what a nice class of women you have there....
>
> "We look to America for tolerance, for freedom, for liberty. What is it you say in your song, 'The land of the free and the home of the brave,'—you certainly couldn't sing that if you refused to let a woman land on your shores just because she is devoting her life to trying to help other women, could you?"

In this conversation with Black, Pankhurst maintains further that militant methods won't be needed to achieve woman suffrage in the United States because American women receive better treatment and have more legal rights than those in England. In reporting this explanation, complimentary to American women and men as are the many other excerpts from their conversation, Black introduces a sane, sensible, and thoughtful Pankhurst through dialogue.[33]

## Vivid Action

As a skilled writer of nonfiction, Black often turned from lists, descriptions, and dialogue to action. Indeed, Ishbel Ross maintained in *Ladies of the Press* that Black's "vivid, personal writing" featured "startling effects—hard jolts," created with active verbs and sentences.[34] In her article about being taken to the city receiving hospital by policemen in their wagon instead of in an ambulance with trained medical personnel, Black relied on active prose, as in this depiction of the police's response when she pretended to faint on the street:

> Then a muscular hand clutched me by the arm roughly and jerked me to a sitting posture. Another jerk brought me to my feet and he soon had pulled me out to the pavement. Another policeman got me by the other arm and together they dragged me across the sidewalk to where a black covered wagon stood. Either man was strong enough to lift me with one arm but they preferred to drag me. They pushed me feet first into the wagon and huddled me up in the corner.[35]

Similarly, at suffrage parades, prize fights, political conventions, and San Francisco polling places, Black employed action to show readers what had happened and how it should be judged.

## Adaptation of Quotations

In moving readers into new worlds, Black often employed well-known quotations, extending or changing their meaning, using the familiar to move readers to the unfamiliar. Many current nonfiction authors, in their titles and arguments, have employed such allusions, like Joan Didion in *Slouching towards Bethlehem*, Jon Krakauer in *Into Thin Air*, and Annie Dillard in *For the Time Being*. Beyond quick excerpts from nursery rhymes that might open articles, Black relied on familiar phrases and quotations throughout her articles to ask readers to consider traditional values and new possibilities.

As Black writes about women involved in supporting the men of the American Railway Union (ARU), on strike in 1894, she presents her story with this subhead: "It isn't a case where 'men must work and women must weep,' but one where men musn't work and women will help—the ARU restaurant and the way the women run it." After providing a long account of the women's creation and administration of a restaurant for strikers, she again uses a line from Charles Kingsley's "Three Fishers" (1851), a poem concerning families faced with tragic loss when men don't return from the sea: "The women of the A.R.U. do not believe in the song which says that 'Men must work and women must weep.' Just now their whole time is spent in telling the men not to work, and as for weeping—they've never thought of such a thing. 'Weep,' said a slim little woman in a tight black gown, and a sailor hat tipped over a shock of bright yellow hair. 'Well, when I get time to weep I'll let you know.'" Through extended dialogue, Black describes the place, the miners, and the menus as well as the women working at the restaurant, who plan and cook the meals, keep the peace among the male strikers, taking revolvers off them when necessary, and lend extra support to the strikers' wives, many of them with young children. These staff members thus appear as active problem-solvers in a crisis, not women who weep.[36]

In another article, concerning women workers at a cannery, Black quotes Thomas Gray's "An Elegy Written in a Country Churchyard": "It is no sensational story I have to write. No tale of dire cruelty or hateful tyranny. It is only a chapter in the short-and-simple annals of the poor. Just the plain story of a day with the working women of San Francisco."[37] Gray's poem speaks of the need to attend to the workers generally ignored by English poetry and respect:

> Let not Ambition mock their useful toil,
> Their homely joys, and destiny obscure;
> Nor Grandeur hear with a disdainful smile
> The short and simple annals of the poor.[38]

As Black values these women and their work, she adds them to the list of subjects that matter. In using this familiar line, she associates her own efforts with a famous poet's attempt to alter traditional judgments of those often ignored.

## Exaggeration and Humor

To involve and persuade readers, Black also employed exaggeration as she depicted common, and ridiculous, prejudices. In one column from 1910, for example, she discusses the shock expressed over a "smutty" *Ladies' Home Journal* cover, which showed a woman in a ball gown being dramatically kissed. Black first claims that younger women are interested in much more than romance and thus that they may not find the cover as enthralling as editor Edward Bok might have imagined or mothers might have feared. And then Black speaks to the young woman in an ironic tone about the silliness of parents who get upset about such an image: "You better not let mamma see it or she will hide it up in the garret along with the Sappho and the unexpurgated copy of Arabian Knights that your wicked Uncle Dudley brought home from Paris."[39]

## Comparison

In many other columns, Black employs the oddest of comparisons to get the readers' attention, to enable them to see connections that they would otherwise miss. In a column from 1908 she describes the cultural power of beauty and youth, which can become destructive if seeking to maintain them takes over. The specific case here concerns a woman of forty who keeps rushing back into a burning house to get her bracelets, rings, and breastpins, and ultimately dies in the fire. Black compares this woman to one who sacrifices everything for the diet and baubles that supposedly spell youth: becoming nervous, exhausted, and unsatisfied at forty, as a result of attempting to imitate twenty, resembles repeatedly choosing to be engulfed in flames.[40]

To create the surprising comparison and comment on familiar beliefs that may not be the best ones, Black often relied on familiar household items. In "Homes Not Wrecked by Women Voting," in April of 1915, she argues that women can take on many roles, not just serving as wives and mothers. And then she provides this comparison using a well-known food: "If there are fifty-seven different varieties of pickles, all of them, they tell us, piquant, and every one of them excellent, why should you want to run womanhood through a mold and make us all exactly alike?"[41] In an article titled "Love and Marriage," with the intriguing subhead "Winifred Black says there is just one sensible, sane reason for getting married," the strongest line concerns pill prescriptions lingering in the medicine cabinet. The article depicts a woman who is flipping a coin to decide which man to marry because she feels that she needs to marry somebody. The man under the most serious consideration isn't good looking and she doesn't have anything in common with him but she hates to waste him—like someone taking old pills left in the medicine cabinet instead of throwing them away.[42] While Black often used extended scenes to make comparisons, she also did so more succinctly, in compound sentences. In an article asking the question, "Is Divorce an Evil?" in 1892, she concludes that "divorce does not make unhappy marriages; unhappy marriages make divorce."[43]

## Turning the (Gender) Tables

Along with other rhetorical techniques, Black regularly used turning the tables, taking the judgment commonly made of one group and applying it to another, using this method to get readers to evaluate what they may have accepted automatically, especially about the appropriate behavior of women and men.

This turning proved efficacious in examining traditional values concerning political equality. In an article about woman's suffrage, from 1890, for example, Blake claims that interviews with women have taught her that interest in voting has been growing. But, she continues, many women think that they should not admit to wanting to achieve this goal: "No less than half a dozen said this to me this week: 'I believe in suffrage, but I would not have any one know it for the world.'" When Black asks one woman why she will not speak for suffrage, she gets a succinct answer: "Men do not like a woman who says those things." And then Black turns the tables by asking another question: "What would we think of a man who refuses to give his idea on any of the issues of the day because women would not approve of him?" In not needing an answer, the obvious one being that "we" would not respect such a man, Black speaks for women's right to activism and independence while she also makes fun of "time-honored witticisms" surrounding suffrage, that women will only vote for handsome men, for example, a claim as ridiculous as women's need to hide their desire for civic involvement and equality.[44]

Black also often uses turning the tables to consider gender and the results of aging. She counters the idea that older women are no longer sexual beings and can no longer be of interest to men by considering how men would feel if such a claim were made about them: "Now, if I should sit up and say that when a man gets to the point that he no longer interests women, he does this, that and the other, what a low moan of fevered anguish there'd be from every poor old dotard who thinks he'll never be old enough, or ugly enough, or stupid enough, but that he can still 'interest' the ladies."[45]

Black also uses this turning the tables to evaluate men and women at work. She argues that it is not ethical to use sex in business, to sell things, and the woman advocating this use of sexual attractiveness knows it. "Tut, tut," says Black here in imitation of Lewis Carroll, employing her common response to the ludicrous. And then she asks what the reader would think of men that use sexy looks to get women to sign contracts. Certainly it's done, she admits, but no one respects such men and they seem foolish just as flirtatious women do. In this piece as in many others, she also makes the gender comparison to reveal the ridiculousness of focusing on love at the office—men wouldn't sit around at work and ignore what needed to be done to chit-chat about the progress of their love affairs or they would look mighty silly doing so.[46]

As Black employs this turning of the tables, she also moves it into more dramatic situations to get readers to reevaluate "acceptable" behavior. In one column from 1930 concerning domestic violence, for example, after describing a woman that kicked and beat her husband, she asks whether the complete power of one human being over another might automatically lead to savage behavior. She begins by employing one of her dramatic openers to engage readers in this situation, which switched the presumed gender of the aggressor and victim of violence:

> She called him names.
> She cursed him.
> She beat him.
> She kicked him.
> Now he has divorced her.
> The papers are full of the story.

Certainly in this situation the man would leave the woman—as women should also leave men who beat them. Here she claims the only difference to be that male violence and the woman's need to get away would not be deemed as news worthy.[47]

## Direct Address

While Black employs a variety of techniques to bring readers into new situations, she also speaks directly to them as well as to the subjects of her articles. Direct address frequently allows her to focus on the foibles of men and women, to frankly discuss typical behaviors that the reader might choose to avoid.

While she addressed readers in many of her articles, this technique provided the structure for her advice columns, which she began to write for syndication in 1914. She thus speaks to a woman becoming involved with a man who is engaged to another:

What do you want with a man who would break another girl's heart. Don't you realize that he'll treat you just exactly as he has treated her? A man who flirts with one girl will flirt with another. It isn't the girl he cares about, it's himself. Can't you get that into your consciousness? Let the chap with the other sweetheart go and it he doesn't go of his own accord you send him about his business and let some other girl break her heart over him, if she's goose enough to do it. You will meet Mr. Right some day, and then there'll be no problem at all.[48]

In other pieces, instead of speaking directly to the reader or letter writer, she employs direct address to express sympathy for some people whose stories she has told as well as to rebuke some experts. In an article about the unrealistic depictions in fashion magazines, for example, she talks to the artists that create these impossible images: "Please, Mr. Artist, won't you be a darling and draw us some pictures of real girls and real men for your fashion plates—Just for a change?"[49]

## Questions for the Reader and for Herself

As an ending technique, Black commonly asked readers to help her judge difficult cases. In advice columns she often followed her own answer to a question with an invitation to the reader to reflect on the situation under discussion. Concerning a boarder who wants to marry the fourteen-year-old daughter of his landlord, for example, she follows her own strong condemnation with "What would be your reply to this strange letter?"[50]

As Black asks readers to consider their own opinions, she engages them in questioning cultural norms. In one feature piece, she writes about marrying for security as a form of being bought and owned and then compares the choice to entering the harem of a Turkish sultan. She then uses a list of hyphenated adjectives to state her own unequivocal judgment and asks a final question, this presentation and thus the presumed answer to her question strongly weighted against giving up freedom in Turkey or the United States: "I'd rather be the homeliest, pug-nosiest, knock-kneeiest, freckle-faciest, most commonplace little cash girl on a platform in the cheapest shop in the busiest bargain season—in the United States of America—than to be the most beautiful creature who ever breathed—if I had to breathe behind the lattice in a horrible harem. How do you feel about it, girls?"[51]

## And Non-Stuntly Analysis

Like other masters of nonfiction, including David Foster Wallace and Michael Lewis, Winifred Black used many techniques to draw readers into a scene or case; like them, she also regularly turned from the scene to various forms of analysis. From the beginning to the end of her career, she was never just performing a stunt but collecting the information that could lead to thoughtful assessments of American institutions and relationships.

In one article from 1921, for example, Black wrote about all the criticism in American magazines of young people of the flapper era. She first engages readers with specific lists of accusations: concerning extravagant vulgarity, laziness, lewd dancing, painted faces, eccentric costumes. All of these "mad follies of the moment ... of wild extravagance and of boundless carelessness" were being "commented on most bitterly by writers of well-known ability." After opening with a list of the supposed traits and citing these questionable experts, Black turns to analysis in a defense of the young. She first argues that the youth of all generations have seemed extreme and less than serious: here she employs essays by Joseph Addison in the *Tatler* and the *Spectator* that commented on follies of youth in the early eighteenth century to make this point. She then reasons that some current excesses stem from the situation in which the younger generation came of age: encountering the solemnity and deprivation of war years, the debt of the post-war years, and new technologies such as high-powered automobiles that were altering social rules. And then she turns to domineering, cruel fathers who judge, control, and even beat their daughters, even as times are changing, and she ends by asking her readers, "Which generation is better?"[52] While Black relies on lists and characters, she also engages in analysis, using evidence in this case to explain why young people may appear unconventional but may ultimately be better than their restrictive parents.

—⁂—

In all of these techniques Black demonstrated that the who, what and where Sam Chamberlain insisted upon as the first lesson was only the beginning of effective prose. Her articles reveal her use of an array of techniques to engage readers in specific situations as well as in analysis of ongoing trends and cultural expectations. As a skilled crafter of nonfiction, Black employed strong and varied creative techniques to reach readers for almost fifty years.

# 9

# Black's Subject Matter: The Changing Definition of "Normal"

By accessing a variety of techniques, Winifred Black developed a set of themes concerning American life. With increasing freedom of subject matter and method as the years and decades went by, she could write about what mattered to her, and many themes reverberated in her opus, with varying points about them made through the decades. In forty-seven years of writing various forms of short nonfiction, which appeared in newspapers around the country each week, Black developed a vision of women and men and of American institutions that gained her national fame and influence. Perhaps the foremost of Black's topics, the one that informed everything that she wrote, was the need to examine life carefully and make individual choices, a possibility and even a requirement because of the changing nature of what was coded as normal or acceptable in the United States through the decades.

Black insisted throughout her career, not just during wartime or the Jazz Age, that American culture was changing. And, like Foucault, she maintained that cultural changes mandated ever new codes of normal, indeed with newspapers as a powerful agent of enculturation. With this recognition of ongoing alteration in what could be considered normal or moral, she repeatedly constructs the worst codes for women as having held power long before. Rhetorically she thus sweeps away, in a current of change, definitions and traditions that she considers restrictive, labeling them as nearly forgotten even when they were still fully operative. For Black, a primary means of abandoning the narrow-minded, the tyranny of local prejudices, occurred through reading. "What a big world it is," she claimed in 1921 concerning not just the effect of travel but of reading, "when we take other people's interests and other people's affairs and other people's joys and other people's sorrows and weave them all into a bright, soft, evergrowing web of memory and of understanding and of appreciation!"[1] With the freedom that Hearst increasingly gave her, for her *Examiner* articles and her syndicated columns, Black attempted to be both insider and outsider, speaking about daily life but chipping away at unexamined daily choices, in the nature of the best nonfiction.

## Changing Images of Women, Always Modern

In many essays written through the years, Black maintained that women were then leading a more active, independent life that naturally separated them from earlier generations, with small changes signifying larger ones. In a column from 1910, ostensibly about the new trend of women playing golf, she maintains that women no longer needed to act sickly or weak to attract and keep men, her vague references to an earlier time providing the opportunity to laud the current day and the future: "You'll never get us back into the camphor and peppermint sisterhood again," she maintains concerning the new normal. "We're just finding out how much fun it is to be alive, we women, and we're going to keep finding out more and more every day."[2]

Over the years, Black continued to contrast the old-fashioned with the modern and thus to argue that the range of the acceptable was changing along with women's freedom and economic independence. In a column from 1912, concerning whether a woman would want to know that her husband was cheating on her, she writes, "The old fashioned woman didn't want the chance. 'Don't tell me,' she sobbed, 'I don't want to know.' Of course she didn't want to know. Why should she? What could she do? The modern woman? That's different, quite different. The modern woman has the whole affair quite in her own hands; she isn't helpless, not the very least bit in the world."[3]

In 1921, Black again asks if women have changed and here recognizes that feminists are right in declaring that they have: "The old-fashioned, helpless, clinging, useless woman, who was proud of being a goose, is gone." If such a woman still exists, Black continues, she will pretend otherwise because older, restrictive definitions are no longer accepted as right. Women don't have to marry, and they can enjoy being single, she argues about life in a changing era; they can be friends with other women and engage in many activities, without fear of a negative reputation.[4]

In examining a change in the desired traits, Black recognized modesty and reserve as older, once assumedly correct behaviors for women that required careful consideration: indeed, these established values might be important to abandon. In 1913, she acknowledges that women who imitate the clothes and behavior of stage and movie stars may seem shocking. Imitating the crude excesses of vaudeville reviews, many of them are "dressed as no harem beauty in any 'British Blond' road show would have dared to dress beyond the footlights two years before"—out on the streets, even in church. But, Black claims, these are in fact "decent wives, honest mothers," not deserving of negative judgment. And accepting modern costumes may help women move beyond older behavioral expectations that involved more than dress: "Perhaps this very breaking down of all the customary barriers of modesty and reserve is the very thing to make no such barrier necessary."[5] Like Mary Wollstonecraft in *Vindication of the Rights of Woman*, Black indicates that the assumed best values, like modesty and reserve, can be a means of controlling women, of keeping them passive or subservient: such older expectations should be set aside.

"Obedience, docility, submission to her elders," in a column from 1916, she lists as other traits that had been gendered female and had proven to be a liability for young women of the modern world. In 1916, when Margaret Sanger opened the first birth control clinic in the United States, leading to her arrest for distributing information on contraception, her subsequent trial generated enormous support for her cause. In "Safeguarding Our Girls," Black praises the resulting new emphasis on doctor visits and sex education for daughters. But, beyond instigating this new form of discussion, Black continued, mothers needed to consider the other values that they taught daily: "The average girl is taught from her very cradle, first to be amiable, next to be good, and last of all to be sensible. Obedience, docility, submission to her elders. What stress do we lay upon them when we're trying to teach our little girls how to grow up to fight a woman's battle? And she'll have to fight, when she grows up, too." After speaking against these older values that engender a dangerous level of passivity, Black ends the column with a key question for a mother concerning her daughter: "Is she learning somewhere, somehow, that she is accountable to herself and to herself alone for what she makes of her own life? She can and must learn these lessons in what Black labels again as a changed world."[6]

After World War I, Black again argued that there was a new sort of modern woman. In a piece from 1919 about work done by volunteers in a welfare shop in San Mateo, she states the change quite clearly:

> The women of this country are never going back again to what they were before the war, never and never. We've taken a great step forward; we've grown mentally and morally and soulfully, and we can no more creep back into the mean, little, selfish, sordid, narrow cells we called ourselves before the war than a great, gorgeous, silvery and gold and purple and rose butterfly can creep back into an ugly old cocoon again and live. We're broader minded and more generous and more kindly and more loving than we've ever been before and we're going to keep on growing, too.[7]

Here she rhetorically brands earlier generations with a negativity that she did not ascribe to them earlier; and she again lauds the change in what was constructed as normal and right.

Throughout the years, Black also claimed that marriage was naturally changing, for the better, as women asserted themselves as they had not in some vaguely designated past. In an article from 1912, for example, she considers a generally introduced man "out west," who killed himself because of the lack of meaning in his life, one of his dire criticisms being that "women marry for money." Here Black launches into a thorough rebuttal, claiming that some women might still make that misguided choice but not half as frequently as fifty or twenty-five years earlier. Women practically had to marry in "those days," she claims, or be condemned as the fifth wheel on someone's couch. Half the women who walked up to the altar twenty years earlier, she continues, had heard the wedding ceremony almost desperately with just one idea in their heads: "Well, anyhow, I'm not an old maid now." Black next asserts the ascendency of a new terminology and new attitudes, perhaps focusing to some extent on what she preferred to be true: "That's all changed. No girl has to marry to keep from being an old maid these days. There are no old maids. There are bachelor women—and mighty free and independent and happy."[8]

While Black continued to write about a more equal vision of marriage, asserting through the years that the change had already occurred and thus that women should not doubt their right to participate in a new normal, she also chronicled changes occurring through education and work, as already having occurred, as instigating appropriate new behaviors and attitudes that young men and parents would simply have to accept. In 1915, for example, she looks at greater access to a college education and to a job as altering what women will be willing to tolerate. Here she gives the example of young women at Northwestern University being asked to sell tickets for a football game that they were not allowed to attend. In the best tradition of nonfiction, she moves from a small, specific matter to a much larger cultural trend that her verbs make clear was already occurring: "Women have been doing that all their lives–selling tickets to somebody else's game—and they're getting tired of it, getting woefully tired of it…. I'm glad the girls have waked up. They've been waking up all over the country, somehow. It's odd, but it seems to be catching, this waking up business."

As the article continues, Black further discusses a growing trend toward militancy among women, toward "waking up," by providing a further example. She depicts a father who is woefully out of date: not willing to let a grown, working daughter set her own hours, a form of control he would not expect to exercise on a son. And then, she presents her conclusions concerning the football game and this family. Both male college students and parents, attempting to ignore a tide that was turning, were naturally leading women to a feminist concern for economic and political equality: "That's why so many women are feminists. That's why so many women are determined they won't live at home another day."[9]

As she wrote through the years about already occurring change, Black repeatedly spoke for youth, for seeing the good in the younger generation and in changing codes. One column from 1916, for example, concerns a college girl saying "damn" and even worse, the shock of it all. But then Black describes herself, at age fifty-three, meeting with a large group of college women and enjoying all their conversation: "What breezy, independent, good-natured, big-hearted, broad-minded creatures these are—these New Girls of ours who go out for a 'bit of a blow' when they feel like it without waiting for any man to invite them."[10] As Black speaks of their conversation and their freedom, their being out without men, she praises the new "normal" behavior, encouraging readers to join with her in a positive appraisal of what had already changed.

## Historical Events That Women Dealt with and Caused

As Black discusses the recurring creation of the normal, she also considers the impact of big historical moments. She recognizes, for example, that World War I led to changes in appropriate behavior. In one column that develops this subject, she writes specifically about two vaguely identified men, looking for brides after they have come home from the front, and she talks about war changing what these men seek as well as what women—by region of the country—have been trained in the past to be: "These two men were brought up in the part of the country where they spoil girls, and make selfish little pets of them, and flatter them and expect them to be helpless and reasonable—but they've been away." These veterans are no longer impressed by silly tempers about hats, dresses, and puppies, affectations that might have charmed in an earlier era: "They want, not a silly doll for a wife, but a deephearted, kind, loving, generous, reasonable woman." And so women who have already changed, who have moved beyond affectations and expect a seat at the football game, are exactly who they should be in the modern world.[11]

As Black wrote about positive change over time, in what was acceptable and normal, she often credited women's efforts as providing the agency that caused modern transformations. As in many earlier articles, in a column from 1919, she again stipulates a time in the past in which human liberty had been restrained, the cause, as she states vehemently, being a tendency to put the wife and mother, the good girl or the true woman of the nineteenth century, on a holy pedestal: "Times are indeed changing. Twenty years ago every man in public life, no matter who he was or what he really thought, or how he treated his own wife or his own daughters at home, always made a point of speaking in public as if the only difference between the heavenly choir and the plain, ordinary, every-day woman of American was that the heavenly choir was winged." Here she recognizes that changing definitions, the movement away from the apotheosis of the true woman restricted to the home, had come from women's own efforts to achieve education, jobs, suffrage, and equal rights. And, Black continues, she would cast her lot with the women "who would like to throw up our hats to think that the time has gone by when a woman had to take a sugary compliment and swallow as if she loved it, when what she wanted was just a little, plain, common-sense justice."[12]

Black's positive though evaluative stance on change, always a major subject for her, continued through all the upheavals of the 1920s. One column, from 1921, concerns the silliness of opposing the new dances, such as the Charleston, since dance has always quite happily been about closeness and sexuality; this dance is simply a new, positive normal.[13] An article from 1923, about a modern woman and her husband who decide to adopt a baby, involves readers through a quick denunciation of ridiculous, old-fashioned nay-sayers who insist that change is ruinous: "What a time we do have telling each other that human nature is changing and that the world is going to the dogs and that the young people of today are not what they were a generation ago. Stuff and nonsense, bosh and fiddlesticks!"[14] Another column from 1923 asks parents to look at the ways in which a new, seemingly shocking generation actually mirrors the excesses and fads of their own and thus to consider the new as not so hideous:

> I seem dimly to remember, fathers and mothers who were perfectly horrified over the roller skate fad, and wasn't there a mummie over there who thought it was a bit too fast for anything for girls to go downtown and have their tintypes taken.... Fashions change, but we never get over being shocked, do we?[15]

With her use of "we," Black indicates that readers might initially be shocked by modern changes, as an older generation of parents had been at the turn of the century, but they should join Black in ultimately deciding to celebrate contemporary choices.

As Black discussed the power and rightness of the new in different historical periods, she also considered it as affecting not just the young but women of all ages who could move beyond the worst of older traditions. One of her articles from 1922, for example, concerns strict rules from the nineteenth century, reflecting the code of Queen Victoria, about how a widow should grieve: wearing dark clothes and her wedding ring, accepting only limited visits, and maintaining a somber demeanor for many years afterwards.[16] Black discusses these older requirements and then segues to a Foucaultian discussion of what was actually currently normal and natural for women, regardless of what might have been expected in the past:

In your grandmother's time and mine, a woman who went out of the house one step in less than a year after her husband's death was considered a bold baggage.

And thousands of women voluntarily made prisoners of themselves for years, not because they felt like doing it, but because custom demanded that they should.

Nature is not cruel. Nature is kind.

The wound heals, the heart beats again to its wonted cheerfulness or should, and the brave woman, the unselfish woman, the woman of real character, puts away her personal grief as she puts away the little garments once worn by the one she loved. She does not take those garments out for every passing stranger or every casual acquaintance to see.[17]

During the Depression, Black continued to talk about change and especially to praise the strength of women in dealing with hard times. One article from 1931, for example, concerns Katerina Rehua of Sydney, an Australian mother of four, whose husband was ill and out of work for nine months. Rehua entered a swimming contest for the prize money, swimming for almost forty-eight hours, breaking a world's record and winning a much needed prize of five hundred dollars. This story, reported in other newspapers in articles that just dealt with these facts, offered Black an opportunity to comment on the abilities of what she again calls the modern girl as she discusses an ever new sort of normal and praiseworthy: "But stop—come to think of it the modern girl can swim farther and ride better and run faster, and play better tennis, and skate more skillfully than her mother ever could."[18] And this physical strength and bravery will enable such modern women facing hard times, like Rehua, to support their families and persevere.

Through the decades, even though Black was aware of the difficulties caused by war and other crises, she looked at change as allowing women and men to continually redefine themselves, to recognize that tradition did not have to bind them, that what was deemed normal was always changing, often for the better, and that it never had to contain the individual.

# 10

## *Gender Distinctions*

One of Black's repeated themes certainly is open mindedness to change, indeed a recognition that what might seem eternal or morally right could alter and be altered, with change emanating from the agency of women as well as men. As she looked at the new, one of her major subjects was gender identity, indeed gender trouble, to use Judith Butler's term.[1] Frequently Black dealt with the biological and the cultural, with what women and men might be encouraged to think was naturally appropriate to their genders and what might be the actual divisions between them. "We deal with you in business as men to men nowadays, you know," she wrote addressing men in 1910, "and we're finding out that a good many of these old theories about the difference between men and women are nothing but theories, and that we're cut out of just about the same kind of cloth all of us, both men and women, after all."[2]

### Taking on Cultural Constructions of Gender

Though Black repeatedly argued that the differences between men and women were biologically few, she also wrote about the traditional behaviors that commonly divided them, about cultural choices and expectations much more than necessity.

In 1892, attending a prize fight in San Francisco gave Black the opportunity to comment on the culture in which men participated, the roles they took on as a group of spectators, which she observed as she sat alone in a private box: "I had not been at the prize-fight five minutes before I saw that I was looking on a race of beings I had never seen before." When the boxers suddenly bloodied each other with fierce blows, she writes,

> I turned sick and dizzy.
> The crowd howled with joy. The bell clanged. The trainers lifted their men and rushed to the corners with them. They sponged them with big soft sponges. They rubbed them down.
> "*Clang!*" They were in the ring again, hard at it. They fought faster and

harder. The Bostonian had the best of it. He struck the other a blow that sent him reeling to the floor. Only for a few seconds, though. He was up at once and rushing blindly at the Bostonian. No use; he was struck again, he went down again.

The crowd yelled like wild beasts. Every man in the hall sprang to his feet. The barkeeper jumped madly up and down, waving his white apron. The trainers leaned forward to the edge of the platform. They were breathless with suspense.

As she comments further on the unrestrained aggression of these "wild beasts," she claims that "I am glad because I have looked upon a new race of beings to-night. New to me. I mean."[3] Here she claims that men felt required to become beast-like in such a site, as they would not at home: their behavior was not biologically necessary.

Black also often wrote about what this "wild beast" behavior, culturally encouraged and often accepted as inevitable, seemed to necessitate in response. In 1915 in "Who Carries the World, Old Atlas or His Wife?" she discusses sculptor Gutzon Borglum, who crafted the first statue of Atlas as a woman, the large world within her hands and resting on her right shoulder. "Only woman has the strength and endurance for such a weight," the sculptor claimed in justification of this controversial portrayal.[4] After discussing the statue, Black segues into further consideration of what men's wild-beast choices required of women. "Men make the world—they change and fashion it to suit their whims and fancies—but it is a woman who carries the burden of it upon her shoulders," she claims. And then she envisions what would occur in a future with just one gender, indeed without men who feel required to act irresponsibly and take unnecessary risks:

> If all the men in the world died tomorrow we should have a pretty bad time of it—we women. We should be lonely and heartsick and homesick enough in all conscience, but it would go on being a rather pretty world and rather a comfortable world and rather a civilized world, after a fashion, for all that, for a time. If all the women should die today, it wouldn't be six months till the men were living in caves and killing each other with war clubs.

For women, the burden involves not just emitting a moral or civilizing influence, as in the traditional "angel in the house" or true-woman depiction, but doing double and triple work each day in their homes, at their jobs, and in their communities, thus controlling the worst of the cruelty and selfishness nurtured in men.[5]

While in many articles Black comments on men feeling the need to act like beasts, or as Neanderthals who would kill each other with clubs, she also believed in their ability to change their behavior, to not be controlled by cultural expectations or traditions any more than women had to be, to recognize a changing normal. In fact, she often advises women to recognize the pressure men experience, to be tough and even brutal, an expectation that does not have to control them. In an advice column from 1914, for example, she talks about a girl whose brother who is always showing off. Black says in response to this girl's embarrassment that "every man in the world has a showing-off side in his life—that's the old primal male in him getting to the front. Haven't you ever seen a rooster strut around the barnyard just to make all the hens cluck excited comments on his glory and splendor? That's what brother is doing, sister. He wants all the ladies to cluck over him; he doesn't know it, but that's all that's the matter with him." And just as women are capable of change, she claims, so are men: "Poor fellow, some day he'll get over the 'rooster' period of his life. Then he'll turn red over every time he thinks of it. In the meantime the only thing that you can do is to grin and bear it—and be sure you grin all the time you're bearing it. That's the important part."[6]

Thus, in raising men, parents need to curb rooster tendencies, recognize them as a cultural tradition, and not as a gender difference: they should give their daughters a chance at independence and their sons equal responsibility in the home. And she often used specific situations to disparage any other possibility. In one column from 1914, for example, she scoffs at the ridiculousness of a boy who runs away from his aunt's home because he is asked to wash the dishes. His sisters chop wood, Black tells her readers, and it's only willfulness and selfishness, mistakenly nurtured in him, that allow the silly boy to deny responsibilities.[7]

## And Gender in the Business World

As Black considered gendered types of behavior, she contended that women and men were not required to adopt any particular type of behavior in the home and certainly not in the office: they could decide about what they wanted to say and do. In one column, she admits that women could be jealous of each other, competing for the boss' attention, setting others back. But she argues that this behavior also occurs commonly in men; indeed plots and competitions may form the nature of modern business. The sexes should not be judged in such large categories, she continues, since men and women can share so many traits, and no one is compelled to have any characteristics: the good and bad traits of office employees can exist in either gender. And she concludes that "breadth of mind, depth of soul, warmth of heart, keenness of perception, tolerance, justice—there is not sex in any of these qualities."[8]

## On Stereotypes Concerning Childbirth and Child Rearing

In considering the having and raising of children, Black makes some of her strongest and most controversial statements about gender and culture. Beyond the one biological reality, of childbirth, Black feels that so much is cultural and performative, beginning with childcare. "Some men love children and some women hate them," she wrote in 1915. "Why try to generalize? Most of the men I happen to know happen to be fond of children, and some of their wives are very anxious indeed not to have them."[9] In a column from 1922, she writes that "just like a woman" had been said since Adam and Eve, along with "just like a man," but neither of these phrases should actually be judged as being an insult or even as having a precise meaning. Here she makes a point about gender with reference to the latest trends and to children: "Some men may be more comfortable with babies; some women may be more involved with sports and they may be the ones smoking cigarettes."[10]

As she limits the biological to giving birth, Black recognizes that what occurs even directly afterwards may be culturally determined. In 1931, for example, she writes that weakness was a prized trait in women, after childbirth for example, but was not necessary, not appropriate for the work they had to do: "The average American woman expects to be a semi-invalid for months after her baby arrives—and nine times out of ten her expectations are fulfilled. What is there about civilization that drags down a woman's physique?" And then she continues with the larger cost of this weakness in women: "And does mental strength depend at all on bodily strength? If it does—well then perhaps we're in a bad way, we and our children's children."[11] And, in another column, from 1922, she argues that though most women want children, they do not want them so badly that they should be expected to do everything for them while men are out and about, here with reference to the latest dance craze: "No woman on earth wants to sit up at night with the baby while husband takes her pretty cousin to a tango party."[12]

In her columns, in recognizing the ability to give birth as the only real gender difference, Black frequently considers false double standards. Indeed, she describes such customs quite sarcastically in a column from 1915: "The double standard was established on the day that Eve bore her children in pain and agony, and Adam went out for a walk to admire the scenery so that he wouldn't be bothered with too much pity." But she claims that fatherhood was becoming an "acquired virtue" and could be given much more attention. As she advises men about child care, she expects not less of women but more of them: "Level up, not down."[13]

## On the Classic "Womanly" Behaviors

In this analysis of the performativity of gender, Black often wrote about many behaviors associated with women, beyond those connected to child care, as learned traditions, not who people needed to be.

One of her common topics was hysteria, the history of which she repeated in several columns. As she notes, Plato's dialogue *Timaeus* compares the uterus to a living creature that wanders throughout a woman's body, "blocking passages, obstructing breathing, and causing disease." Such a diagnosis, of a female instability that warranted rest and careful monitoring, became a symptom of, or even a credit to, the civilized and contained true woman of the nineteenth century. During the early twentieth century, as more women left their homes for school and work, as women played more sports and rode their bicycles, the number of women diagnosed with female hysteria declined sharply. Thus, Black argues, it was clearly a gendered trait that depended on the century or the decade, not on biology.[14]

Black discussed hysteria frequently in her columns at the beginning of the century when such a medical diagnosis was beginning to wane. She depicted not just the passage of time but the agency of women in creating this change: "Sick women are out of fashion; for that much we have to thank the modern woman. It used to be the thing to faint and have hysterics, and no perfect lady ever tried to walk a whole mile without swooning before she got to the end of it." In 1910, she notes that women themselves had once engaged in the extremes of hysteria to appear as the normal and approved, but they no longer had a use for it—womanhood had begun to involve sports, school, and work, and not fainting.[15]

Perhaps shocking her readers, Black also frequently wrote about men's use of hysteria, a word rarely applied to them. In a column from 1922, for example, she discusses a man who pretended to attempt suicide to get his wife's attention; he was jealous of her activities and friendships. Black calls his choices, using what was by then an old-fashioned term but certainly one applied just to women, as a form of hysteria, adopted to manipulate, a trait not viewed here as gender-specific, but as a technique employed by those who perceive themselves as deserving deference and acting enfeebled to get their way.[16]

To further engage readers with the subject of gender, Black often wrote columns about men who possess other traits commonly attributed to women. In an article from 1919, she describes the nagging employed by men, indeed by senators, to create an endless barrage that can net them what they want. A man might exploit this technique, as Black describes in her humorous tone, to shape his wife's behavior and to keep her from expressing her own opinions: "He criticizes and disagrees, and modifies and corrects, until every other woman in the room either feels like slapping him or else pities the wife." No one will wonder why, Black continues, if the wife decides to leave him.[17]

Similarly, in her discussion of vanity, Black depicts this traditionally gendered trait as applying to men. As evidence, in 1916, she considers a man of fifty, thinking that a young woman would marry him not for his money but for all he could teach her. He is thus demonstrating the utmost of vanity: no woman of fifty would make that assumption concerning a man of twenty-five.[18] This male vanity, Black asserts further, operates as an often unexamined cultural tradition when husbands expect to control their wives. In other articles, she speaks plainly about women as being vain primarily during their teenage years but men as becoming more vain, with social encouragement, in each decade of their lives. The average man, Black asserts, believes that even a queen or princess would be grateful to have him: "Did you ever see a man of any age, size, complexion, looks or ability who would be in the least surprised if a queen stepped down from her throne and begged him to let her go and live in a little two by four flat with him and be blissfully happy darning his socks the livelong day?"[19]

In an article from 1919, she discusses the ever new normal by labeling vanity as an old-fashioned attribute of men, one that they need to rid themselves of in the modern world. Concerning a husband who has mandated that his wife cannot take a job, in fact saying, "You shant," Black depicts his assertions as vanity, and as a throwback to another time: "Perhaps the little man's vanity is just the last link that is holding him and his wife to the old ideal—the ideal which made the woman the clinging vine and the man the oak."[20]

## Reviewing the Language of Gender

As Black judges assumptions concerning gendered behaviors, she also asks her readers to consider the word choices applied to women. Appearing on editorial and magazine pages, her articles on this subject were intended for men as well as women readers. They were especially focused on inappropriate body discourse, which readers were meant to recognize as ridiculous once they considered scenes in which it was employed. In one column from 1915, for example, she describes a man speaking to a woman's group, making comments about "birds, and flowers, and the evening breeze" and about the women's attractive looks, instead of speaking to them seriously. Here Black makes clear not only that such language is belittling but that these women are too confident to be actually wounded by it, and certainly they are not complimented: indeed, they did "the best they could to keep from laughing outright." And then she goes on to a more extreme example to make her case about the demeaning language of body compliments: if a woman were leaving a battlefield with her dying son in her arms, would a man comment that her eyes were beautiful and expect her to be pleased? Her title "Why Should Men Talk 'Up' or 'Down' to Women?" asks the question, with the answer clearly that there is no reason for them to do either.[21]

In another column from 1915, "Woman Wants Brains, Not Beauty, Praised," Black creates another scene in which gendered language and judgments appear as ridiculous, here concerning a concert by a professional pianist who plays Strauss, Debussy, Wagner, Beethoven, and Liszt. After the performance, a man goes up to her, and his comment is "'What delicious little hands you have! How in the world do you manage to reach an octave?'" Here again the man is clearly out of synch with what women are: "The old-fashioned man is wondering yet why the new-fashioned woman turned her back and did not even answer." Black continues in this article by moving to the larger topic of body remarks that women are no longer willing to pretend to find pleasing, again an indicator of change in normal behavior: "How can they live and not see that the world they live in is changing like the pictures on a screen and that nothing in the world is changing as fast as the woman who lives in it? Old and young, pretty and ugly, clever and stupid, the modern woman has begun to ask to be admired, not for what she can't help, but for what she can." Focusing further on changing codes, Black maintains that thirty years earlier women with fewer opportunities might have been satisfied by the hands comment, "but the man who tells her of her beauty when she's trying to convince him of her sense does not please her any more." In fact, she continues, women at a summer resort made a skit of all the silly things that men said to them—here all women seem to be aware of the insult inherent in vapid body compliments.[22]

In this discussion of gendered discourse, Black moved beyond personal interactions to the political. At the 1920 Democratic Party convention, held in San Francisco, party leaders claimed that they fully supported women suffrage even though they had not done so in 1916 and Woodrow Wilson did not give his support until passage seemed an inevitable outcome in September 1918. Even as these leaders sought to increase support by women, as Black reported, they repeatedly employed inappropriate body imagery that the women there were supposed to find thrilling. Indeed, every time a woman went onto the stage, the band played "Oh, You Beautiful Doll." Maybe this song choice was cute the first time, Black tells her readers, but it soon devolved into idiocy, as judged by the women there.[23]

Moving from personal and public interactions to the assumptions of other newspaper writers, Black further developed her analysis of traditional discourse in an article from January 1917 concerning Jeannette Rankin, member of Congress, whose qualifications for office she begins this piece by summarizing. Rankin attended the New York School of Philanthropy, later part of Columbia University, from 1908 to 1909, then moved to Spokane. After briefly doing social work, she went to the University of Washington and there became involved in the women's suffrage movement. Then, in Montana where women gained the vote in 1914, she was elected to an at-large seat in the U.S. House of Representatives, the first female member of Congress. Here Black claims that in covering her career, newspapers repeatedly skipped these qualifications and instead bragged that she "makes her own clothes, trims her own hats, and bakes the best biscuits in Montana." Black then examines the hubris, the utter vanity, of a common belief that Rankin would not stay long in Congress because these housekeeping skills would cause some man to want to marry her, and she would give up her ambitions and political principles for that opportunity. Maybe, Black continues in a highly sarcastic tone, Rankin wasn't elected because she has "brains and character and energy and ambition"; perhaps people felt sorry for her because she wasn't married and thus elected her. It is a masculine conceit, Black further maintains, to believe that women would give up everything for marriage. Will Rankin continue in Congress or leave to darn socks, Black asks, her answer to the question certainly clear.[24]

In making the argument "that we're cut out of just about the same kind of cloth all of us, both men and women, after all," Winifred Black repeatedly claims that the usual definitions of gender normality stem from cultural expectations, not biology. For Black, a reconsideration of the normal could influence opinions about the traits of both genders and the language used to compliment or accuse. Ultimately, as she often stated vehemently, this knowledge altered expectations of women as bodies and as partners: "Why! Man alive, a woman isn't just a sex, with a curl or a braid and a ruffle or a swish with which to fascinate the male. She's a human being, and she has a mind and a soul and a heart, as well as imagination and a body."[25] Although Black certainly recognizes that men may perceive themselves as needing to be "wild beasts" while women may think they should become sexual conquests or doting mothers, the specifics of her nonfiction characters, scenes, and analysis create a more complex landscape of gender.

# 11

## *Prejudice Against the Other: Concerning Race, Sexual Preference and the Women Who Aren't Like Us*

Beyond gender differences and the changing landscape of the normal, one of Black's common topics was prejudice against groups deemed as Other by middle-class and wealthy white Americans whose lives were generally chronicled in newspapers. "It is nothing less than a shock," she argued in 1921, "when you run into the hard crust of prejudice, when you are hearing a clever man or woman talk. Curious, isn't it, how the letting of the mind accept, without question, foregone conclusions sterilizes and kills all spontaneous thinking and speaking."[1] Black frequently employed nonfiction scenes and characters as she wrote about various forms of prejudice, and especially about so many stereotypes of women, and she asked readers to come along with her by examining their own values. In an essay from 1929, about a visitor who helps a homeowner to clear out the closets, Black advises some "house-cleaning for our minds" to move beyond unexamined prejudices, a type of house-cleaning that occurred commonly in her writing.[2]

## Considering Stereotypes: The Gay American as Other

In her writing, Black seemed generally to assume that her readers were involved with marriage and children, that they were planning or engaged in heterosexual lives. Certainly being gay was not a major subject in her writing, but she did give it some, albeit guarded, attention, as almost no other newspaper writers did. To involve readers in this topic, as with many others, she employed lists, description, and scenes; she also relied on her technique of stating and altering her own prejudices, thus attempting to alter the prejudices common in her audience.

In one column in 1922, with so much change occurring at the time, she comments on what she calls "gentlemanly girls," which she describes as "smart and well-groomed with their hair bobbed, short skirts, neat boots, regulation puttees, golf sticks, cigarettes." She speaks first of her own quick judgment of them: "I'm afraid I'm old-fashioned enough to like the regular type best." But as she records their interactions and their fun but thoughtful conversation, she moves beyond her initial judgment and writes that they are "frank, clear-eyed, unaffected creatures," a judgment that she encourages readers to share.[3] These women may be heterosexual flappers, trying out all the new styles, or they may be part of what Lillian Faderman discussed as the "fledgling lesbian community" of the 1920s, but what matters here is these young women's good sense and friendship.[4]

In another column from the early 1920s, she uses description and an examination of her own prejudices as she writes about men who appear to be less than all-American masculine, who might be gay. She describes on the train "a strange lady-like person who buys face powder and talcum powder and monogrammed socks—a being who likes shaded lights and soft colors and can't bear to hear the word 'baseball.'" And she continues that "there were five or six of them in the observation car, chattering away like so many magpies, lifting their eyebrows and tossing their heads and going into the barber's to be manicured and massaged." Next she admits the strong prejudice that she felt at the sight of them: "I wanted to creep away some place where I couldn't possibly see them, or hear them—or even hear of them again." But then she narrates a scene in which a young mother struggles with her baby while trying to get out her train ticket; no one comes up to help her except for one of these men. She concludes that she finds herself open to the discussion of what makes a good man or woman that the younger generation has initiated: "Just like a man—just like a woman—go on with your nice little discussion, boys and girls. I like the sound of it. There is something natural about it."[5] In such an essay, Black aligns herself with the prejudices of many readers and then uses specifics to encourage them to at least consider changing their opinions, of the right and natural, along with her.

## Considerations of Race

Race was not one of Black's more common topics; the characters in many columns can be presumed to be white, and she did not seem to write about the situation of the Chinese Americans in San Francisco. But race was not something that she totally avoided either, her nonfiction emphasis involving a close look at individuals. Other column writers of her era either ignored the subject or exploited the worst of stereotypes. Dorothy Dix, for example, wrote regular syndicated columns as her character Mirandy, this character speaking in heavy dialect occasioning jokes about African Americans. In a New Year's column for 1906, for example, Mirandy reveals herself as someone who had rarely told the truth, had been staying out all night while her husband stayed home, and had heaped abuse on her children: "Den my mind misgive me dat maybe I kinder held a too tight rein on Ike, an' dat dere was a little too much knock-down-an'-drag-out policy in de way I manage de chillen." When she vows to be more truthful, as the story continues, she no longer fits with her neighbors, who all lie about everything. In Black's nonfiction, she certainly didn't create any such "humorous" characters, but instead tried to engage with the facts of actual Americans.[6]

In her investigative articles as well as in her columns, she was willing to ask harsh questions about race in the United States and provide her own answers for readers to consider. For the *Philadelphia North American* in December of 1899, not a Hearst paper, she wrote about a lynching in Maysville, Kentucky. An African American, Richard Coleman, had been seized by a mob while being transported to a courthouse for trial in a rape and murder case; he was then burned to death. Here she employs dialogue to move from her discussion of the murder to local citizens who instill prejudice and violence in their children. She tells of being in the parlor of an honorable Maysville family, known across the state. The wife reads that a grand jury is investigating the lynching. A family member, a county administrator, comments that the court is "obliged to do that" and indicates his own complicity by further stating that "I certainly wouldn't like to testify in court about who helped at that little bee." Black then turns to the children growing up in that house. The little girl says, "I saw the nigger burnt, didn't I, mamma?" "Yes, honey," replies her mother. And then Black moves on to questions that construct the reader as repulsed by what happened in Maysville: "Do you remember that little Maysville affair, you who are reading this? Do you remember how your heart died within you at the very headlines which told how a miserable wretch was burned alive in the presence of a joking mob of men, women and children, who laughed aloud?" And then Black asks her readers another key question: "What kind of men are bred in such an atmosphere?" And she answers with specifics about the result of fostering violence and hatred: "Teach a boy from the time he can toddle that his natural weapon is a six-shooter or a knife, and you must not be surprised if he gets into trouble for using it someday. Educate a girl to believe that a man must be ready to shoot another man on any sort of trivial pretext or be branded as a coward and you can pave the way to a nation of assassins."[7]

Similarly, in November of 1900, Black chose to write about a case in

Limon, Colorado, another lynching of an African American boy, age sixteen. Preston Porter, Jr., who had confessed to the murder of a white girl, was led by rope through town, and then tied to a stake and burned to death. He screamed out to be shot, but onlookers only heaped on more fuel. Black's harsh condemnation appeared in newspapers throughout the West, both her complete article and excerpts from it. The law should have been allowed to administer justice, and thugs who would drag a man out and burn him to death had to be punished: "So Says Winifred Black," as she was widely quoted.[8]

Beyond legal cases and trials, Black wrote about individuals that she knew. In an article about stereotypes of rich and poor, for example, she attempts to overturn economic and racial prejudice by looking at what specific people do and not what they might be assumed to do as members of a group. Not all wealthy people are greedy; not all are generous and kind. And, similarly, she continues, "there are so many poor, and every one of them a different kind." And then she moves to the example of an African American employee: "There's my washerwoman, for instance, as black as a human being can be, ill and asthmatic, taking care of three grandchildren." This woman tries to help others in her neighborhood, especially those who are unemployed; she does her work well; she plans for her grandchildren's future. She is an individual worthy of the reader's consideration.[9]

As Black looked at the complexities of actual people and of prejudices, she also wrote about native Americans. One of her interviews, from 1892, concerned Chief Standing Bear of the Sioux, who referred to Black as White Squaw with Talking Paper. He was in San Francisco as part of a wild west show when she interviewed him with an interpreter, her long article published with the provocative title of "A Woman and a Savage" and with a subhead that spoke of his roaming the plains before the arrival of the pale face. In a theatre with German musicians and an English troupe of performers, she labels him as "the only real American in the place." He tells her that he often had to fight to protect his land from white soldiers, and she speaks of him in an exaggerated fashion as a "ferocious old fighter in every single war the whites have had with the Indians." Noting the prejudice that white men feel for a fighter with his past, he fears that they may take revenge, as Black notes: "Why, you know, he won't walk on the sidewalk for anything. Walks right in the middle of the street and makes every one of his braves come after him single file. Says he can see around better." Here she discusses his choices as what he had to do to survive, as fighting for his group and their land, what anyone would do to protect his own. While she has chosen the provocative label of "savage," she also chooses to look closely at the choices that circumstances required him to make.[10]

## Probing Women's Judgments of Each Other

As Black wrote about prejudice, she was also willing to consider women's prejudices towards each other, judgments that they make especially when they have no acquaintance with various types of women. Black often maintained that for women to enlarge their worlds, they needed to engage in the lives of others instead of turning away, exhibiting an openness that could begin in reading nonfiction.

In 1905, when she wrote for Hearst's *Cosmopolitan* about small gold-mining towns in Death Valley, Black considered a world in which women were not so judgmental, her story of an odd locale pointing to the possibility of communities among women. In small towns like Bullfrog and Tonopah, she describes gambling and quick money loss and gain, involving what she labels as "up-to-date Argonauts." Even as she discusses frontier mining, she also focuses on the women in these towns: "Women there are in plenty, all kinds of them, from the little Boston bride who is trying her best not to let her husband know how desperately homesick she is, to the elderly widow from Nebraska who has come to make her fortune selling homemade pies and shortcakes." And she also comments on the "democratic way of doing things in the desert camps." With no distinctions by class, she finds women willing to speak to each other, to be part of a group, to not judge another woman's means of making a living: "The haughtiest woman in the community will stop to listen to the words that fall from the lips of the woman whose pink wrapper flutters in the ever-blowing breeze, so be it the tale she tells concerns strikes or leads." In this frontier community, women did not find themselves separated by class or neighborhood; instead, they could move beyond the stereotypes or divisions that ruled in cities, united in a shared situation and interests like gold and land. Just as such a space could move women beyond traditional judgments, so could the wider experience of learning about various situations and communities through nonfiction.[11]

Though she wrote about the oddities of Bullfrog and Tonopah, Black recognized that in most cities and towns women could be judgmental, certainly upper-class women could be so even as they tried to help women of lesser means. Black repeatedly spoke in support of women working in factories and as servants: they were proud of themselves, and they did not need to be redefined by upper-class efforts to provide aid. In "Ladies, or Women," from March of 1910, she writes about the West End Woman's Club in Chicago, which was campaigning for working women to be called "young ladies employed." These club women wanted to provide the "young ladies" with a place to go, for recreation and instruction, extending the growing settlement movement founded in 1887 by graduates of Smith, Bryn Mawr, and Wellesley. To provide "uplifting influences" in the slums, these activists established homes that could serve as meeting centers for young working women, dividing them into "clubs" and giving instruction in homemaking skills, in the arts of singing, gymnastics, and dancing, and in high-school subjects, with involvement from many women's clubs.[12]

While Black does not disapprove of practical offers of help, she will not agree that working women are downtrodden, that they need help more than anyone else, or that richer women should assume the right to prescribe for them. "Women who work are usually women with sense," she argues as she turns from settlement classes to her larger subject of the respect due to women workers. "They have to be, or they couldn't work for a living—and earn it." She even claims that they are probably happier than the average society girls who might seek to help them, with more brains, more sense of purpose, more to do.[13]

## The Telling Example of Prostitution

To get the attention of readers, Black often chose the extreme case. In her quest to encourage women to consider the lives of women deemed as Other more thoughtfully, she frequently wrote about prostitution, using that least acceptable of occupations to write further about women's prejudices toward each other.

She frequently wrote about the power of women as well as men in labeling a woman as a whore, a topic that she especially pursued in the 1920s as young people experienced more freedoms but might be judged for embracing them and indeed might become embroiled in more than they intended. She recognized that women could be labeled as prostitutes for loose behavior, whether they were taking money for sex or not. In 1923, she wrote that no matter what a young woman might prefer to think, the man who "picks up" a stranger has a sexual opinion of her from the minute she steps into his car. A woman who would leave a club with a stranger, Black says directly to her readers, may get the reputation of a whore: "No matter what he says or how many romantic stories you read, girls, or what you see in the movies, the man who asks you to go for a ride with him when you don't know him must just as well call you a good old-fashioned Biblical name right out in plain English and be done with it."[14]

In writing about women who did take money for sex, Black provided stories of individuals. In one column from 1912, she tells a story about a poor man and his wife endeavoring to help their child who fainted on a mountain road, a place on a difficult trail where someone had recently died from exposure. Black counts the tourists that pass by in their cars: "No: five, six, seven, all passing, not one of them even slackens speed. Oh, yes! they see the girl well enough; see them crane their necks to miss no part of the sensation." And then the painted woman, "coarse featured, bold eyed, loose mouth," is the one who stops and helps very efficiently: in her big car she takes the entire family to the hospital, where she pays for the child's treatment. Black talks with her at a campground later to ask about the child, but the other women there still will not speak to her, their judgments of her occupation, her place in life, too rigid for them to acknowledge the painted woman's selfless compassion, but Black expects her readers to do so.[15]

In her many other articles on prostitution, Black certainly did not ask her readers to embrace this choice, and she could be very critical of the decision to become a prostitute. But she did ask them to consider what might cause a woman to make this choice. One column, for example, concerns a woman who went into the red light district to sell her body, not out of desperation or bad judgment or domination by an evil man, but for fun and for extra money to buy a new hat and clothes, things that her father would not buy for her. For Black, the reason that a woman would choose such a life bears careful consideration as her "sister woman" makes judgments of it:

> The woman who makes a mistake in life—the most terrible mistake a woman can make—and makes it because she is young and light-hearted and light-headed, or because she is in love with love or with some one particular man, oh, who can treat her with enough kindness and pity? What sister woman is there who dares call her too cruelly to account?
> But the woman who throws away her good name, the woman who sells herself body and soul for a new hat or a new frock or a pair of diamond earrings—well, poor fool, she gets the things she wants and the things that belong to her and to her sort of woman.

The woman thus seeking money for extra things doesn't deserve the shedding of tears, the offer of sympathy, but clearly for Black a young woman who desperately needs money or who is manipulated or forced into the work would deserve a different type of response: indeed she may have made the only available choice.[16] By forging these distinctions, Black asks her reader to think fully about these women's lives and not to place them all in one category: not all piteous, not all evil, not to be immediately judged without a consideration of their circumstances.

Black responded similarly to a international campaign to save young prostitutes, launched at the beginning of the twentieth century under the powerful label of "white slavery." During the Progressive era, whether prostitutes were abducted, manipulated, or resorted to "the life" to earn a living, reformers, including many leaders of women's clubs and settlement houses, began to class them as "white slaves," a term stipulating that women would never adopt this life voluntarily and that they needed to be rescued and brought back to some semblance of moral American life. Many African American writers, concerned about black women's migration to northern cities, cautioned against evil companions that might propel the unwary to prostitution, but as the term "white slavery" suggests, most of the publicity concerned white women forced into this life.[17] For newspaper editors like William Randolph Hearst, this campaign could foster stunt-girl articles offering both erotic physical details and moral purpose. Nellie Bly and Nell Nelson, both at the *New York World*, wrote exposés on the manipulation of individual women, victims of cruel men, their degradation rendered with piteous detail, but Winifred Black would not take on such an assignment.

Instead, as a cultural critic, Black wrote about the concept of white slavery. In response to this publicity, she asked readers to consider not just the women working in this trade but the women and men trying to save them. For Black, women involved in this trade did not automatically need judgment and protection, by clubs or governments: they could make their own choices. "Working girls are not unhappy, downtrodden, heartbroken creatures at all," she maintained in 1915, and said they were making their own choices, not necessarily involved in any form of slavery if they worked as prostitutes, able to seek help if they needed it. For Black the important message was that women acted through their agency even if others would not understand or approve: she did not like to view women in any situation as passive victims necessarily in need of saving.[18]

Black eschewed severe judgments of any working women as victims or as harridans, their individual situations deserving thoughtful attention instead of instant decrees concerning guilt or innocence. In these articles about prostitution, she also turned her attention not only to the women who refused to speak with them at a campground, but to the women and men who endeavored to save them. One such piece concerned women reformers who turned prostitutes away from a meeting in which they went on and on about ending the white slavery trade, about the need to save other women. Describing a distraught prostitute whom they ignored and then escorted to the door, Black uses "we" to depict the group response: "We turned out the poor thing who was facing woman's hour of supreme torment—turned her out to suffer and to die, alone, and prided ourselves on our virtues and our principles when we did it." This "we" of activists on the white slave question, who might construct themselves as so sympathetic, here appears completely judgmental, without interest in or knowledge of these actual working women. Such an activist "we" needs, in Black's viewpoint, a "good dose of some medicine of common sense" to avoid being "maudlin, hysterical faddists on the white slave question."

Black also wrote about movies that this white-slavery reform campaign fostered, advertised as providing a helpful warning to young women but actually just an exploitation of sex, in her estimation. These films included, from

1913, *Traffic in Souls* and *The Inside of the White Slave Traffic*. Black argues that such depictions could have no moral influence since, as she often maintained, "every girl in her teens knows right from wrong" and will make her own choices—and thus needs no film to explain the possible paths to her.[19] Another column concerns a play about white slavery, containing what she labels as "sexplanations" and depicting these sex workers, as she describes the play's exaggerated content, as victims dragged "through flood and famine, through fire and brimstone, through neglect and cruelty, to the end of the world." Black doesn't cite a title here but many such plays appeared in 1913 and 1914, with titles like *Trapped in the Great Metropolis,* and so she may have wanted her judgment to apply to the group, many of them being made into films. Such sexplanations, she argues, had become a topic of conversation, something for polite society and clergy to get excited about, but with little real knowledge of reality or the reasons for the choices that women made.[20]

Though Black generally supported Hearst's reform efforts, launched through the pages of the *Examiner* and backed by his own fortune, she sought to avoid involvement in his campaign to close The Barbary Coast, a red-light district, nine blocks of San Francisco bounded by Montgomery Street, Washington Street, Stockton Street, and Broadway. With Hearst's anti-vice campaign and then the passage of the 1914 Red Light Abatement Act, the Barbary Coast was effectively diminished and vice activities not suspended but for a time hidden from view, but not with help from Winifred Black. Instead of contributing to this effort that judged all prostitutes alike, Black used the nonfiction interview to examine particular realities of this choice of work. One of her dramatic openers introduced a woman trying to kill herself because of the closing of the Barbary Coast. "She jumped into the bay, in despair, out in San Francisco—one of the women who has been making her living in a Barbary Coast resort," where she had worked as a prostitute for eight to ten dollars a night. In an interview that took place right after the woman was rescued, she told Black that she has no other means of supporting her two daughters, ages ten and twelve. Thus the morals police who would close down this area have rendered her unable to support her family, impossible, she has found, by washing floors or taking any other job that she can secure. The city government, or the city's newspaper, or even this reporter who would wish for her to find better employment should not make decisions for her.[21] As Black would do concerning many issues, she here expressed her trust in the adult woman's right and ability to make her own choices. About prostitution, she creates a double judgment that she offers as a possibility for her readers: they do not have to find prostitution an acceptable choice, but they should engage in considering the circumstances involved and in respecting the fact that women have made these choices.

In many of her columns, Black took on the subject of prejudice, examining the treatment of those deemed to constitute the Other, a subject that few writers tackled in newspapers. Along with considering traditions concerning what was normal and abnormal for women and men, she wrote about other sites of prejudice, among them race and sexual preference. In even taking on women's customary judgments of each other, Black asked readers to move beyond stereotypical visions of the Other and to think more individually and critically.

# 12

# *Independence and Dependence/ Parents and Children*

Beyond constructions of gender and race, beyond prejudices at the heart of American life, another well-developed theme in Winifred Black's nonfiction is certainly independence, depicted for both genders in an array of ways, but especially concerning women as they made decisions through the decades about leaving home, securing an education or a job, and getting married or divorced. In the 1910s and 1920s, with more possibilities available, she especially concentrated on older expectations of parents and newer choices for young women. She often depicted key moments of separation as symbolic of the determination that would be required throughout life, this theme perhaps reflecting her own path forward, which included leaving home to act in a traveling theatre troupe, searching for her brother in the West, becoming stunt girl and journalist published across the country, marrying twice, and then owning homes and raising her children on her own.

Concerning the adolescent and young adult, Black often wrote specifically and derisively about children that remain in their parents' shadow. In a column entitled "Winifred Black Writes about Roses and Daughters," to describe a daughter impeded by her mother's care she uses the image of a woman who pounds nails through rose bushes, attaching them to a wall, making them look neat but stunting them instead of helping them to grow:

> She has a delightful home—of her mother's choosing. Pretty clothes—made to her mother's taste. A circle of friends—all carefully picked out for her by her mother.
> She never reads a book her mother has not read first.
> She never sees a play her mother hasn't seen first.
> I always wondered why she looked so discontented. Since I've known about the roses I begin to understand.[1]

Viewing such domination as unnatural and cruel, Black wrote frequently about the natural drive for independence, the positive move into adulthood for young women as well as men. In "Winifred Black Writes about a Daughter's Problem," from 1923, she advocates for independence and greater choice for daughters by reminding their mothers of the freedoms that they themselves had sought, distressing at the time to their own parents, about which she addresses one mother directly: "She had to bear with you, your mother, you can look back and see it now, and she probably thought you were just as impossible as you think your girl is today." As she further addresses the mother, Black speaks for the desire for independence as ongoing, as binding the generations: "Let her fuss and fume, and preen her feathers, poor little thing. She is just following out a great, natural law.... She will settle down in time, and you and she will have many a laugh together over the things that seem so tragic to you now." Black ends the piece by further arguing for the independent life required by women: "Don't be so hard on Little Daughter—don't think so much about her—she is something beside your daughter—she is a human being, with her own heart and her own mind and her own soul. Help her all you can, but don't criticize her so bitterly, even in your own heart. Daughters are mind-readers sometimes, and then resent what you think almost as much as what you say."[2]

Part of independence comes in young women as well as men moving out from home and supporting themselves, an especially complicated choice, Black makes clear, for girls growing up in the homes of domineering fathers who also control their mothers. Where the young woman is uncomfortable, straining under imposed restrictions, she should leave and she should do so by herself unless the mother, another woman making her own choices, seeks to leave with her. Here Black addresses the daughter: "What a mean little miserable business it is—this living under one roof, when you hate each other, so that you can hardly bear to breathe the same air! Why don't you go to work and take care of yourself? No, don't take your mother away from your father—not unless she finds it absolutely impossible to live with him."[3] Another column concerns Louise, age nineteen, with a cruel father who contains her, admitting of no joy though she gets out to be with friends as much as she can, behavior for which she is frequently admonished. With an angry father and a beaten-down, nagging, unhappy mother, both "crushing life and joy out of their house, and at the same time taking the careless sweetness of youth out of their children," the daughter must find some means of escape.[4] If such an unhappy daughter remains at home and thus financially and emotionally dependent, she should not complain: "As long as you take money from your father or any other human being, you must be loyal. This man, rough and disagreeable as he is, who keeps the roof over your head and food in your mouth and clothes on your back, has a right to some kind of gratitude and some attempt at understanding."[5]

In Black's analysis of fathers, the cruelty did not have to be quite so obvious, a subtle perhaps as dangerous as a more overt form of control. One column from 1914, for example, depicts a kindly and concerned father, frantic

## 12. Independence and Dependence/Parents and Children

because his daughters want to grow up and leave. One wants to teach dancing, one to be a painter: both seek to leave their small hometown and live in New York City. He can't believe that these young women want to leave his lovely big home and involve themselves in the arts and the city. Black's interview with him reveals that he had no problems with the daughter who wanted to marry or with the sons who left to pursue their own ambitions. And then Black asks the father a question comparing these approved siblings with the two who long for freedom: "Why haven't the others the same right to their own independence as she, or as the boys?" And her final appeal to the reader reveals her insistence that control stifles young women, making of them something that "we do not love to think of."[6]

Similarly, in "Winifred Black Writes about Why Girls Leave Home," a column much reprinted, its title reiterating the name of a popular melodrama about young adults with restrictive parents, Black again speaks of the stunting of young women: "Starved for beauty, starved for peace, starved for quiet, starved for room enough to turn around, starved for company of their own age, starved for sympathy and starved—this is the worst starvation at all—starved for love." And here the love she discusses is not the love of a young man but the true love of parents who respect what a young woman might want to make of her own life.[7]

Such independence, for Black, involves not just leaving home but finding a life's work. She recognizes that young women may have crazy plans, impractical, but they also have the right to make their own way. In one column, from 1914, she discusses young women taking off to study art in New York and in Europe, and she admits that they might be a bit silly and self-indulgent: they might desire to become stylish bohemians not hard-working artists. But here she also argues that only with such opportunities and training can the true artist emerge. In this piece, she speaks directly to the mother of such an artist: "You can't keep your genius at home, little mother with the anxious eyes. She's an eagle and all your cluckings will never make a little brown hen of her." The answer to her titular question of "What Threatens the Girl Art Student?" concerns parents more than any other difficulties.[8]

When the daughter has left the home and is supporting herself, Black asserted in other columns, she should not be immediately pressured to marry, the next form of Foucaultian family pressure and social discipline. One column on this subject concerns a happy working woman, living in her own home, who makes up boyfriends to please her mother although she has no attention of ever marrying. Here Black again addresses a mother directly: "You're obsessed with the old-fashioned idea that a woman can't be happy unless she's married." And she then presents her own data about the potential happiness of various choices: "Of course we all know that a true marriage is the greatest happiness in the world, but a single woman is 10 times as independent as the happiest married woman in the world, and she's twice as happy as an unhappy married woman." Black then claims further that several of the daughter's married friends are tired and ignored, one having been abandoned for a chorus girl and another having endless mother-in-law problems. "Let daughter manage her own affairs," the piece concludes.[9]

In all of these depictions and arguments, Black advocated for the independence of young women and men and argued that it was more prevalent than perhaps it was. Dependence, she maintained on the women's page, editorial page, and front page, should not be expected of or chosen by adults. Guided by the stories and analysis of nonfiction, both women and men could initiate a quest for a personally chosen life, supporting themselves and achieving freedom, not a selfish choice in Black's estimation, but what human beings were meant to do, an argument ultimately not about one gender but about adulthood.

# 13

# Working Women

In her *Good Housekeeping* autobiography in 1936, Black wrote about so much change that had occurred during her lifetime in the American view of women as workers. "And I have seen the whole status of women change like something in a pageant," she wrote, and then explained further:

> When I was a girl, a woman who worked was pitied. A man would not let a wife or a sister or a mother or even a maiden aunt work to support herself, not while he could keep a roof over their heads. If he had let one of his womenfolk work, he would have been an outcast from his fellow men. I have known in my time those sad widows of the world who have never married and who were the unpaid servants of their married relatives. I am glad there is no necessity for women of that sort in the world any more.[1]

From the beginning of her career, Black frequently chronicled women at work, a subject perhaps of particular interest to her as one of the few women in the field of journalism in 1889 and one of the most successful at her death in 1936, her emphasis repeatedly on what had already changed and could change further to improve the workplace. Her affirmation of independence and the changing sphere of the normal would continue in her coverage of work.

## Women on the Job

Throughout her career, Black wrote about the attitudes of women and men concerning the growing trend of women on the job. During the years of her career, the participation of women in American labor increased steadily. In 1890, 17 percent of women age fourteen and over had gainful employment, this designation including any work for pay or profit at a business or on a farm for more than fifteen hours a week. From 1890 to 1910, the percentage of men in such employ was over eighty, and a percentage or two below that in 1920 and 1930, but though it was much lower, the percentage was increasing for women: in 1900, 18.1 percent; in 1920, 20.4 percent; and in 1930, 21.9 percent.[2] With a growing population, of course, this increase meant much larger numbers. From 1900 to 1920 the number of women in white-collar jobs, for example, surged from 949,000 to 3,353,000, the biggest jump within this category occurring in clerical positions but also with a much greater level of participation across the other employment labeled as white-collar, such as professional, sales, technical, and management.[3]

With this marked upsurge, many issues arose concerning working women that Black examined through nonfiction. For a series in the *Examiner* that also appeared in papers across the country in May of 1914, Black was asked to name the world's greatest woman, but instead of choosing a well-known figure in philanthropy or social service or the suffrage campaign, as other writers did, she decided on regular working women as her object of respect.[4] Throughout her career, she would employ that respectful tone even as her specific subject matter changed in her ongoing attempt to consider workplace realities.

## Positive Constructions to Begin Her Coverage of Work

In describing women at work, Black wrote repeatedly—and with different emphases—about why they were there. In her first decade as a journalist, she spoke positively about women taking jobs, about their ability to do the work and their laudable reasons for doing so, perhaps simplifying a complex space to enact a positive situation that she depicted as already fully in existence.

In 1894, Black wrote that men deemed women's work to be acceptable when women had to support themselves and their family members and when they worked at something for which they were well suited and qualified. In those situations, she claimed, and perhaps she was attempting to render this judgment true, women did not have to face accusations concerning their "proper sphere": "Who ever hears of a practical, sensible woman, in any business or profession whatsoever, being called to order by the 'sphere' question. If a woman must earn her living nowadays she goes out and earns it, in any decent way she thinks fit. The most profound woman-hater of them all never dreams of finding fault with her for that." Black claims further that proper-sphere criticisms surfaced primarily when women sought suffrage and equal rights; then men suddenly judged that they were needed at home. But women could work at anything they could do, even digging ditches or taking on other physical labor, without such derision occurring, without "the most profound woman-hater" having any impact on a woman's choices at all.[5]

In many other articles in the next decades, perhaps assuming what she wanted to be true, Black wrote further about women's opportunity to do a job for which they were qualified. In "Some Advice to Women," from July 1908, she responds to a claim made at a Women's Wage Earners Convention that women employees needed to fight the tyrannical man. Her answer might have encouraged women to work though it was not quite accurate: "The man who wants a competent stenographer doesn't care whether that stenographer is black, white, green, or yellow, old or young, man or woman. Half the time he really doesn't know. All he knows is that his work is well done, in which case the stenographer gets a good salary and holds on to a good position.... There is and should be no such thing as sex in business."[6]

## Moving to a More Complex View

Black maintained at the end of the nineteenth century that women could work without negative reaction, perhaps to encourage them to enter into employment if they wanted to do so. As she continued with this subject, she crafted a more complex view of women in the work world, recognizing barriers to their working as she also carefully introduced a wider range of reasons for their doing so.

With increased participation in the work force, Black began to argue not that there was no prejudice but that women should not be subjected to the prejudices then occurring, especially concerning their reason for working. In 1917, for example, she recognized that many men judged women as just at the office or store to somehow entertain themselves. She knows no women, she replies, who work for fun or for vanity. Here, in a list of appropriate reasons for work, she links independence and self-respect with the more acceptable care of others: "They want money, they want independence, they want self-respect, and in nine times out of ten they use more than half of the money they earn taking care of somebody."[7] In 1928, with the provocative title "Yes, Women Take Men's Jobs Despite All Social Theories," she again discusses the common belief that women worked just for amusement. She begins here with men who, angry because women took their jobs, say that women should stay at home and not take needed money from responsible men: they are missing the fact that women may do the work as capably or more so than men and that they may be supporting themselves and their families as well as developing their own abilities and interests.[8]

During the Depression, also, Black wrote about the need to work, about women's right to keep their jobs though she acknowledged the opposition to their employment engendered by sharply increasing unemployment. "On the whole the business woman is a pretty good sort of human being," she maintained in 1934. "She's usually intelligent and she's usually generous with her limited means, she'd like to see every other woman have as good a job as she has. The business world today could not do without her."⁹

## Arguing for Workplace Change by Positive Examples of It

As a greater percentage, and certainly a much larger number, of women sought employment, Black continued to speak respectfully of their efforts, but she also began to write about changes needed in the workplace. She often employed the positive example, in articles on the women's page or the editorial page, to advocate for a more widespread workplace equality.

During World War I, for example, she wrote about women working in hospitals and in factories and about their need for pay equality. In manufacturing jobs, in 1914, the average weekly salary for women was $7.75 for a fifty hour week and for unskilled men was $10.71, with skilled men earning $14.99.¹⁰ When the typewriter came into common office use in the 1890s, women had rapidly moved into clerical jobs, for which there might be a decent income, certainly more than for teaching, but not with salaries equal to those of men.¹¹

In dealing with inequities, Black often led with positive examples, making an attempt to extend their influence. In one column, beginning with "Hurray for Uncle Sam!," she reports that the Navy had begun paying women clerks the same wages as the men, that Uncle Sam, actually Navy Secretary Josephus Daniels, had made this promise to Carrie Chapman Catt, along with giving the order for women to have hiring preference in office jobs.¹² In March 1917, with the United States entering the war, the Navy's need for clerical assistance had been far greater than anticipated. Daniels enrolled women in the Naval Reserve to work as clerks, thus releasing enlisted men for active service at sea. As a result, 11, 275 Yeomen (F) were in service at the time the armistice was signed, the largest recruitment of women by the armed services: only about three hundred "marinettes," as the Marine Corps designated women, were on duty during the war. In addition to performing clerical duties, the Yeomen (F) served as translators, architectural drafters, fingerprint experts, camouflage designers, and recruiting agents, in the Panama Canal zone, Hawaii, and France as well as in the United States.¹³ As Black discusses Catt's involvement with Daniels and his decision concerning pay equity, she celebrates this incidence of common sense and justice: "Work should be paid for by what it is and not by who does it." She then uses this patriotic appeal involving the armed services in wartime, and Uncle Sam's (Daniels') choices, to argue that this principle should apply equally in other parts of government and in the private sector.¹⁴

This concentration on examples of equity, presented in an attempt to extend their influence, continued through the decades. In 1929, for example, Black reported in a column syndicated around the country on teachers in San Francisco who had recently begun to be allowed to remain on the job after marriage, to which she responded with "Hooray, hooray, and three times three!" Though many women lost their jobs during the Depression when they were judged as taking employment needed by men, the supposed supporters of families, policies forcing women to quit teaching jobs if they married, and certainly if they had children, had been instituted much earlier. When Black wrote about San Francisco in 1929, close to 75 percent of U.S. school districts had bans on married women teachers, not married men teachers, enforced differently by the decade and even by the individual school administrator, with policies changing as schools had more and less difficulty finding qualified applicants.[15] For Black, writing for a national audience in 1929, the end of a marital ban in San Francisco was, or should have been, national news, an example of what should occur across the country. In discussing the justice of allowing married women to keep their teaching jobs or to seek them, Black does not question whether married women should be working. Instead, she argues that schools are not there to support single women, or single or married men, but to employ the most qualified teachers. Marital status should not matter any more than any other fact, like eye color or city of birth, she continues. What matters for hiring in teaching, as in other industries, is whether a person is good at the job and of good moral character, thus not gender and not marital status.[16]

## And Writing About Sexual Harassment

On the women's page, on the magazine page, and on the front page, as Black wrote about women's work and pay, she was also the one writer regularly discussing sexual harassment.

Concerning this topic, especially in early columns so focused on a positive work life, she sought to recognize the problem but not to discourage women from entering the work force because of it, a difficult balance to maintain. In one column from 1907, written for the *New York Journal,* she states that Maude McChesney, from the Englewood Woman's Club in Chicago, claimed that women on the job had to put up with sexual offers from bosses and thus perhaps they should not be seeking employment. In one of her classic uses of the expert, Black counters that the average stenographer works for a businessman whose goal is business, not causing such problems. Women who work can be happy and respected, the woman behind the counter at a store as much as the woman making the purchase.[17]

In another column, from 1912, with a carefully constructed and surprising structure, she presents the fact that a reader had criticized her for denying the problem of sexual harassment as she encouraged women to work and as she claimed that such inappropriate and threatening circumstances were the exception. "The Hungry Stenographer" opens with a woman writing angrily that sometimes to keep their jobs women had to put up with a boss's inappropriate speech and action, that Black, "secure in her position," didn't recognize this reality of work life. Indeed, this letter writer claims that she is unable to find a job because she won't acquiesce. This harsh criticism of Black, as either naïve or unconcerned, part of a letter that Black could have ignored or may have even fabricated for rhetorical purpose, would certainly engage readers. It ends with "I find it in my heart to hate you for condemning something you know nothing of" and sets up Black's reply.

Here Black creates a conflict requiring that she explain herself further. In reply, she admits that sexist, aggressive parasites in business do exist, the "doddering old fool, or a feather-headed young one ... absurd creatures." But she will not admit that women who seek to work will encounter or must submit to such overtures: these men, not the regular sort, should be laughed at, disarmed, or simply refused. If the woman finds herself in an office that cannot be improved, Black argues, it is a rare one and thus there is no reason for her to discontinue her working life: she should go somewhere else. In this column, she continues by presenting a conversation with a group of women workers who echo her opinions, thus associating her values with those of a larger group of working women.[18]

## Women as Changing Their Own Work and Home Behavior

Though Black wrote about prejudices against and hardships encountered by women on the job, she also wrote about difficulties that they were causing for themselves, of their need to change as they became workers, creating an analysis that contradicted what was thought to be "womanly" at the time—and thus she argued in these pieces, as elsewhere, for change in the definition of what was normal or approved behavior. Like Deborah Tannen, she wrote that workplace misunderstandings often stemmed from what men and women viewed as the appropriate way to interact with each other, in words and body language, their errors at the office often beginning in codes of romance. As she discussed these misunderstandings, Black argued that the construction of women as living for romance and family could be, and should be, altered as they entered the work world.

Part of women succeeding on the job, Black argued, entailed getting over some of their home-cherished sensitivity. In one column from 1910, entitled "Foolish Pride," Black writes about a young woman who is upset because of the way she is treated while working as a housekeeper: she is not called by her name or asked about her own family and home. Black's answer to her, as it would be frequently on this subject, is that it's business and men wouldn't care about a close personal relationship with the employer. Women need to become more professional as they enter the work world and not judge as an insult what was not meant as one, but instead was part of a separate code.[19] Indeed, in another column, she asserts that bosses need to treat their employees equally, and in many situations that may involve being tougher, less polite and accommodating, with their women employees. "The fact is," she writes, "men in business are not tyrannical enough to women in business. The average man is so much kinder to his woman stenographer than he is to his male clerk that the idea of calling him a tyrant in his dealings with women is a joke." At whatever level of tyranny a boss may operate, he needs to do so with both his female and male clerks, and women need to respond without the sensitivity encouraged at home.[20]

Black also writes about women needing to be more serious about their work, to look at it as a career, and thus not to be letting their family or love interests interfere, a difficult achievement for women, Black argues, given societal expectations placed on them. In this discussion, Black often uses groups of women talking, especially about love as something to control at work. In one column from 1916 reporting a conversation about concentrating on careers, an older woman asserts that putting work first is "unwomanly." And here the group is shown turning the tables, denying that women should always identify themselves with love and family. "We don't call a man unmanly," they reply, "who tends to his work first and makes marriage a secondary consideration." Men learn their trade seriously and discuss it seriously, the group of women assert, certainly in confirmation of Black's viewpoint, without detracting from marriage and family, and women can do so also.[21]

Just as women should not be discussing love at work, they should not be using sexuality or flirtation to advance their position. "Going into business," Black claimed in 1922 concerning women's abilities to be themselves at work, "never turned a feminine, attractive woman into a masculine, unattractive imitation of a man." But these looks or this sexuality should not be used "cold-bloodedly": women should not flirt in the office, just as they should not discuss their love lives or their children.[22] In another column, she discussed the types of women who don't deserve their jobs and especially concentrated on the inappropriate use of "good looks" and "sugary words": "There's the spite woman and the jealous cat and the incompetent stenographer who makes up for her incompetence by her good looks or her sweet and sugary words to the boss."[23]

Beyond needing to examine and alter their behavior at work, women workers had to change their behavior at home, in neither site allowing the expectations of the "womanly" normal to make a work life impossible. She wrote frequently about working women asserting that they could not do every chore for their parents, their husbands, or their children, recasting what might have seemed like selfish or unnatural behavior as they refused to take on every task. Five studies done between 1926 and 1929 indicated that on farms and in towns, women's work in the home each week including food preparation, housework, and care of children and adults, involved a total of 51.5 to 62.7 hours, which might be combined with hours of farm work or a part or full-time job.[24] Black argued repeatedly that there was nothing unwomanly in the working woman, married or single, attempting to reduce those weekly numbers in an attempt to live and do work well.

In "The Business Girl" from December 1916, she discusses the choices she would make if she were expected as a "womanly" young person to do everything at her parents' home: she would have a "plain understanding with the folks at home," that she could not run their errands or concern herself with all their small needs.[25] Into the 1930s Black continued to develop this topic in strongly stated advice about rest as well as work. With the comparative title of "Loaf Like a Man," she argues for women to pay somebody "to do all the mean little, nagging, worrying things in life," thus marshalling their energies for what really mattered. She here speaks to women workers directly: "You are throwing energy away on today's fussiness. You can't fly an aeroplane and pick strawberries at the same time.... If you are in business, be in business as a man is in business." She thus advocated for the extended family to help the wife and mother, not for this woman to always exhaust herself for them.[26]

In a column from August 1916, Black lauds a friend who rests when she gets home while her non-working mother and sister take care of the housework. She acts like a man at work, Black quotes this woman as saying, and has learned to do so at home, and she doesn't care about what anyone thinks: "I have to do a man's work and it's got to take a man's strength to do it, and the only way I can conserve that strength is to save it and not throw it away on a lot of little fiddling things that somebody else can do just as well as I can."[27] Indeed Black was writing about a serious situation for working women living with their parents or with their own husbands and children.

## The Myths and Realities of Particular Professions

Besides writing about the language and behavior of offices generally and advocating for change in attitudes concerning women at work and at home, Black also focused her attention on particular professions, especially those that would generally be considered out of bounds. In considering the woman as worker, she often wrote about jobs not generally covered on the women's page or the any other page of the American newspaper.

Black wanted readers to be aware that women worked seriously, even in the oddest of environments. When she describes gold mining towns in Nevada, in an article for *Cosmopolitan* in 1905, she concentrates not just on the men making claims and entering the mines but on the women working in local businesses:

> "Public Stenographer," declares a placard on a tiny dugout in the side of a steep hill, and inside the dugout there are glimpses of the public stenographer herself, very trig and trim indeed, sweeping out the dugout and dusting the typewriter which stands inside the door.[28]

Black also wrote about women in even less traditional roles, such as a woman pilot who flew eight hundred miles to break an American record, this aviator reticent about bragging or discussing her achievements, as it is often true of those, Black asserts, who achieve so much.

Black also described women whose professions caused them to be looked on negatively, as though members of another species. In December 1889, for the *Examiner*, she wrote about working as a ballet girl at a "big spectacular" at the Grand Opera House. Though this article begins with subheads focusing on the stunt girl—"The 'Examiner's' Annie Laurie Becomes a Nymph of the Ballet and Appears for One Night Only"—Black's focus is not on herself but on women at work. Most people, Black argues, seem to believe that nymphs of the ballet lead a life of elegant leisure featuring frequent banquets of champagne and truffles, their escapades interrupted only by quick trips to the stage: "There is a great deal of nonsense talked about the 'happy, happy chorus.'" Here she sought "to join the serried ranks of the 'extra ladies,' and find out just what life behind the scenes really is." She considers the means that these women use, including thin tights and various sorts of padding, to improve their looks and thus their income. She praises their frank speaking, that they "have a large vocabulary of plain Saxon at their command" even though their talk about income and employers does not particularly engage Black: "The conversation of these nymphs of the ballet was not particularly edifying—at least not to me." She concludes the discussion with a positive evaluation of their work lives: "They earn every dollar of their money, these hard-working girls, and if they are a little rough and plain spoken who shall say that they have not their trials and their battles to fight!"[29]

Black also wrote about even less savory or accepted occupations for women, including prostitution in so many articles, not just to discuss judgments of this extreme choice, and local and national campaigns against it, but to consider the life and the work.

## The Effects of Work on Those Engaged in It

Many of Black's articles about work, placed on women's pages and throughout the newspaper, consider the changes it caused in women—and in what they expected in marriage. "Twenty years ago," Black wrote in 1916, "the working woman who married usually left her job. Today she holds onto it as long as she possibly can. Many of the women you see working in offices are married women who've come back to the shop to help out their husbands."[30] Only 4.5 percent of married women with a husband present worked in 1890, 5.6 in 1900, 10.7 in 1910, and 11.7 in 1930, this number increasing to 15.4 in 1940, and so a greater percentage and many more women were indeed keeping their jobs after marriage.[31] Writing in 1916, Black was encouraging as well as reporting on this choice. And as she asserted frequently, this work before, and during, marriage was altering who women were as wives: normal or natural behavior was culturally determined and certainly could change—and would be changed through work.

A job, indeed, Black maintained, could change whether the woman would choose marriage at all. In "A Man Who Wants a Wife but Needs a Housekeeper," a column in the *Examiner* in April of 1906, she creates a nonfiction scenario involving a man who lost his wife that year. He is looking for another to care for his children and for his house, as Black describes what he seeks: "Some discouraged woman of a certain age who is so tired of earning her own living that she'd do anything on earth to get what she calls a home." She continues by asserting that he wants a "sublimated hired girl—without the wages." But this type of desperation, Black argues a bit optimistically, no longer exists because of women's ability to earn their own way. A woman could buy her own farm and get her own furniture and piano, "and not sell herself body and soul" for such items. This man should hire a housekeeper and wait for love, Black concludes, for he should not want any woman who would be so desperate as to accept such an offer: no self-respecting woman would do so.[32]

In a column from 1911 as in many others, Black continued to argue that women who worked did not need to marry for financial reasons. Here, a woman who works as a shop clerk declares that she likes the independence that stems from earning her living: she doesn't envy the women coming into the shops with their children, completely dependent on their husbands for even the money to buy gloves. Black praises the shopgirl and criticizes women, what she deems a minority, that would seek a husband just because they are tired of earning their own living.[33]

While women might delay or avoid marriage because they could support themselves, work might also change their behavior within their marriages, creating a new normal. As Black bluntly maintained in 1916, "You can't push women out into the world to earn their own livings and keep them the same kind of creatures they were when somebody shielded them."[34] Work had caused women to expect to make decisions for themselves.

In many other columns, Black contends that an income provided options that wives did not have when they were completely dependent on their husbands. In one column, using a scene and dialogue, she introduces a "clever socialist" who contends that men will not be as likely to use up a wife and move on to the next one if their wives are more independent. The woman's ability to live independently creates a balance in marriage that Black humorously indicates is not just a socialist's plan and not just a dream of the future, but what working women were achieving at that time:

> "Women will soon learn to control this marriage business," said a clever socialist to me the other day. "Just as soon as a women can earn her own living there'll be no more of this desertion and this new love idea. 'You be good or I'll leave you,' the new woman will say. 'I can support the children myself.'"
> "Dear me," said I to the socialist, "that isn't a threat, it's a promise."[35]

Black also wrote repeatedly about the changes work created for older women. In 1920, she wrote about a grandmother whose children and grandchildren were moving to another town to which she was not accompanying them. As described in this article, "Grandma Goes to Work," the grandmother earns her own way, working at a library, feeling happily independent, with her choice of books to read, movies to see, and friends to share troubles with: "She's found out how to be happy."[36]

―――

Through regularly published nonfiction, Black brought American women workers not just before the few who might read a business or women's magazine but before the American public, across the nation, in various sections of the newspaper. She considered an array of topics about working, her work respectful of women and their employers, though she also advocated for change in opportunities and in behavior, relying on nonfiction scenes to open up this world to readers and speak for a new normal of hard work and equal treatment.

# 14

## The Power of Beauty

In considering so many parts of American life and the lives of women, Black also recognized the pull of beauty, the self-definition depending on it, and the difficulty of losing it. Through the people and places of nonfiction, she crafts a powerful rhetoric of the body, creating a perspective that countered so much that appeared on the women's page. While other articles on the women's page or Sunday magazine might concern what to wear and how to look, she frequently wrote about not bending to the pressures of beauty and fashion, thus minimizing the need for following the dictates delineated in articles that surrounded hers. She often discussed the judgments contained in beauty news and advice as fashions began to change more quickly and women felt more pressure than ever before to buy the latest style.

### Mass Production and the Fashionable

At the nineteenth century's end, catalogs, department stores, designers, and manufacturers sought to attract customers to ready-to-wear. As women bought mass produced and cheaper goods, for which the profit margin came from sales volume, advertisers encouraged them to discard last year's fashions and purchase skirts at new lengths and shirts with new tucks, the kinds of changes that were easy to make on a production line. Charlotte Perkins Gilman commented in 1905 on the new advertisement-fed desire to adopt new styles each season instead of each decade: "In modern cities the proud lady wears robes of brown and burnt orange, or of green, blue, violet, indigo, and all additions to our fabricated rainbow, because 'this year they are wearing it'! And there is no more to be said."[1]

The mass consumer breakthrough garment for women's ready-made was the shirtwaist, a blouse resembling a man's shirt. Mass produced beginning in the 1890s, this shirt peaked in popularity between 1909 and 1914, driven by the iconic Gibson Girl, the omnipresent model woman, first drawn by Charles Dana Gibson, an illustrator working for *Life, Collier's, The Century, Scribner's,* and *Harper's*. In 1895, there were no more than a half dozen shirtwaist factories in New York City, but in 1900 there were 472. With workers toiling in factories instead of doing piecework in their own homes, patterns and fashions changed regularly.[2] In 1900, skirts were gathered in the center back and then gored so that they fit closely around the hip area, flaring toward the ground. Some women shortened their hems in response to a scientific claim that street-length skirts might enable microbes to climb up onto and attack women's bodies, a claim never made about men's long pants. In 1905, the S-curve provided the reigning shape, the bustle of the 1890s having gone out of style. In a shirtwaist and skirt, the corseted female figure, with the shirt bloused over at the waistline and the skirt gathered in the back over a slightly protruding rear end, resembled the letter S. The "swan" corset design required for this look was not for a weakling: it forced the wearer to push the bosom forward and bring the hips back. Below the waist was a very slim hip and stomach area, making a strange combination of features—and a body that looked like it might tip over.[3]

A new longer and leaner look became popular in 1909, introduced by French designer Paul Poiret. It included an Empire waist, with a belt right under the bustline (not a good look for women with larger busts). This look reached its apex in 1910, when dresses featured a hobble skirt, so tight at the hem that women could barely walk. Ballroom dancer Irene Castle helped to end that particular vogue: "I could not dance in a hobble skirt (though I tried at the beginning); therefore I wore simple flowing gowns that would leave my legs free."[4] Fashions changed radically again in the spring of 1915, with dresses featuring a fuller bell-shaped skirt, wide collars, and sloping shoulders, a feminine look often featuring flowered patterns.

To sell a seasonal approach to fashion, advertisers relied on changes in newspaper production. For most of the nineteenth century, newspapers had refused to print ads that included illustrations, large display type, or layouts more than one column wide because these designs were difficult to reproduce.[5] By the 1890s, however, because of the new halftone photoengraving process and other innovations, many papers had dropped such restrictions and had begun creating the more vivid visual presentations that manufacturers sought. With the line drawing, artists for magazines and newspapers could present striking images of women, changing the body type as designers changed the clothes. Like the computer-generated images now seen on fashion magazine covers, these drawings could standardize the approved features, presenting a look that reiterated a particular year's view of perfection.[6]

By the 1920s, so much of what a woman sought to wear mimicked the latest attire of movie stars. The favorite magazines of the period, like *Vogue, Harpers*, and *Life*, featured Clara Bow, Louise Brooks, and Mary Pickford. In the flapper era, in the clothes worn by model and actress alike, the corset had been cast aside; the typical dress featured a tank top, low waist, and short hemline, diaphanous fabrics, and little adornment, the emphasis as never before on youth as well as sporty good looks, rail thinness, and a slight bust.[7]

By the end of 1930, as the Depression affected the public, a more conservative approach to fashion took over. Skirts became longer, the waist-line cinched, and darker colors and thicker fabrics came back into style, all creating a more traditional "womanly" look. Fashion from films still appeared in magazines and still mattered: the leg-o-mutton sleeves designed for Irene Dunne in 1931's *Cimarron* inspired the broad-shouldered look.

Hairstyles were also changing drastically with the years, with various judgments made of the new. Masses of wavy hair were fashionable at the beginning of the century, swept up to the top of the head and gathered into a knot, the style worn by the classic Gibson Girl: a woman let her hair down only at home. Bobbed or short hair appeared in Paris fashion in 1909 and spread to avant-garde circles, and to women working in hospitals and factories during the war. As the twenties began, cutting the woman-defining long hair and perhaps getting a perm could make news: Pickford's decision to cut her famous long ringlets became national news. The bob was associated, positively and negatively, with shorter skirts, face paint, smoking, drinking, dancing, and being out without a chaperone. Some schools banned this hairstyle and offered bonus pay to teachers who kept their long hair. In the 1930s, curls and waves and shoulder-length hair were all the rage. Some women opted for soft waves set close to the face while others arranged their hair in tight pincurls.[8]

Not just clothes and hair changed quickly with constant marketing during Black's career. Over these years, make-up also went through radical alterations. As the century began, upstanding women generally eschewed such "paint" as the sign of an immoral woman. More socially appropriate, though sometimes dangerous, choices included light powders and moisturizers with ingredients such as alcohol, mercury, glycerin, borax, and bleach. Tinting the skin became common in the first decade of the century to achieve the desired "pale, delicate translucent skin," the harsh bleaches often having dire results. Into the 1920s, powders, rouges, and mascaras became more accepted, with make-up made and advertised by Max Factor, Elizabeth Arden, and others. Lipstick became widely popular after Maurice Levy's 1915 invention of the metal lipstick tube.[9]

Although all of these alterations appeared in fashion magazines and in stores, they also came to dominate and expand the women's pages of newspapers. While many articles concerned improving and decorating the home, a growing number helped the perfect affluent woman to adorn herself with the latest of expensive wares. In the fall of 1910, for example, in the *New York Times*, the regularly appearing articles that combined fashion with society news included "The Decrees of Fashion for the Autumn," "Wide Variety in

Furs of the Finest Kind Seen at the Social Events at the Close of the Year," "Some Striking Examples of the Season's Medley of Frocks and Frills," "Simplicity in Style and Absence of Vivid Colors More Than Ever Noticeable Among Women Who Dress Well," and "Soft Petticoats Should Be Worn With the Tight Skirts That are Now Being Worn." These pieces frequently appeared along with large line drawings, of stately women in aristocratic clothes, which might take up half or more of the women's-page space.

## Dissecting Cultural Expectations of Beauty

Winifred Black was certainly writing in years of constant fashion change, in decades in which women were expected to make quick and expensive shifts in their clothing styles, influenced by the drawings and photographs in magazines and newspapers. The latest fashion and hair necessities appeared along with advice on how to get the newly required body size and negative articles about being out of style. In nonfiction articles through the decades, often with her work located near to all of these paeans to fashion requirements, Black dissected cultural expectations and the power of fashion experts.

In 1891, Black published a long article, almost an entire page, with the title "Valueless and Poisonous," along with a reprinted affidavit from a chemist to whom she sent the moisturizer and skin whitener products of the era for analysis. The piece starts with the story of a woman who sought to buy an array of beauty products to make her skin youthful, vibrant, and wrinkle free, marketed along with pamphlets touting claims about exotic ingredients and magical alterations. Black quotes these claims at length and compares them to the chemist's analysis: some of the mixtures he finds harmless, containing common elements like salt, chalk, and cotton-seed oil though nothing that would justify the exorbitant prices. Other products, like a face bleach much sought by women at the time, contained dangerous corrosive elements.[10] In this researched nonfiction, Black demonstrates her readers' ability to move beyond must-have products, to consider them thoughtfully, an attitude that she encourages about all the accoutrements of beauty.

In some of these early pieces, Black employed her criticism of experts to consider the influence of American designers, magazines, stores, and even doctors on what women might choose to wear. In 1900, as she reported, the society of physicians, meeting in Rome, spent a long session denouncing the evils of the long street skirt, which reportedly was encouraging microbes to crawl up onto a woman's torso and injure her health, a better choice for street wear being the ankle length skirt and boots, anything shorter of course being too erotic. A slew of experts had discussed this supposed health issue in *Harper's Bazaar* and other magazines.[11] In this column, Black uses sarcasm to respond to the sudden concern about germs and skirts: "If you listened to the doctors nowadays you'd go out to some secluded spot and do your best to die in peace, just to get rid of the deadly microbes." Here she speaks further for common sense and for independence, employing an exaggerated example of what she might choose to wear: "If I wanted to wear a chain armor and a pot helmet to a garden party, I'd do it and say no more about it, but I should consider myself aggrieved if my sorrowing friends took it upon themselves to remonstrate with me on the singularity of my taste." She next moves to her larger point, about women not letting nervous experts control what they do: "What's the use of living at all if you're going to be scared to death all the time?"[12] Black's article appeared in the *Atlanta Constitution* around ads and articles that advocated for the kind of specific requirements that she disparaged: the newest of ladies' shirt-waists, "glove-fitting" corsets, and diamond brooches. Here Black creates what might be the anti-fashion-page as she speaks against the need for the latest or for the expert and equates an automatic following of fashion dictates to a type of fear that can take away an adult's confidence in her own choices.

With the ascendancy of the Gibson Girl and then the hobble skirt, as well as new wraps and shoes, Black wrote in 1910 about the ever growing concern for "clothes, clothes, clothes, money, money, money." One column discusses a "smart New York tailor," another expert, who has determined a minimum for women to spend on that year's wardrobe. Black responds that large sums are not required, that women can sew, adapt items, and make their own style: they can look just fine without succumbing to the newly assertive fashion world. "I wonder what we'll do to amuse ourselves when we leave this world and get somewhere where there aren't any spring fashions," she writes, suggesting that women can find many other amusements and many other ways to spend their money. In the Syracuse newspaper, this article appeared along with the newest styles for college girls, the newest in millinery, and trend toward hand-embroidery on that year's clothes.[13] Similarly, in March of 1910, Black wrote that worse than poverty for hurting women was all this concern for dressing from the time they were very young, with mothers insisting that their daughters care about the latest fashion and men judging them for their looks. The belief seemed to be, Black argued, that fashion should fill a young woman's head all the time.[14]

In the second decade of the century, Black frequently recognized the power of the Gibson Girl in mandating creamy white skin and upswept hair as well as the latest of shirtwaists and skirts. Her prettiness had become an all controlling addiction: "The average girl spends over half her time, energy and nerve force trying to look pretty. She spends every penny she can beg, borrow or steal—or put it mildly—buying puffs and curls or rats, and high heels, and powders and complexion lotions, and remedies for tan and freckles, and things to put on her hair to make it grow, and stuff to use on her hands to make them white, and she ogles herself in the glass, and struts and poses and 'affects this' and tries to 'look like that.'"[15]

With the growth of fashion magazines in the 1910s, as drawings and photographs sold the latest versions of the Gibson Girl, Black wrote further about the power of these images, making women want to be what they were not. In 1917, for example, she described what women looked like in magazines, an unreality: "So tall and so slim, so proud and haughty, and they wear such perfectly good clothes without ever a wrinkle or crease or a thing!" She claims that she doesn't know anybody like that, and she doesn't think that any of these women would make good friends: "They're all so far away and so up in the air, the magazine girls." And she also critiques the American man thus represented, her point made by one of her hyphenated adjective chains: the men in these magazines are "high-shouldered, long-armed, long-legged, long-nosed, long-chinned creatures," with whom no one would feel quite comfortable.[16]

Before 1920, as Black continued to write about changing fashions and the power of experts in determining how women should appear, she also recognized the power of men in dictating the few right choices for women's weight, height, and hair as well as clothing. In one column from 1910, she begins with a reverend from "somewhere" in the middle west, one of her vaguely identified experts, assailing women for their love of fashion. Though she agreed with him that fashion spending and anxiety were out of control, she places blame not just on magazines or designers or women but on men who, regardless of what they might say about good values or personality, respond instead to classy boots and clothes.[17] Similarly, in a column from 1919, she asserts that men often look for the currently approved type without concern for "either the mind or the heart or the morals of the 'perfect girl.'" She continues here in comedic form, describing the games played by employing "the right kind of clothes": "Why, a girl from the Home for the Feeble Minded can win the fatuous attention of 50 men, any hour of the day, if she wears the right kind of clothes, and looks adoring and adorable enough!"[18] But she also argues, as she often did about gender not necessitating one type of behavior, that not all men evaluate on any one basis, and she then moves to direct address of a woman reader: "The best sort of men do not marry for beauty—they marry for character. Hold up your head, Big Sister. There are a few sensible men left in the world."[19]

Before 1920, Black also wrote frequently about the growing power of fiction, plays, and film in determining what women felt they needed to wear. Emma McChesney, a fashion buyer and Midwest traveling sales representative for T. A. Buck's Featherloom Skirts and Petticoats, had appeared in three popular collections of stories by Edna Ferber: *Roast Beef, Medium: The Busi-*

*ness Adventures of Emma McChesney* (1913); *Personality Plus* (1914); and *Emma McChesney and Co.* (1915). *Our Mrs. McChesney* appeared on Broadway in 1915, a popular play with Ethel Barrymore in the lead, and in 1917 was being made into a film also starring Barrymore. Given the popularity of the character, books, and play and with the film coming out, department stores stocked and sold the products that this character marketed. In one column, Black declares that down to a particular color on the border of a wash rag, buyers were trying to get women to choose what they did not want. This popular character, Black maintains further, had "made everybody buy heatherbloom pettiskirts when they really want to wear bloomers." Pettiskirts are ruffled, soft tiered, layered skirts of fine net or mesh, originally worn as petticoats but that year remade as very fancy skirts in which it could be hard to sit down. Athletic bloomers (also known as "rationals" or "knickerbockers"), baggy knee-length trousers fastened to the leg a little below the knees, not Amelia Bloomer's longer original, would be much more comfortable than the mesh skirt, but they were not what the current marketing blitz advocated. But when buyers and department stores work at creating a public preference, Black continues, few other styles will appear in magazines and newspapers and few other styles will be available in stores. Black recognizes that if she wants a round hat when the floppy ones are in style, she doesn't stand a chance of finding one: "You might as well try to wade the Atlantic ocean as to imagine you can have anything the Buyer thinks you ought not to have."[20]

Into the 1920s, Black chronicles the power of the changing popular body, the ever thinner and taller model, no longer the hour-glass Gibson Girl. She sometimes employed humor to comment on how unnatural these models appeared, how tall and skinny, floating in their diaphanous fabrics, as in a column from 1925 in which she asks readers what they would do if they met one of unnatural women on the street and concludes that the best answer might be to run into a doorway and hide: "Why they are six feet tall, at least, every one of them and they haven't an ounce of flesh on their poor bones and their knees are so sharp that you can see them through their poor little skinny skirticoats." Here she also critiques the ridiculous clothes created in the 1920s for models and their imitators to wear on vacations like a trip to a dude ranch: the real cowboys there would be hurting themselves with laughter when such fashionistas arrived. And then with direct address, she speaks to the illustrator of such fashions directly: "Please, Mr. Artist, won't you be a darling and draw us some pictures of real girls and real men for your fashion plates—Just for a change?"[21]

In other columns on the power of fashion, Black showed that even the intrepid reporter and social critic could get caught up in the power of the approved new. In a column from 1924, she writes about choosing a hat, a newly popular turban style with big bumps on both sides and raisin-like appliques at the top. She then admits quite forcefully that this style didn't look good on her: "It makes me look as if I had murdered my grandmother and wouldn't think anything of putting poison in the baby's milk." She continues with the discussion of the fashion power to which she acquiesced: "It's the latest, the very latest, didn't the saleswoman tell me so, and who am I to have sense enough to wear what I really like when the milliner tells me it's not the thing."[22]

Though Winifred Black repeatedly recognized the control exercised by the fashion industry, she would not ever totally deny women's agency. In 1923, she wrote that bobbed hair, so avant garde just a few years before, was supposedly out of style and women were being told to get rid of it for something shorter or more angular or for long hair. But busy women, professionals, had found this cut convenient, Black claimed, and did not have to listen.[23] Similarly, in 1925, when fashion writers declared that corsets were back and with them "whalebones and steel and little waists and everything," she replies to them passionately about how a woman will respond: "Turn your nice loose, comfy shape into an hour-glass figure—not for anything in the world." Mama could "lace herself till she fainted," she continues, but Mama couldn't dance or play golf or do anything outside.[24]

As Black wrote about fashion and hair, about moving beyond the much encouraged obsession with the latest and most stylish, she was critiquing American beauty culture. Often her articles appeared on women's or magazine pages where everything around them described the need to follow the latest fashion trends. While critiquing fashion and fashion magazines, she moved beyond the specifics of expensive and ever changing mandates to a critical examination of these expectations as well as women's power of response.

## The Power of Diets

As Black certainly recognized, in the years in which she wrote, changes in the approved body shape and weight accompanied changes in fashion, hair, and makeup. The Gibson Girl ideal of femininity, featuring "voluptuous" bust, small waist, and wide hips, could be achieved by corseting, but the flappers' appearance, of androgynous youth clothed in thin materials, engendered a new mania for quick weight loss. Many women adopted the grapefruit diet to boost their metabolism and drastically reduce their calories; others bought jars of tapeworms advertised to help women drop pounds without effort. Lucky Strike Cigarette Company used the appetite-curbing property of nicotine in an ad campaign, "Reach for a Lucky Instead of a Sweet," and sales increased by 200 percent during the 1920s.[25]

In her articles about new clothes, Black emphasized the changing nature of the appropriate size. In October 1919, she writes about a friend who used to eat chocolate and had wanted to be plump to have the hips and breasts of the Gibson Girl. But lately this woman looked at Black as though she was discussing cyanide when she mentioned ice cream. "She's banting to get thin," Black tells her readers, "and to my eyes she's so thin now, that I don't see how she gets her clothes to stay on at all."[26] Here she describes the swift changes occurring as the Gibson Girl gave way to the flapper, the new normal or appropriate body size leading to the worst of diets.

In an article from 1930, as in many others, she continues her analysis of acceptable size by comparing American body expectations to those in England. An English vaudeville actress, no name given, claims that she has to diet so much more to work in the United States, that the body considered beautiful here is so much thinner than in Europe. As Black describes this actress' reaction to working in this country, "She's sick of starving and picking and pecking and counting the calories and getting weighed." The reader's grandmother, Black continues, could certainly confirm that the required look and size had changed, that a larger size, to 185 pounds, had been stylish in the United States in the 1890s but certainly not after the world war and into the 1920s. This article about the actress' sudden need to lose as much as sixty or seventy pounds appeared, in a Texas newspaper, next to "Today's Fashion" and "A New Manicure Idea" as well as a full-page ad for a fall style show, Black's column serving there as an anti-fashion statement, against following the trends that the other articles helped to enforce.[27]

In May 1936, the last month of her life, Black again commented on women of all ages being unsatisfied with their weight, going on crazy diets and denying themselves, because of the latest fashion dictates. Here a woman who is not seeking love and not interested in becoming a movie star eats only salad and drinks only tea because "she just can't stand it to go into shops and have the managers say so politely: 'So sorry, madam, we have nothing in your size.'"[28] Again, as she so often did, Black argues that women can demonstrate their self-respect, and teach their daughters, by making other choices.

## On Beauty and Age

In this discussion of beauty, fashion, and diet, Black also wrote about how the "requirements" affected older women. She certainly recognized that a woman might like to look young again:

> She put on a cherry colored house gown of quilted silk and the gold shoes, and stockings that were a charming contrast, and then she sat and put her feet up on a chair and had a lovely time feeling rich and admired and beloved, and young—again.

And the silver in her hair changed for a minute into the gold that it used to be and all the lines of sorrow and the marks of grief, disappointment and humiliation seemed to fade like something in a dream. She was eighteen again with a quick brain, and a warm eager heart and a gay love of laughter that kept her from dying of sorrow, years and years ago.
Foolish woman, wasn't she?
But somehow—[29]

Though she recognized the attraction of youth, she wrote, in different ways through the decades, sometimes in quite strong statements, about the mistake of doing way too much to maintain it.

From 1910, with the fashion industry and the young Gibson Girl having taken hold, her article entitled "Woman's Vain Fight" relied on one of her startling leads: "Three women, in good financial circumstances, of excellent character and very good social position, killed themselves the other day." The details that follow place them in different parts of the country with ages in their forties, extreme examples of women who judged that their attractiveness and purpose to have ended with their youth.

In further developing this piece, Black contends that instead of becoming less secure, women should be at their happiest between forty and sixty, with friends, husbands, and grown children. "But along comes a beauty culture fiend," she then asserts, "and the poor woman of 40 odd loses all her serenity, and gains what? The beauty fiend tells her that she is getting wrinkled and that she is too fat and that her hair isn't as bright as it used to be." The "fiend," Black continues, leads her to fear younger women, causing even the forty-year-old to "turn green" every time her husband speaks to any woman under seventy and leading to ridiculous, frantic beauty behavior: "And poor 40 odd massages and shampoos and exercises and dresses and totters around on high heels." Nearly fifty herself, Black again opposes the beauty fiend by arguing that being comfortable with yourself is better for keeping a husband than pretending to be twenty-five.[30]

In 1912, as she continues to consider beauty and aging, Black asserts that, within the United States, seeking to always remain young is a fairly new tendency, a symptom of the rapidly changing normal. And she asks about what has happened to an earlier type of aging woman: "What has become of all the good comfy women we used to know, women who were 40 and glad of it, women who let out their corsets and put on loose shoes, and tied their hats on with a rubber, and let it go at that? All gone, disappeared, vanished into the beauty parlors to be made over into 20." Then she goes through all that can be better with acceptance that a woman is no longer twenty: no more weepy hours caused by not being chosen by a man, no more desperation over not having all new clothes. Instead this woman can eat good food, read books, enjoy the sun and outdoors, have friends, and make no petty enemies because of looks.[31]

As she continued after 1910 to write about age and beauty, she spoke further about the various stages of a woman's life. In an article from 1915, concerning an old friend of hers who is forty-five, Black celebrates the movement in life past children and past so many uncertainties. This interview includes extended quotations from this woman concerning what she worried about at various stages of life: beauty, dates, one particular man, career, children, success at family and her job. And this friend looks at moving past forty-five as bringing on the best sort of independence that she lacked before. "My heart is giving my brain a chance, and I've begun to live," she tells Black.[32] Another interview, also from 1915, employs the image of the best parts of each season as a metaphor for various ages of women. This woman doesn't need to turn back the clock to earlier seasons, to pretend to be twenty or sixteen or worry about the requirements of perfect youth, but to fully engage in each season of life.[33]

In 1916, Black uses humor to consider the woman who has not accepted the best of each stage and instead insists on having her hair dyed yellow to look good in her coffin. This piece starts with a quotation from this woman's hairdresser, who is involved in all the extremes of hair dying and marcelling. Black then speaks about moving beyond crippling vanity and brings in her own example: "The longer I live the longer I want to. Isn't it so with you? Life gets fuller and richer, and more possible and more delightful, the more we learn how to live it. Things that would have worried me to death five years ago I pass over with a smile today."[34]

As she further developed this subject matter, she argued that some women never recover from the attention paid to beauty, with her example in 1917 of a woman, moving into middle age, who had been the great beauty sought by every young man. Sadly, she is now "always angling for compliments and tossing her well-coifed head, bridling and smiling, or as often pouting and frowning after an infantile fashion which goes ill with her age and position in life."[35] In 1922, as part of the flapper culture of thinness and extreme youth, Black wrote about women of sixty trying to look thirty through plastic surgery. Here her expert is Dr. Leon Michael, suggesting a "severe operation" for which he then sends his large bill. The first tummy tuck had been done in 1899, face lift in 1901, and eyelid surgery in 1906. Plastic surgery developed further as a means of treating soldiers in World War I, the new procedures available for beauty work after the war. Between the 1920s and the 1940s, breast augmentation surgery became another popular option, involving the transplanting of fat to the breasts from other areas of the body, such as the legs or buttocks.[36] Black here argues that instead of trying to erase decades, paying for what was called a "mask of youth," risking health and money on surgery and wearing ridiculous clothes, a woman should enjoy the age of fifty or sixty and all the accomplishments that come with it.[37] She again spoke against surgery's mask of youth in an interview with Eleanora Duse in 1924 when this actress was sixty-six: "Duse, sixty years old and over and doesn't care who knows it. What a relief. No paint, no rouge, no 'mask o' youth,' no hair dye, no 'you see I married so young,' and 'no, of course I can't remember that' camouflage."[38]

In 1931, as part of her insistence on cultural contrast, on considering the normal as actually temporal and regional, Black compares older women in Germany, dressed cleanly and comfortably, with older women in this country caught in the American view of beauty and of worth. In hard economic times, while some older Americans "paint, powder, and make up their mouths, and they wear shoes that are too small for them, and they starve themselves to keep a girlish figure," German women do not feel the same pressures and do not have to waste their money in this manner. Beauty and its requirements could certainly vary by year and place, and any requirements that might seem eternal or necessary could change and could be avoided.[39]

By 1931, Black had become a recognized advocate on beauty and age. Columnist Leola Allard, a journalist from Chicago whom Black had helped to get a job at the *Denver Post*, wrote in her own syndicated column that even during the worsening Depression women were wasting money on beauty creams with little real effect, $187 the price for two jars of one product. And then Allard segues to Winifred Black, the quintessential role model who is past her youth and owns this fact and looks gorgeous: "Winifred is past her youth and tells you so. Why shouldn't she? She's got more pep than any woman I've known in twenty years. I asked her how she kept her skin so lovely and soft, so pink and white." Black tells Allard about a cheap old-fashioned cream that she uses, which costs fifty cents, not $187. And Allard continues with an interview of Black and her own commentary in response: "'And don't you ever fall for fancy jars of new things, beautifully advertised?' I asked her, and she laughed loud and long. I'd pay $187 for a jar of something that would make me laugh like Winifred." Allard then continues: "And if the lady who bought the anti-wrinkle cream at $187 could see Winifred's skin, she'd give away the two pounds of hokum. And it is just that."[40]

---

In her writing on the women's page and elsewhere, Black critiqued the tyranny of beauty and youth. While she recognized the spell-binding power of men, magazines, stores, experts, and even surgeons, she also thought of women of all ages, armed with nonfiction examples and analysis, along with their own good sense, as fully able to make their own choices.

# 15

## *Dating, Domestic Violence and Marriage*

Throughout her career, along with gender, normality, and beauty, Black frequently wrote about American dating and marriage. She married and divorced Orlow Black, married Charles Bonfils but rarely lived with him, and expressed strong opinions about what women should and should not do concerning romance and husbands. Certainly she could discuss marriage as lasting and loving. To do so in one column, she begins dramatically by presenting one man's hideous, sexist view of the older woman:

> "When a woman's 40 years old," said the man, "she ought to be killed, or put in a convent or somewhere, and her husband ought to have the right to go out and get a new wife."
> "All right!" said the man's wife, and she went into the next room and took a pistol out of a drawer and shot herself through the heart and died.

Then Black immediately alters this view that the older wife would no longer be wanted, that she should do the husband a favor and off herself: she discusses, instead, a marriage that can change and grow along with the woman and man, part of the full life she envisioned for older women: "She's learned that marriage is a partnership and, even at that, only an episode, in a really full and rounded life. She isn't perfect herself, and she doesn't expect her husband to be perfect. She doesn't watch the clock, and go into hysterics if husband is five minutes late, and she doesn't call him up on the telephone four or five times a day to find out if he still loves her. She has her own friends, her own interests, her own life, and she isn't trying to make herself over to suit him, or to make herself over to suit him, or to make him over to suit her—any more."[1]

In pieces appearing on magazine and women's pages among positive pieces about weddings, marriage, housekeeping, home decorating, and children, Black often struck an evaluative tone, asking women and men to look thoughtfully and independently at marriage. Over time, she created long lists of reasons not to marry and of many types of men to avoid, giving more time to this task than to praising the tendency of Americans to wed.

## Does a Woman Need to Marry?

One of Black's strong arguments through the years of her career was that women did not have to choose marriage, that indeed many marriages were not worth having, certainly not a common judgment on women's pages or elsewhere in the newspaper. In the years that Black wrote, most young people headed quickly into marriage. The average age of first marriage for women was twenty-two in 1890 and twenty-one from 1900 to 1940. Only 6 percent of women over age forty-five in 1890 had never married, a figure that increased to a little over 8 percent in 1920, holding steady through 1940.[2] Given the near universality of the choice, Black was speaking skeptically of a highly accepted American institution.

Even with marriage being a fundamental choice for most Americans, Black maintained that the normal in terms of choosing it was subject to cultural change. In 1916, she wrote in her dramatic manner, "Though it was popular to marry at one point to avoid being an old maid, that reason is gone, gone, gone." Many women in England, she argued, were choosing to marry and take care of men that returned from the war, but they did so out of love, for the days were gone when women had to have a husband and married mainly to secure one.[3] She meant for women to understand that traditions and expectations could change, and women and men had the right to carefully consider what was best for them.

In 1921, she again writes about a younger generation being less controlled by the need to marry. A woman of thirty, she goes further, might brag that she was unmarried: "The New Woman wants clothes and books and music, and golf and hiking trips—and she doesn't give up all these things very easily—not just to get a husband." Black continues comparing time periods by declaring that "the girl who danced and flirted and laughed her way through life up to 20—and then got married and put on a Mother Hubbard and long-sleeved flannels and let it go at that—doesn't exist today."[4] As she did for other topics, Black may have been reporting about marriage what she preferred to be true.

## Waiting to Be Sure

In all types of columns, continuing through the 1920s, Black wrote about waiting to be sure, about not rushing into marriage or assuming it to be necessary. While she argued in her opinion columns that women should consider marriage carefully and maybe avoid it, she used advice columns to refute the claims of particular readers, and through them to reach all of her readers, concerning the appropriate age to wed and the need to do so at all. One advice column, for example, considers two friends judging themselves to be old maids, at age twenty-five. They are thinking about becoming housekeepers to farmers that they don't love for the chance at marriage to these men. "Ridiculous," Black replies. "Keep young! Stop thinking of yourselves entirely—become interested in people—books—events—things!" and their interests would lead them to a future involving a good marriage or a good life without it.[5]

Indeed, Black often argued that being single is better than being in a marriage that involves settling. In 1919, one advice column concerned another twenty-five-year-old, worried about not being engaged and considering an involvement with a man who flirts with her and with everyone else. "Get out of your heads that marriage is the aim and end of life," Black replies here bluntly and then continues by comparing single and married life: "Unless a woman is happily married she is far more likely to be happy when busily earning her own way. Happy married life is the happiest, of course, but why sigh? Why not become busy and grow happy?" The real trouble is that this letter writer is not occupied with work, friends, and activities, the keys to real happiness.[6]

## Men to Avoid

While Black often argued that women could happily put off marriage or avoid it all together, she also frequently and emphatically listed bad reasons for making the choice. Indeed, she reviewed all the types of men not to marry and employed extreme examples to document their varied means of chaining up women, physically and psychologically. She regularly placed articles, on the women's page and throughout the newspaper, surveying an array of relationship types that could cause a woman to lose her self-respect and independence.

In 1915, Black used a surprising cultural comparison to segue to bad reasons for American marriages. In an investigative piece, she goes out to speak with Japanese men waiting for a boat to arrive that will deliver their brides, women chosen by their pictures and a list of traits, their families guiding the decision, the men paying for the passage. And then she proceeds to a group of reasons for American marriages that may lead to less of a chance at a successful relationship:

> I do hope they'll be happy. They stand about as much chance of it as do our friends who marry each other because somebody thinks they should, or to keep some other girl from getting him, or to show the other fellows that he can win her if he wants her.
> What do you think about it?[7]

## 15. Dating, Domestic Violence and Marriage

In her columns, Black wrote frequently about social expectations as a totally inappropriate reason to marry. In an opinion column from 1917, she created a character who had told a young man that she would marry him, her family and friends maintaining that she needed to find a husband and leave home and that this would be her chance to do so. But, given that she did not love this man, Black urged her to get out of the engagement right away and not be miserable. And she continued, speaking for independence: "Have pity on the man if you have not on yourself. Write him a letter and tell him the truth, the whole truth and nothing but the truth. When you've mailed the letter go out and get a place somewhere as dishwasher or bedmaker or scrubwoman or anything else on earth that will make you independent and take you away from the place the people who seem to be so anxious to get rid of you are kind enough to call your home."[8] No woman should settle for what she called in an advice column a "cheap imitation of love," spurred by family or social pressures, or expect the man to do so either.[9]

Beyond avoiding a man who might be chosen for security or family connections or anything but love, women needed to shun the adulterer and not accept any argument that men had a natural propensity or the right to stray. The advice column genre frequently gave Black the chance to address a respondent whose boyfriend had been seeing someone else, as in a reply from 1919: "Shame, shame, little girl, where is your American independence? Surely you wouldn't allow any boy to behave in this way and still care for you, would you? How can you think of him except with disgust? Forget about him."[10]

As she considers the adulterous man, she also writes about the young woman who actually believes that the adulterer will leave his wife and be a fine husband to her. In a column from 1915, she writes about a young woman who has allowed an older, married man to support her in a cottage outside of town, in fact has already been on the honeymoon with him. They entertain friends and travel together. And he has promised to divorce his wife, leave money for the children, and marry the girlfriend. But for this girlfriend to expect a future of marriage, Black argues, involved engaging in a "cruel, wicked, miserable fiction": ultimately, the man doesn't leave the wife, and he argues that the younger woman is at fault for having believed him since he is actually a dedicated family man. Here Black recognizes that her advice can only go so far: other young women reading this article will think their case is different though they may actually be in the same vulnerable situation.[11]

Though Black's articles almost always construct the boyfriend or husband as the unfaithful one, she felt that a woman who cheated was no better. One column from 1910 concerns a man with a nineteen-year-old wife who left him and the baby and ran off with a married man. Her husband wants her back, but getting her back, Black replies, would be a terrible mistake. He may be heartbroken but that doesn't last, and the mistake of reuniting with her certainly would. She is a "weak, selfish, self-centered, cruel woman" and wouldn't change.[12]

While Black thought that no woman, or man, should choose a cheater, she argued also about avoiding a man evidencing jealousy as a lifestyle, a trait that would only get worse and could signal the end of a woman's independent adulthood. On this topic she speaks repeatedly and especially strongly in her advice columns. In one of these columns from 1914, for example, she replies vehemently to a woman whose boyfriend wants to keep her from her friends:

> What do I think of a fellow like that? Why, I think he's an impossible person, that's all, and a very rude and unpleasant one at that. If he's going to act like this before you are even formally engaged to him, what on earth would he do if you were married to him. He'd have you locked up somewhere like a criminal and carry a stick to beat you into submission as if you were just a dog or some other sort of slave to him. He isn't civilized. Maybe he can read or write, but that's just about as far as civilization has struck in with him. Let your cave man go, little sister, back into his cage. He'll find some poor half-wit to go with him and live there cowed and terrified and trying to make herself believe that she is happy.[13]

In another advice column, from 1917, Black speaks to a letter writer about not waiting a minute longer for an offer of marriage from a selfish, unkind, and jealous man, one who keeps hinting at marriage and never proposes, who wants to separate his supposed beloved from her friends and have her with him whenever he wants. Instead she should immediately stop seeing him, a piece of Black's repeated advice about getting rid of the bad man, not trying to fix or understand him: "And when you stop, stop all at once, don't prolong the agony, will you? You'll get over it, dear—we all do. It will be hard, but it will be splendid, some day, to think what you escaped."[14]

Black also presents more extreme examples as she advises women to avoid the jealous man. In one column from 1910, she discusses a Frenchman who had kept his wife chained to a wall for two years because he didn't want her out and about where she might see other men. "Of all the miserable, selfish, outrageous forms of insanity," Black argues here, using this extreme case to examine the tendency, "jealousy is the most terrible." She then addresses the enchained wife, a striking version of the woman controlled by jealousy, and says that she should not let such a form of persecution continue: she needs to escape and restart her life.[15]

In her thorough enunciation of all the types of men to avoid, Black moves beyond the adulterer or the jealous man to the one that might plan to dictate a woman's every decision and every movement, perhaps not jealous but certainly controlling and harsh. In one column from 1921, she writes about a woman living with a "coarse, hard, cold-eyed, loose-lipped" husband, not a gambler or drinker but someone who just parks a wife and goes on with his own life outside of the home. After three years, Black writes, the wife has been changed by the experience, has become "irresponsive." "Day by day and hour by hour," Black continues, "he poisoned her innocence and dragged down every beautiful instinct in her nature, until now." The long-term effect encompasses who the woman is—the price she has paid involves her own self.[16]

In other columns, Black chose extremes to get her readers' attention concerning women withering away after being abandoned within their own homes. With the evocative title of "Buried, though Alive," she published a column in 1921 that did not concern a man who actually buried his wife alive, but instead kept her in the house, employing abuse about her looks and age to discourage her from ever venturing out on her own. Such a man, Black declares in one of her adjective chains, is "pompous, over-bearing, self-sufficient, egotistical," and then she provides more details of the couple's situation. After he was promoted from office manager to general manager, he began ignoring his wife who no longer seemed to him pretty and up-to-date enough; he began to find her aged parents embarrassing; she didn't play golf and wouldn't smoke cigarettes with his smart friends. He went to the theatre without her and, in her few times in the company of others, "he thought nothing at all of bursting into the conversation and utterly squelching her if she ventured timidly to express even a shadow of an opinion." And then Black admits that something similar can happen to men whose wives and children don't respect them, who spend all their money, and who think negatively because they don't make more.[17]

Black wrote in other columns about men that want to control women, keep them in the home, keep them from working, decide what they should weigh and wear—keep them from having their own viewpoints and lives. "The man who thinks a woman is too good to work thinks she is too good to think," she argues in 1914, "too good to have any will of her own, too good to suffer. And he thinks these things just as long as he is under the spell of passion, and not one second longer. When a man says that he doesn't want the woman he loves to think, he is always afraid that she might get to thinking about him some day, and find out how little there is to think of."[18] Similarly, in 1927, she argues that some men seek what she calls "dumb-bell ladies" or women who will pretend to be so: "A small man hates to have a wife who is as clever as he is, and he simply will not endure a wife who is really more clever than he is, and lets him know that she knows it. He can't stand it, that's all."[19]

In a column from 1930, Black uses a conversation among women to further develop her judgment of men who seek to belittle and control women. Here a wife tells the group that she loves her husband but "he doesn't want me to go a step anywhere on earth without him." As the women consider their friend's options, they list the choices to cope with the "jailer-husband" as three: to knuckle under and "be a doormat," to leave him, or begin to lie to him, this last one labeled as Alibi Road.[20]

Beyond the jealous and the cruel and the unfaithful man to avoid for their lack of respect for and desire to control women, Black isolated other types of men to avoid, sometimes employing a humorous tone to do so. In 1926, for example, she writes about a man who gives lectures concerning Americans' love of money, speaking on and on for higher values: whatever an audience may think of his proclamations, his wife knows that he is tedious and pompous. And then Black addresses her reader directly on having to live with this man: "What would you take to be his wife and have to listen to his rigmarole five or six times a day—honestly now—what would you take?"[21]

As Black reviews all the types of men with serious liabilities, she gives the advice of leaving them if they become truly unbearable, and she never concentrates on methods of re-winning or changing them, as did so many pieces on women's pages. If the situation could be judged as tolerable, with leaving thus not required, the other possibility would be to begin to ignore him. One column from 1910, entitled "Unhappy Eleanor," describes a woman abandoned at home, to whom Black replies with questions: "Why aren't you indifferent to him?.... Why don't you put him right out of your heart?" This wife can be nice when he's home and then forget all about him and go on with her own life since he isn't the whole world, a fact that many other women, Black claims, have discovered: "You won't be the only woman who smiles amiably to a man at whose presence or absence she is absolutely indifferent." As this wife gardens, sees friends, goes home to see her mother, or learns French, as Black advises her directly, she can "let the man who is neglecting you walk in his own road, in his own way, and never affect you by the quickening of a single beat of your heart."[22] Whether the woman ultimately decides to stay or go if she becomes involved with a man evidencing a significant liability, what she must avoid doing is to reevaluate her own worth if he denigrates it, to lose contact with her own values, to lose herself.

## Of Economic Dependence—on Men

Much of Black's frequently negative analysis about marriage concerns money. Creating her own Marxian analysis, she tied an understanding of finances and the ability to support oneself to the best sort of courtship and marriage. As in her analysis of children with their parents, she warned repeatedly about the cost of lacking awareness of money and in depending on others for it and for security.

## 15. Dating, Domestic Violence and Marriage

In one column from 1912, Black uses baby talk to describe women who marry and then become completely dependent on their husbands' money, stealing from the men's pockets for car fare, being treated like children and soon enough acting like them: "Such sweet 'ittle bitsy bridey-brides, all in their new clothesie-osey, and with their pitty 'ittle hatsies on." Although entering into such a relationship may seem like an appropriate means of surviving, ultimately even the husband will be unsatisfied, Black argues, because it is a fact "that no man respects what he can tyrannize over and that no man wants a human door-mat for a wife." The marriage for which such a woman has given up her own adulthood may not last, and this woman will not be prepared financially or otherwise to move out into the world alone. "Wake up, bridey brides," Black advises. "You must have some place in the world yourself."[23]

Black wrote repeatedly about the actual costs of being supported, often stating the worst of results quite directly. In a column about a woman who leaves one husband and is looking for another who will pay all her bills, Black strongly judges the tendency to give up on self-development and take what a man offers: "She will pay for that support in the ancient coin of such bargains."[24] In some articles, Black went further in examining the dependent wife. One piece concerns a husband who holds all the money and will not give any but tiny amounts to his wife, whom he expects to work endlessly in the house. Black here strongly argues, with one of her adjective chains, that this "greedy, stingy, arguing, selfish husband" has instituted a form of slavery in his house, making her into a "creeping, crawling, hiding, fibbing, hunting, ransacking thing."[25]

Black also frequently warned women who thought that not having to work, that being supported by a husband, would definitely be a better life than going to an office or store or factory each day. In one article, for example, she describes a stenographer who feels that her lot is much harder than that of a supported married woman. Their conversation gives Black the chance to again discuss the lot of the married woman, with no money of her own, with nagging or begging as her only access to anything, and then to address the stenographer directly: "Some of them have to wheedle an hour to get what you earn in a day."[26]

Beyond a woman's striking out on her own or maintaining a job, Black argued that another, always available, remedy to ending complete financial dependence was to learn about how family finances worked. For a woman to insist on understanding the family's budget and its role in decision-making, as she quotes Tennyson's "Oenone" to indicate, could create a route back to "'self-reverence, self-knowledge, self-control—these three alone lead life to sovereign power.'"[27] In an article from 1910 she writes about a woman who is mad at her husband for all he is spending and for his extravagant care of his own mother. Though Black certainly agrees that life with an angry mother-in-law can be intolerable, she takes another tack here, claiming that every wife should understand the finances of her own household, what is spent and what is needed, and perhaps earn her own share of the money, instead of just complaining about what her husband spends and won't spend. If she disapproves of the current budget, she should suggest a better plan: she should take responsibility.[28]

Beyond her analysis of financial independence before and during marriage, Black also examined widowhood, as a difficult adjustment of course but also as a chance for a woman to control her own finances. In one of her columns about becoming a man's possession, Black speaks of the death of an older husband, whom she describes as "the man who owned the woman," after which she happily took up with a younger, long-haired musician that the husband would have detested. This wife had put in the time with the man that she "belonged to," who kept her from friends, from singing, from having her own thoughts: she had "belonged to him body and soul and heart and brain and breath and breathing—and he never let her forget it for one minute," his money ceding him the power and right to control her life. Her friends feel sorry for her, believing that she has fallen socially by becoming involved with the musician, but this couple shares interests, and she deserves kindness and fun. In Black's economic terms, she has "earned" the money on which she now lives with her sweetheart.[29]

## And Discussion of Domestic Violence

As Black considered dating and marriage, certainly often expressing a negative viewpoint and always stressing the price of dependence, she also wrote about domestic violence—on the editorial page, on the women's page, or on the first page—when few other people were discussing it in any of these sites with any degree of seriousness. Though Black certainly condemned men for the violence and deplored the courts' lack of concern for it, she also spoke quite forcefully to women about their responsibility and agency in making it stop.

Especially in the first decades in which Black wrote, the American criminal justice system did not perceive domestic violence as a crime. In the 1910 case of *Thompson v. Thompson*, the United States Supreme Court upheld a District of Columbia statute that barred a wife from recovering damages for assault and battery by her husband upon her person. *Thompson* placed men's rights and "privacy" above wives' physical safety. Many states, such as New York, Maine, Pennsylvania, Illinois, Michigan, Minnesota, and Iowa, had laws that constrained a woman's right to protect herself against marital violence, making a conviction unlikely except in the harshest of cases.[30]

At the beginning of the twentieth century, when Black brought the subject of domestic violence before her readers, seriously and repeatedly, along with recognizing that the police and courts generally ignored this reality, violence within a marriage was often treated as little more than comedy in American journalism, as can be seen from a few examples in the *New York Tribune*, a major newspaper at the beginning of the twentieth century. The humor distanced readers from the events reported, inviting them to assume a position separate from the fracas, to peer into an underworld whose violence could appear as entertainment, ridiculous and fun. The article "Threw Wife Out of Window/She Puts in a Good Word for 'Mike' When Patrolmen Finds Her on the Sidewalk," from the *Tribune* in August of 1908, turns on ethnic stereotypes to render violence against a woman comic. When a patrolman sees a wife "hurtling through the air from a second story window," her first words, which begin the piece, are "'Mike' was always a good man. I won't make a complaint against the lad, sure." Mike has thrown his wife out the window during a party "in the spirit of fun" and "she was not fatally hurt." She is, through the dialogue, portrayed as an Irish woman for whom incidents like being tossed out of a second story window are a familiar component of life with men, nothing for readers to become overly concerned about.[31]

As part of the comic underworld of violence against women as described in the *Tribune*, small details often become the focus of titillation and entertainment. "Woman, Gagged, in Burning Room," from October of 1916, presents the shocking but supposedly humorous sight of a woman tied up by a violent stranger: "A window on the third floor had been shattered and through the splintered gap protruded a pair of dainty feet, that kicked spasmodically, yet in unison. The ankles were lashed together."[32] In "Bloodstain Causes Fatal Shock," from May of 1908, with the subhead "Woman Wounded Slightly by Knife Prick Dies from Fright," readers find that a woman who had been stabbed actually died from seeing the blood, which was "too much for the woman's weak heart."[33] "Two Slain over Woman," from May of 1908, with the subhead of "Double Tragedy at Coney Island—She Is Shot, Too," depicts the fun of an unfaithful and immoral woman, a singer in Coney Island clubs, being attacked by three jealous men: a professional wrestler, a gangster called Lump, and an East Side gang leader, the notorious "Kid Swift." The details in these pieces of dainty feet, weak hearts more dangerous than knife pricks, wrestlers, and gangsters clearly differentiate readers from the subject: there's no compassion or concern here, just the zany fun of distant, cartoon violence.[34]

Given this treatment of domestic violence in the *New York Tribune* as well as many other American newspapers, Black spoke fairly in 1915 when she recognized that members of her own profession did not take violence against women seriously. Her description of the stories reported in newspapers reflected what could commonly be read in the *Tribune* and elsewhere: "Most people seem to think there's something funny about a divorce. Many newspaper reporters can't write the story of a divorce suit without trying to be humorous. I read an article in one of the great and influential newspapers this very day. It was supposed to be humorous and it was all about a woman who had had to run out of her own home in her night dress because her husband had threatened to murder her." Reporters often went even further, she claimed, by asserting that women cause these beatings, the most minor of issues being cited as leading naturally to a man's violence: "It was a lovely story. It had all the old things in it about the mother-in-law, and the hard biscuits, and the bill for the new fall hat, and the lodge night absence—not a thing was left out."

In this article, Black then asked readers to examine the violence in their own homes and those of their friends, to get beyond the common judgments, enforced by media representations, that cruelty is humorous, the woman's fault, an unavoidable part of marriage. And then she ended by returning to this "lovely story" of the woman running from her home in the night: "I suppose some people laughed at it. I didn't. I keep wondering how that article looked to the woman who married because she believed that the man she married loved her and would take care of her and protect her, and help her bear the disappointments and griefs of life." As Black focused further on the wife, she argued that the reporter should have actually considered the woman's circumstances, moving beyond the prejudices that Black and her readers do not share with him: "She had a baby in her arms when she ran out into the night, and the baby cried—'squalled,' the reporter wrote it. I wonder if the man who wrote that story ever held a child of his own in his arms and tried to think what would become of that child if she died and it was left alone in the world."[35]

In some of her earliest articles, like one from 1892, Black writes about the difficulty that women had in even admitting the situations in which they lived, enveloping the entire family in duplicity and danger. Women often didn't want to admit that they were in unhappy and abusive unions in which they were humiliated and mistreated, a tendency she describes fully: "Women talk a great deal of nonsense about the disgrace of a divorce. They seem to think it is no disgrace to live with a man whom they despise. They seem to think it is no degradation to submit themselves to abuse and humiliation. They have what they call pride—but they have no self-respect. They care for what other people will think more than they care for their own dignity and womanhood. Such a woman as that is vain. She cannot bear to have people know that she is not an idol in her husband's heart."[36] In another column from 1906, Black says again that women often lie about domestic violence, staying with the abusive husband because of the shame involved in telling the truth to family and friends. As she describes this dangerous tendency, she claims that a woman with a violent husband might "let him whip her to death before she would admit to her dearest friend that he ever laid a finger on her."[37]

In other columns Black tried to carefully lay out the facts of life in a home dominated by domestic abuse. One column concerns a husband, described as a "selfish, evil-tongued brute," who took it out on his wife and family every time another man stood up to him. And the shame caused by this violence, always occurring only within the home, motivated the entire family to dissemble: his young daughter felt forced to run out and meet him so children in other homes with real fathers would not recognize what was going on.[38]

In other pieces, instead of presenting the cartoon details common in the few news articles that concerned abuse, Black continued to consider the circumstances of women who felt trapped in violent marriages, always to encourage readers to get away. One column, an interview from 1909, concerned a man who beat his wife and would not allow her to see friends or family. When Black asks her why she doesn't leave, she replies that she cannot support her children and herself. Black here acknowledges the difficulties of getting away but is ultimately not supportive of the choice to remain in the home. "Poor little foolish, trembling, cowardly rabbit," in fact, is Black's stringent commentary about a woman who would cower in the corner and perhaps be killed, or allow her children to be killed, rather than find some means of getting away. Here her ultimate message concerns the necessity for courage.[39] In other columns, Black continued to insist on the woman's ability to get away: "The American woman cares too much for her children and for her own self-respect to live with a drunken brute or a cruel degenerate, just because he happens to be her husband."[40] And in many of these columns, Black directly addresses the woman under attack: 'Be not the property of any one human being, but an intelligent, independent member of society. And when you are that, no man will dare attempt to abuse you or your children. Or if he does, you will know what to do about it." Black also frequently wrote about women's responsibility to aid each other in the worst of situations: "Why do these poor little women allow themselves to become so isolated? Why do they permit themselves to be cut off from all communication with other people? Isn't there a neighbor woman somewhere who can go to the nearest priest or the nearest preacher and tell him your sister's story?"[41]

As part of her ongoing campaign to get women away from their abusers, Black wrote often and critically about social pressures on women to remain in violent situations. Using one of her experts who needed correction, for example, she begins a column in 1920 with the Society for the Upholding of the Sanctity of Marriage, which opposed divorce under any circumstance and was attempting to amend the Constitution to outlaw it. To refute this society's thesis concerning marriage's sanctity, Black speaks of a young woman who married because she was expected to do so and began living with "a brute who abuses her and her children, and spends all her money on another woman." This wife undoubtedly needs to leave, for herself and for her children, their lives certainly lacking sanctity in a brute's lair, any other "expert" judgment being narrow-minded and unrealistic, ultimately damaging to women.[42]

Though Black often writes about women as victims of violence, she also frankly considers the character of the woman who would stay. In an article from 1915, concerning a case of domestic violence in Texas and the wife's defense of the brutal husband, Black describes the wife's decisions to remain in the home, defend her husband in court, leave the clerk's chambers with him after he pays a fine, and nag him down the street. Black certainly judges such behavior harshly: "Any woman may be struck once by her husband, but the woman who lives with him after he has struck her once is as bad as he is, and that is why she stays with him."[43]

In harshly denouncing women who live with violence, Black argues that taking a beating will only bring more of it, that women do not calm or change men by becoming their punching bags. In one column, addressing the reader directly, she employs strong words about remaining in such a situation, the wife's worse crime in this case being not that she ultimately shot the husband but that she had stayed with him:

> Have you been reading about the woman in Kansas City who went without food so that her husband might eat—and then when the husband threatened to leave her she shot him dead? The husband beat her, abused her and laughed at her, and neglected her. He imitated the way she walked and the way she talked. He was, so they are saying in court where the woman is being tried, a drug addict.
> Well, of course, there's something odd about the woman. No one can help being sorry for her—not because she shot the man, but because she wanted him to stay with her, no matter how he treated her.
> If what they say about the dead man is true, you don't wonder he wanted to get away from a woman who would follow him around the earth just to be starved, neglected, and abused.
> No man in his senses could have anything but contempt for a poor-spirited creature like that.

In this column, Black then uses questions to involve her readers in considering the woman's motivation, in further evaluating her actions: "No, I don't admire this woman for going without food so that her husband could eat. Was she trying to buy his gratitude? Why couldn't the poor blind creature see that the more she did for a man like that the more he would despise her?"[44]

In another article, about a woman whose husband drank and then became violent, the mother and grown daughter crying about the situation but not leaving, she again focuses on the individual's responsibility to solve the problem, to get away from such violence—the advice applying to both women, who must end the habit of pain. But the mother stays and dies there, and the daughter marries a man who drinks, which such victims often do. But after this cruel man dies, the daughter chose to stop viewing herself as a victim: she supported her children, made money and friends, and enjoyed her life, having finally considered the best options for moving forward and having broken the pattern of participating in abuse.[45]

As Black wrote about domestic violence, in articles appearing around the country, she often segued from the need to leave to the law that would apply if the wife did so. Laws changed slowly concerning spousal abuse, with variations from state to state, as she indicated in detail in her articles. "Rule of thumb" laws in many states in the 1800s allowed a husband to hit his spouse with anything smaller than the width of a thumb. The case of *Calvin Bradley vs. the State of Mississippi* in 1824 was the first of many major cases of domestic abuse decided in the state Supreme Court, allowing a husband to administer "moderate chastisement in case of emergencies," the restriction of "moderate" viewed as positive change. It was not until 1871 that the first state, Alabama, rescinded the legal right of men to beat their wives in even a moderate manner. In 1882, Maryland passed a law that made wife-beating an actual crime, punishable by forty lashes or a year in jail. But, in 1886, to defend the rights of men, North Carolina courts declared that a criminal indictment could not be brought against a husband unless the battery was so extreme as to result in permanent injury. In the late nineteenth and early twentieth centuries, women campaigned for both Prohibition and woman suffrage as part of their effort to curb violence towards women; their attempts to gain control over their own income and possessions, through Married Women's Property Acts, also stemmed from a concern over having the means to assert themselves and leave the home if necessary.[46]

In many columns, Black used stories of individual women to acquaint readers with not just this history but the current inequality before the law, bolstered by the 1910 case of *Thompson v. Thompson*. In one column from 1913, for example, she tells the story of a man in El Paso who had been arrested for whipping his wife. The neighbors called the police and when they came he acted like he had the right to whip her. And he says that he had come from the Midwest, and that in Kansas and Missouri he could hit her. He asks the police if Texas has other laws: the officers don't seem sure about whether the damage done to the wife would warrant an arrest since both state and federal rulings protected men.[47]

Black also reported in 1913 that in North Carolina a man could place a notice in the paper declaring that his wife had left him and dictating that no one should help her. When she investigates this right, which stemmed from the state's head of household laws, a lawyer informs her that anyone who helped the wife could be locked up and fined because, as the lawyer indicates, "she belongs to him just as his dog does." Indeed, someone who came to a wife's aid would be "enticing" her, a term adapted from laws requiring the return of a slave and into the twentieth century of an African American servant.[48] Black makes the comparison quite explicit, labeling one wife, in a particularly dire situation from which she is unable to extricate herself, as a "beaten slave."[49]

In another article from the next year, entitled "Peculiar Laws of North Carolina," Black reprints the type of ad that a husband could place in the newspaper requiring the return of his wife and threatening prosecution against anyone who was harboring her. She again also records the response of a lawyer, who tells her that the husband could issue a public injunction that "I hereby enjoin all persons to refrain from giving aid, comfort or employment under extreme penalty of law," with fines or jail time possible, because "she belongs to him like the rest of the livestock." Black judged this situation dramatically: "Skin deep, some civilization, it seems to me."[50] In 1919, as she considers the coming of national woman suffrage, she again returns to domestic violence and laws that often do not protect the abused and desperate wife. Here she claims that many of the states that will refuse to ratify the suffrage amendment are ones that don't have or won't enforce laws against violence—and thus the fierce need of a federal law ceding all American women the right to vote.[51] In another column, from 1922, concerning a woman considering suicide as her sole means of extricating herself from of a violent home, Black writes that only in a few states does a woman still belong to a man. Her point here is that a woman in one of those states should instigate reform or move to where she would have the right to leave an abusive home and take her children with her.[52]

When Black went to England in 1910 to research the suffrage campaign, much of what she wrote about concerned violence and the law. Women there were putting up with a Saturday beating, viewed as part of regular life, as Black claimed, something to put up with but not discuss in public, something for which a judge might levy a small fine but not much more. She made sure readers understood that wives had no power in England, no right to divorce without both adultery and violence being proven, an expensive and difficult endeavor, a worse situation than in the United States even though American women had varying rights from state to state.[53] In this article and elsewhere, Black expressed her belief that women had to assert their rights, in their homes and in politics, to protect themselves and gain security and justice.

## The Hard Decision to Divorce

Winifred Black differed from most journalists by writing frequently about domestic violence, its causes in a man's desire for control, the suffering engendered in the home, the necessity of leaving, the difficulties of doing so. Unlike most newspaper writers, she also devoted her attention to the array of other reasons for divorce, perhaps a topic of interest to her after her divorce from Orlow Black in 1897.

In 1900, in the *New York Times* as in many other papers, the articles concerning divorce focused on its strangeness: society and celebrity divorces and serial divorces by European counts and countesses. The women's page, in the *Times* as in almost all other newspapers, focused instead on making marriages work, on making husbands and children happy. Most advice columnists, like Dorothy Dix, repeatedly advised women on how to keep their husbands at home. Data from the period certainly confirms these writers' attitude that divorce was outside the normal purview of the American woman. The percentage of divorces, out of the total number of marriages, was just 5 percent in 1890 and 7 percent in 1900. Though rates began to slowly increase, to 10 percent in 1915 and to 16 percent in 1930, a divorce could not be obtained without proving abuse, adultery, or abandonment, the requirements differing by state, and the social and religious judgment of this choice was certainly harsh.[54]

Given the low rates of divorce and stigma concerning it early in Black's career, she especially wrote about it then, constructing it as obviously necessary in many different situations of discord. For Black the most crucial message was for her readers, women and men, to be open to the need for divorce in difficult circumstances, a subject that she did not seem to need to write about as frequently into the 1920s as the choice became less rare. Certainly, Black argued for divorce when any violence occurred in the home. Concerning adultery, in a column from 1914, she argued that if the man had once been swept off his feet by the wild fancy of a moment, perhaps a marriage did not have to end.[55] But a woman would need to assert her self-respect and independence if this tendency continued. As she argued in 1912, some "men are so perverse" that they will never be trustworthy.[56] Repeatedly Black argued, quite logically, that a woman should honor a contract made with a good man, who keeps his vows of love and respect, but not fret too much about leaving any other type or worry about how others would judge the situation. For her, the choice involves women's ultimate independence as adults, a repeated theme in her work that she applies to the need for divorce as an option: "The husband? Let him go. He'll find a 'good' woman to marry him and make her work for him. You are not responsible for him; you are responsible for yourself—and that's all.... No man may ruin the life of any woman no matter how 'good' he is or how bad she has been."[57]

But Black also believed that a marriage could be dysfunctional, ultimately not worth the work and the sacrifice of personal freedom, without it involving violence or adultery. In one column from 1901, as a lone voice in the American newspaper, she argued that the one real joy in life is a loving marriage, but nothing much as hideous as a loveless marriage. The tragedies found in divorce court are not as piteous, she claims, as the "ever wearing, ever maddening mystery" of the hum-drum, bad marriage, and the partners in such a relationship might rightly consider getting out of it.

In many other articles, Black looked further at incompatibility, arguing that men and women might come to a humane understanding that their relationship should end, a more controversial choice with children in the home but perhaps the right one. In 1914, she presented a story of two unlikely people who married; interestingly the poet is the man and the business person is the woman. They were unhappy, and she comments not really on their divorcing, as though it was certainly the right choice for them to make. But here she views the marriage as a success because of the children, with no ill effects seemingly of the amicable divorce and with their offspring demonstrating a fine mix of traits.[58]

As divorce became a bit more common in the 1920s, and as states began to include incompatibility as a justification, Black spent less time advocating for the acceptance of divorce. Indeed, she began to caution that true incompatibility should be a grounds though not just a failure to agree on small things. In one column from 1922, she tells the story of Carolyn from Los Angeles who kept her skirts down near her ankles because her husband wanted them long, but had gotten her hair bobbed because her long hair would not fit within the new hats. When the husband saw the cut, as quotations from Carolyn explain, "he gave me one look, picked up his own hat and walked out of the house" and vowed that he would not return until she cut it, which she would not do, as she declared: "I won't let any man tell me how to dress my own hair, so we might as well get through right here and now." As they head into divorce court, Black's comments concern the ridiculousness of it all, the need for both parties to heed each other's preferences, to make compromises, to communicate.[59]

In the 1920s, she also wrote about the more independent woman, indeed like herself, coming into a fuller life and perhaps not needing as much from a husband, thus not suing for divorce if he doesn't meet her every need but instead viewing marriage as only one element of life, not the supposedly perfect fulfillment of every need. One column from 1925, indeed, asks the question: "Do We Expect Too Much from Marriage?"[60] In 1927, she presents census data about divorce, along with "cruelty" as a common plea for women, often used to cover disagreements or even boredom. "I wonder if we expect too much of each other," she asks here, and posits that people may be giving up too quickly on each other instead of viewing marriage as just one element of a full life.[61]

In the 1920s and 1930s, Black also wrote further about the more independent woman and divorce. Arguing again that it is best that couples separate who truly can't live in peace and amity, she claims that some women think that it is wrong in that circumstance to take a man's money. But decent men realize that they have an obligation to support their children and wives, and women should insist on this protection since they may be responsible to make a home for the family for years afterwards.[62] Instead of refusing to act because they fear the law and the courts, women need to stand up for themselves, for their rights, and not be overwhelmed by a man or his family: they can prevail in getting a divorce, Black argued, keeping what they have and gaining support for their children. "If she's any sort of woman at all the courts will stand by her to the very end," Black wrote in 1912. "She can have her children, her income, and her self respect—just by asking for them before any decent judge in the country."[63] And she should certainly take the money that her ex-husband has the responsibility to provide.

But Black doubts the efficacy of divorce when women bring their problems or insecurities into the next marriage. They may choose other men that will abuse them and will again have to take on the responsibility to get away: "I do not respect any woman who lives with a man who humiliates her in any way." It may be better to get free and not quickly enter into the next relationship with the same insecurities.[64]

In her articles in all parts of the newspaper, Black considered relationships through the lens of independence. Women did not need husbands, she repeatedly argued. Many men were certainly not worth marrying, many American reasons for choosing a particular spouse being worse than having one selected from another country. Women in all states needed the right to divorce because of cruelty and adultery as well as real incompatibility, not just odd differences of opinion. And women needed to secure the support necessary for their children. In all these articles, Black chipped away at the received wisdom of getting married and staying no matter what. Through her characters, scenes, and arguments, presented in articles placed near to so many about perfect marriages and homes, Black took on domestic violence, divorce, and life without men, preparing her readers to think clearly and to advocate for themselves within the complex space of marriage.

# 16

# *Feminism and Suffrage: Women as Citizens*

In one column, Black uses turning the tables to discuss the ridiculousness of men having made all the laws that impacted women through the generations: "Is there a man in this country who would be willing to let women make all the laws governing him, without his having any voice at all?" Through the years that women sought suffrage in California, through the fight for a federal amendment, and through the subsequent years in which the results were often denigrated, Black repeatedly wrote about suffrage and the legal power that it created for women. Having lived in Colorado while working at the *Denver Post*, Black could write authoritatively about the results of a state suffrage amendment: in 1893, four years before Black moved there, Colorado had become the second state to cede women the vote. In California, with the backing of strong supporters and a few dedicated journalists such as Winifred Black, women achieved state suffrage in 1911 by only 3,587 votes, after a long campaign involving a vote by the legislature and veto by the governor, and California would ratify the federal amendment on November 1, 1919. Black spoke for suffrage all throughout this long campaign, one of the few respectful advocates of it in a mainstream American newspaper; she was also one of the few that spoke positively about the impact of the amendment after it became law.

## Newspapers and Suffrage

Throughout the campaign, both newspapers for and against woman suffrage often spoke disrespectfully about it. In New York City, the *New York Times* was staunchly anti-suffrage. In its editorial against a state suffrage referendum slated for November of 1915, the *Times* claimed that supporting suffrage in the western states, with their "vast areas and sparse population" and desperate need for independent workers, might be appropriate, but in crowded eastern states "cold and critical male judgment" had deemed it inappropriate and unnecessary—and even dangerous because of the large populations of volatile and poorly educated immigrant workers who would thus assume greater power.[1]

In contrast, the *New York Tribune* supported a suffrage amendment, with encouragement from Helen Rogers Reid, whose husband became editor in 1912, running the paper along with her. But Reid could not control the tone of the pieces that appeared regularly in this newspaper. From 1908 to 1915, many articles portrayed these campaigners as violators of the true-woman code: as hysterical, petty, selfish, overly aggressive—and inappropriately aligned with the lower class. In 1908, the year that a visit from English suffragist Bettina Boormann Wells spurred interest in a more militant form of campaign, the *Tribune* contained several articles about unnatural and aggressive English women, assailing them for a radical inappropriateness that no American woman should adopt. In August of 1908, "Hunting Big Game: The Misses Herberts' Exciting Exploits in Africa," a story about two English sisters on an African safari, begins with the following paragraph separating English suffrage aggression from American common sense even though there is no indication that either Herbert sister was a suffragette:

> Nothing ever brought home to American women the differences between them and their English sisters more than the suffragette methods. But the ability of English women of wealth and position to march in the streets for a ballot is only a public sign of differences more innate, though less widely known. The newest woman in America, for instance, would hardly contemplate the trip of the two Herbert cousins, Agnes and Cecily, to Somaliland. They went alone, wore khakis, men's clothes, shot one rhinoceros, many lions, leopards, hyenas and jackals and numbers of deer and antelope of various species.

Here English women take on aggressive male roles that no sane and natural American woman would ever contemplate. The ending reinforces the contrast: "The impossibility of unmarried women from any race on the Continent doing things like this, and the remoteness of such achievements from the American girl, indicate how very new the new woman is in England." American women might take on new values and causes, this piece implies, but they should never begin shooting antelopes, sleeping in tents with black men, or taking to the streets to secure the vote.[2]

While the *Tribune* marked English suffragettes as dangerous, it did not generally portray middle-class American suffragists in such a shockingly negative fashion. As the paper depicted an escalating American campaign, these women involved with it appeared as mischievous and silly bad girls, in articles creating entertainment for readers while delivering a gentle rebuke to these women who would never actually alter the status quo. In the *Tribune*, suffragist meetings become silly ladies' tea parties, extravagances of a pampered upper class. In June of 1910, in an article entitled "Suffragettes at Outing," a meeting of Alva Belmont's Political Equality League garners the following description: "Refreshments were provided, and everybody skipped the rope, sang and romped around."[3] Another piece, from September of 1910, entitled "Oratory Flows Freely," again stresses the entertainment value of these meetings:

> With horse racing to the right of them and a merry-go-round to the left of them, with drinkables fizzing in the rear and "barkers" on every hand making dreadfully frivolous announcements in stentorian voices, public spirited women of New York held forth on the wrongs of their sex and a few dozen other things yesterday at the Interborough Fair at Donegan Hills, Staten Island.

As they rant on about suffrage "and a few dozen other things," these women resemble carnival barkers, their free-flowing oratory evoking the silly hype of a circus or fair.[4]

The *Tribune* also reported on suffrage parades, which were quickly growing in size and frequency, as spectacular scenes of silliness. On February 3, 1908, "Women Will Parade" creates the impression of entertainment, not revolution, by describing the helter-skelter planning for a parade in which there would be "oratorical outpourings from the fair marchers." Their giddy excitement and lack of organization both provide sources of stereotyped humor: "There will be a big brass band, but whether the leaders will precede the band or whether the band will precede the leaders is a question not yet definitely settled. Whether the paraders should carry banners, horns and torches, and whether they should march in column of fours or twos are other details to be determined." In this as in many other *Tribune* pieces, suffragists are portrayed as upper-class women in possession of more time than sense. Even though the paper's editorials supported women's right to vote, its articles continually downplayed the commitment of suffragists and their possible effect on American life and politics.[5]

## An Active Life in Politics According to Winifred Black

In contrast, Winifred Black, in syndicated articles that appeared across the country, always took the campaign for suffrage seriously. In California, she witnessed all the vicissitudes of state campaigning. The state legislature in 1893 approved women's voting, but the governor vetoed the new law and declared it unconstitutional. A large majority of voters rejected a state referendum in 1896. A group combining laborers, socialists, college students—and some journalists like Black—kept the fight going. Much of the publicity for the movement came from special publications, such as Katherine Reed Balentine's *The Yellow Ribbon*, but in newspapers throughout the state, Black frequently lauded women's ability to enter the political arena and provided common sense reasons for their doing so. From the beginning of her career in California, Black had considered herself as able to understand politics, part of her job to explain the political system to readers, both women and men, and she also applied this stance of knowledgeable involvement to the suffrage campaign.

In a series of articles written before women had secured the vote in California, for which she interviewed the mayor and the governor, she attempted to demystify government processes. As readers heard about the difficulties and the tedium of these state leadership jobs, Black engaged them in a space that they too should be able to enter, with leaders that they should have the right to choose and that should certainly also have the right to be. In other articles, she also brought readers behind the scenes, beyond any mysteries, into how politics actually worked. In "Annie Laurie in Politics," she writes about the men who plan the parades and create the banners—and whose job it is to get politicians elected. She concludes by describing politics as a business: "All this noise and fuss are calmly planned just like any other business scheme. You go to work and get out a brass band instead of advertising a bargain sale, and you have a flambeau parade instead of a cut in prices, but it's quite the same thing after all, isn't it?" And given this manipulation, this creation of what will win, given politicians that utter stirring phrases even when, or especially when, all they care about is being elected, no woman needs to feel overawed by this world: they can evaluate political rhetoric and choose, or be, the best candidate.[6] Similarly in an article "Politics as They Seem," about a state political convention, Black notes that no one heeds any candidate's literature, no one listens to anybody's speeches, everyone follows the dictates of their faction led by "wordy gentlemen" that rose in all parts of the room and "charmed the air with honeyed compliments."[7]

While Black wrote many articles that brought readers behind the curtain of politics, she also carefully constructed herself as suffragist and activist. She depicted herself as an engaged citizen, like her readers, sensible, not extreme, in her belief in human rights, thus her advocacy of suffrage being an appropriate choice for her readers as well, both within the state and across the country.

Black could be very complimentary about what activists were doing while also demonstrating her independence from them; readers could thus trust her reasoned judgments and advocate the passage of a suffrage referendum along with her. She writes, for example, about a Woman's Congress in San Francisco in May 1895, for which the announced subject was the home and education but all of the talk was about the vote, as activists considered various means of overcoming the governor's veto. Here she speaks of the importance of such a Congress to get women of all sorts to talk together about the vote: "It's a good thing, too, to learn that there really is a new woman and that she's come to town."[8] But she also claims that in advocating for suffrage, these speakers were exaggerating women's lack of rights in California, especially about divorce. For this article, she interviews a lawyer and then quotes California laws, in contrast to those in other states, that guaranteed that women seeking a divorce could keep their possessions and their earnings and had a strong right to child custody. In this article, she assures readers that she reports accurately what she hears and sees—and thus as she advocates for the vote and equal rights, she could be assumed to be doing so fairly.

While she argued for the vote, Black continued to note the exaggerations of feminists and suffrage supporters, often naming controversial activists as experts in need of correction. In one column from 1910, for example, she quotes Alva Belmont, prominent multi-millionaire American socialite and a major figure in the suffrage movement, as saying that American men treated their wives like slaves. As Black disagrees, describing this reality as the exception not the normal, she provides a disapproving response to a feminist expert, her criticism rooted in common sense and her own experience.[9]

As Black denied the extremes of the suffrage argument, she carved out a middle that could involve most readers. Indeed, in a speech that she gave to a press club in Chicago in 1912, reported in Illinois newspapers, she argued that to fight for their rights women did not have to become extreme radicals, here labeled with the English term of "suffragettes": "'In whatever program we outline,' Mrs. Bonfils concluded, 'We must go at it in a sensible womanly way. We must not be afraid of public opinion and must dare to stand for the things we know are needed in the world. I don't mean that we must be suffragettes. But we should not bother about gaining the applause of other people or worry in they disapprove because they do not understand. We must only strive to please and keep the good opinion of our better selves.'"[10]

As Black worked on carving out this middle, she often addressed men directly. Certainly, suffrage could not come to California or any other state without men voting for it, and from the beginning of her career Black repeatedly tried to appeal to them with her arguments. In "Do They Want to Vote?" from 1890, Black writes that she has interviewed many local women, who attest that interest in voting is growing, and here she uses turning of the tables to speak of adults, women and men, as having the right to participate fully in their country:

> One strange feature of the situation is this. No less than half a dozen said this to me this week: "I believe in suffrage, but I would not have any one know it for the world."
> "Why not?"

"Men do not like a woman who says those things."

What would we think of a man who refuses to give his idea on any of the issues of the day because "women would not approve of him"?

Here she makes fun of the "time-honored witticism" that women would only vote for handsome men, as ridiculous as women feeling the need to hide their opinions on key issues, including their right to vote in a democracy.[11]

In this article, after Black establishes women's right to speak out on issues, she quotes them as they advocate for the vote. Here an array of women argue that voting is a human right, that it will not render women hard or coarse, that they already engage in society as workers and active citizens and thus will be well prepared to vote, that being denied the vote classes them with criminals and the insane: every woman should claim that "the refusal to give me that right is an insult to my intelligence." Black ends by asserting that whereas the majority of women want the vote, she is not so impressed with this particular right since "the stream of politics is so turgid." And so she constructs herself as not pushing for suffrage personally or selfishly but just reflecting what women want.

While she spoke against extreme arguments, Black also used the family to argue for suffrage, especially as women began voting in some states. She reported the thinking of fathers and sons, in 1915, to show men of different ages, in different relationships with women, who realize that they were wrong in opposing it in their states and at the federal level. She begins by discussing the 1912 elections in which California women could vote and they changed the opinions of "the men who opposed suffrage":

> I was there during the last election, and every woman I knew voted, and voted with all her heart and with all her mind, and with all the soul she could find.
>
> And the men who opposed suffrage looked at each other and said quietly: "Maybe we were wrong about this after all."
>
> And husbands talked with new interest of old questions, and mothers and sons talked together earnestly about issues that were as old as the voting age to the son, and as new as new bread fresh from the oven to the mother.
>
> And so found that mother could do something besides laugh and cry, and worry and love. Mother could think, and mother enjoyed thinking. And son began to take an entirely new interest in mother.[12]

In "Homes Not Wrecked by Women Voting," in April of 1915, Black counters negative arguments made by women and men, including supposed experts, by considering what was happening in the suffrage states. George W. Wickersham, who had been attorney general of the United States, had claimed that suffrage would ruin the home. She answers him with direct address: "Wrong, Mr. Wickersham, wrong again, and wrong all the way through.... Do politics make up neglect your business? Do you ever give up a game of golf to go and see that the right man is elected? Possibly you should do so—but do you?" Then she moves to the experience of women and men in suffrage states like California and Colorado where nothing changed in the home as husband and wife went to the ballot box: sensible people can vote and not be ruined by it. Expecting her readers to agree with her, she moves to countering further arguments made by the faulty Wickersham, who believed women should have no interests or responsibilities beyond the home: "Isn't she a human being first, a woman afterward and a housekeeper after that?" And then Black further creates a telling comparison between women and men as she addresses Wickersham about people having relationships and allegiances beyond their families: "Are you always a nobody but a father, or a brother, or a husband, or a son? Don't you ever think, or feel, or hope, or despair, except in couples? Why should you think women are any different from men in this respect?"[13]

In constructing men and boys as siding with the suffragists, as understanding that voting is a human right that would not harm home or business life, Black uses her technique of portraying the American normal as already having changed, with women prepared to vote and men accepting that fact. Indeed, she argues, what feminists advocated for as change might have already been accepted. In a column from 1914, she uses a developed scene to describe a feminist coming in to speak at a women's group: she wears masculine clothes, smokes during tea service, and thinks that she is shocking the others as she claims that women do not have to behave themselves, to be good and patient and remain within the home. The feminist speaker then maintains that before marriage or instead of it, women should choose the men that they like and not wait to be chosen, and they should see more than one man at once. And then, as the narration continues, the activist looks surprised when no one appears shocked: "The thrilling moment passed—unthrillingly." The shock here is not what the "little feminist" advocates but that she does not realize that all of these women already share these values: "Of course, nobody can live in the real world nowadays without realizing that the whole point of view of the average woman is changing, and changing fast. The woman who, ten years ago, would have sat down and cried when her husband misbehaved gets up nowadays and packs her trunk. She doesn't have to be miserable with any man. She's learned how to take care of herself without one. I was rather glad about this state of affairs myself."[14]

Though during the suffrage campaign, Black spoke for equal rights and for women's ability to enter the political arena, she also maintained that differences in laws concerning domestic abuse and divorce would come with women assuming political power. Indeed, Black argued that the key to curbing domestic violence was for women who had secured the vote to then continue the fight by getting on juries, especially necessary in the 1920s when a freer set of social rules put women at greater risk. She uses a story in 1927, entitled "Taking a Motor Ride with a Stranger," to portray what could happen with misplaced trust: the subtitle is "One Girl Tells Her Experience with a Handsome, Smiling Young Man Who Turned Suddenly into a Brute." Here Black introduces the young woman, Alice, as "soft and appealing and gentle," someone old-fashioned who likes to cook, sing, and embroider. Black quotes Alice as saying that she had gone out to dinner with a friend and had begun to dance with a handsome man that asked her, the friend encouraging her to go ahead. This very handsome man, a good dancer, offered her a ride home: the man beats Alice up and knocks her teeth out.

And then the story goes on to the difficulties for a woman when such a case becomes public, to the differences that women voting and advocating for the rights of others can create. Here Black describes a past in which police would not make arrests and male juries would not convict, in which women were encouraged to blame themselves for what had occurred. But in this case in 1927, as she argues further, with women having gained the right to serve on juries in California in 1924, there was more sympathy, more help, a conviction. When women won the vote, they were still routinely barred from serving as jurors, but they began vigorous campaigns for a place in the jury box: the California example, and Black's article, concerning the practical difference that women could make, through the justice system, in other women's lives.[15] In her many articles concerning a wife's right to child custody and alimony, varying by state as did women's right to vote until 1920, she spoke for the power that suffrage supporters could wield in protecting women going through the process of divorce: "Why don't the suffragetts start to work and get that phase of the question before the legislatures of every state in the country?"[16]

## The Effects of Voting

While Black spoke for suffrage before it became law in the United States in 1920, she continued to write about its impact afterwards, taking on other topics beyond laws concerning divorce and domestic violence, even as women's voting became a target of media critics. Indeed, immediately after women gained the vote, many American magazines and newspapers denigrated the impact of women's voters. Reporters often argued that women had abandoned their goal of equality and had just gone home. In the *Atlantic Monthly* in February 1924, in "American Women and Public Affairs," George Madden Martin claimed that "American women generally are not interested in public affairs, national or local, in the concrete or in the abstract."[17] In March, the anti-suffrage *New York Times* noted that at least, given the error of ceding women the vote, "one bright ray of sunshine illumines the drab picture": women are "still as gentle, as feminine, as lovable as ever."[18] In March of 1924 also, in a *Century Magazine* article entitled "Is Woman-Suffrage a Failure," Charles Edward Russell concluded that "no wonder the politicians are happy" because "women would not vote for women."[19] In an article in *Literary Digest* on April 12, 1924, called "Woman Suffrage Declared a Failure," the author began with key questions that the title answered: "Is it true that 'women will not vote for a woman'? That they are a negligible quantity in local politics? That voting women have done nothing but double the votes of men? That they are apathetic regarding public matters?"[20]

Before woman suffrage became national law and afterwards in response to such arguments, Black asserted her own view of what the vote should and could achieve. Given her belief in women as having so many different traits and interests, she did not expect women to vote in a bloc or to only vote for each other though she did expect for them to support divorce and child-care reform. In 1915, she forecast what indeed would occur after 1920 and what in fact seemed like the best outcome to her: women would vote for other women but not just on the basis of gender, and they would not all have the same political views. Black used one of her surprising openers, "They're going to run a woman's ticket in the next campaign out West, I suppose," to lead into a discussion of her own support of woman's suffrage. Here she writes about various states and municipalities in which women had recently gotten the vote and where separate women's tickets of candidates had not succeeded—in Butte, Montana, where a group of women formed a separate ticket for school board elections; in Colony, Kansas, for city elections, including mayor and police judge; in Elizabeth, Illinois, for a slate of municipal elections. But Black argues that the strength of suffrage in these states should come from women acting as and being part of the whole. Separating by gender, she argues, is always wrongheaded, as certainly men's parties, which denied the rights of women, had been: "A woman's ticket and a woman's party? The women who propose this idea are the very ones who protested so bitterly because the men had a man's ticket for a man's party."[21]

Given her belief in men and women as so similar, Black did not view women as creating some sort of separate moral conscience; thus she argues that the results of women and men voting proved her views concerning the falseness of so many gender distinctions: "I have never been one of those who believed that the world was going to be made over when women got the right to vote. I never could see any great difference between men and women, anyhow, when it comes to intelligence and character."[22] In 1910, when Coloradan women had been voting for seventeen years, Black argued, in contrast to many activists, that though women had the right as citizens to vote, their participation had not initiated huge changes in the system and would not necessarily lead anywhere to any one particular sort of reform:

I live in Colorado, where women vote as naturally as they crochet, and where we have women patriots and women politicians and women bosses and women ward-heelers and women who are bought and sold on election day as their brothers are bought and sold. Oh, woman-suffrage isn't the realization of a poet's dream in Colorado—it is fact, hard, cold, unromantic, rather disenchanting fact. I cannot see that woman-suffrage has done much for Colorado, though well I am aware that I take my feeble life in my all-too-nerveless hand when I say it. Neither can I see that it has done anything in particular for women. But for humanity, for the great, broad, tolerant, just outlook upon life and what life means to both men and women, it must, in the very nature of things, have done a very great deal.[23]

For Winifred Black, it is inevitable and positive that woman suffrage is not "the realization of a poet's dream." Instead, it indicates that women are varied American citizens.

Black continued with her analysis of the effect of suffrage repeatedly after 1920. In a 1928 article about the Democratic convention, she notes that the Democratic Party, which had opposed women's suffrage as had Woodrow Wilson, had "gone over boots, horse, saddle and trench cap to the women." Here Black asks whether women will be swayed by this sudden support, and she again brings up her belief that women vote as separate, thoughtful individuals: "Will women next November vote as individuals—but as women? What an interesting question."[24]

Also in 1928 she had a similar response to Eleanor Roosevelt's claim that suffrage did not have the impact that it should, that it had not done anything for women. Black praised Roosevelt's get-out-the-vote campaign and her concern for women's issues, but she again argued that women did not need to organize separately, that they were not all alike. They could disagree about Prohibition, about foreign policy, about the economy, about many other matters. They could also choose to be activists or not to be activists, just as men could.[25] In 1931, as she described the attempt by women in China to gain the vote, she wrote about what it had not made occur in the United States, indeed the mistake of thinking that it would: "They used to tell us there would be fewer saloons and more schools, better hospitals, and fewer jails, happier homes and better-nourished children the minute women rose up and took the affairs of the nation into their nice, gentle, intelligent, conscientious, well-manicured hands." As they would in China, American women had different priorities as did men.[26]

Black did believe though that seeking the vote and asserting themselves, regardless of their voting habits, had helped women to discover all that they could do if they campaigned for change, regardless of the issues or the work that mattered to them. In 1921, she writes that a college president, one of her unidentified experts in need of correction, had declared that women hadn't changed even though their clothes and vocabulary might be new. And here she says that feminists hearing this pronouncement wouldn't agree, and she engages in a bit of satire of these women: as they state their viewpoints, they comb their fingers through their bobbed hair, light cigars, say "Damn," and quote Havelock Ellis, author of *Sexual Inversion*. She again satirizes extremes as she asks readers to move beyond negative evaluation of the new—to a recognition of how women had changed positively, embracing more freedom while also maintaining their self-respect and intelligence, with the ability analyze cultural traditions, pursue their own goals, and move forward.[27]

Through the years of her career, Winifred Black advocated for equal rights for women and men and praised the results as women assumed more political power, but she did not assume that they had essentialist traits different from those of men, that they would necessarily reform civilization, or that they should work separately from men. Ultimately Black judged that women deserved the vote and equal rights simply because they were American citizens, able to fully contribute to their nation as a group and as individuals, exactly as they would choose to do.

# *Conclusion: In Short*

When Winifred Black wrote letters to the *Chicago Tribune* in 1888 and went on to the *San Francisco Examiner* in 1889, she was becoming involved in journalism at a time of expansion in the types of writing included in newspapers. Black took advantage of this opening to initiate a lifetime of work in creative nonfiction, relying on her own developing skills and interests to become a beloved writer in San Francisco and a fixture of newspapers across the country.

In her writing, she depicted herself as the stalwart daughter of a general, as a dedicated mother, as an advocate of women's rights, as a San Franciscan rooted in the power of place—and as a thoughtful critic of American cultural traditions. Her genre was not the autobiography most often thought of a woman's genre of nonfiction, nor was it the straight who, what, when, and where of news articles found on the front page. In the shortest of prose formats, not ceded the respect given to longer genres, Black demonstrated the power of one strong voice considering the world around her, a woman with the ability and right to do so. Black understood the need to engage readers in key issues through specifics, not the general, flatly stated facts of the news article, but an entrance into other worlds and lives, created through details of character, dialogue, and place along with a reliance on direct address of readers to further draw them into various realms. In a career of writing short pieces, Black thus developed modern nonfiction technique that Tom Wolfe and many other practitioners would continue to develop, always discussing her choices as she made them, speaking for the development of her genre.

Like the best of current nonfiction writers, Black pursued realities that her readers may have never witnessed and indeed may have endeavored not to witness. With a changing, ever enlarging view of what topics should be covered for American readers within the newspaper, the most read genre in the years in which she participated in it, Black considered cultural tradition and cultural change. Her articles, her characters and scenes, engaged readers in drug addiction, domestic violence, the treatment of lepers and of the mentally ill, the work situation of women in canneries and in theatres and in many other work sites. She also considered the reality of regularly approved institutions: of American dating and marriages, of parenting, of the legislature and courts. She also wrote about prejudice in an array of forms, concentrating on race and certainly gender. And she took on the changing nature of normal and thus the possibilities of personal choice. Whatever the topic, she always wrote about the glory of life, lived independently, with women and men responsible first for themselves, choosing the connections that they might like to make, advocating for their rights and their freedom.

Black took on these topics with a strong persona, one which varied by topic and decade. She cast herself as totally engaged as reporter, involved in a calling—able to examine details, judge with an open mind, and guide the decision-making of other independent, well-informed adults. While she addressed women and girls most frequently in the advice columns, her other writing addressed both genders. Women did not need just to read about dresses and homes; men did not need just to read about the city council or foreign policy. Both needed to consider the best choices in a changing world.

Certainly women now have more freedom than they did through the years in which Black wrote, but women and men always deal with the pressures of making whatever choices may be deemed as normal at any given time, in gender definitions, relationships, work lives, politics, treatment of illness, even in response to violence. Winifred Black, in short, showed what nonfiction could achieve in creating engagement with a changing world and with the choices made by the adults within it.

# Chapter Notes

## Introduction

1. "Beloved Writer Devoted Career to Worthy Causes," *San Francisco Examiner*, May 26, 1936, 8.
2. "City's Official Tributes Given for Annie Laurie," *San Francisco Examiner*, May 26, 1936, 8; "Leaders Mourn Annie Laurie," *San Francisco Examiner*, May 26, 1936, 10.
3. "Tribute Is Paid to Writer," *San Francisco Examiner*, May 27, 1936, 6.
4. Willis O'Brien, "All S.F. Mourns for Annie Laurie," *San Francisco Examiner*, May 27, 1936, 1+.
5. "Annie Laurie Pall Bearers," *San Francisco Examiner*, May 28, 1936, 7.
6. "City's Grief Expressed by Supervisors," *San Francisco Examiner*, May 27, 1936, 6.
7. "Annie Laurie Lies in State at City Hall," *San Francisco Examiner*, May 27, 1936, 5.
8. Louella Parsons, "The Passing of Winifred Black," *Fresno Bee*, May 27, 1936, 10.
9. "Annie Laurie, Noted Writer, Dies in Calif.," *Evening Star and The Bradford Daily Record* (Bradford, Pennsylvania), May 26, 1936, 1.
10. "'Annie Laurie,' Beloved Writer, Taken by Death," *Times Picayune* (New Orleans), May 26, 1936, 1.
11. "Winifred Black, 73, Journalist, Dead," *New York Times*, May 26, 1936, 26.
12. Florence W. McGehee, "Orchids and Onions," *Woodland Daily Democrat* (Woodland, California), August 29, 1933, 6.
13. "The Real Annie Laurie," *San Francisco Examiner*, December 18, 1892, 13.
14. "The Colonel's Little Doctor," *Washington Post*, October 8, 1905, 84; "Annie Laurie Says We Are on Right Track," *Springfield Missouri Republican*, January 26, 1922, 10.
15. "Right off the Jump: 40 Big Reasons," *San Bernandino County Sun*, August 28, 1921, 3.
16. "Most Widely Known Woman of American Journalistic Work Will Write for This Paper," *Coshocton Tribune* (Coshocton, Ohio), March 30, 1922, 9.
17. "Rose from Its Ashes," *Emporia Gazette* (Emporia, Kansas), September 19, 1911, 1.
18. "Good Old Laura Jean," *Hutchinson News* (Hutchinson, Kansas), November 17, 1910, 4.
19. Florence W. McGehee, "Fie upon Winnie," *Woodland Daily Democrat* (Woodland, California), August 25, 1934, 8.
20. Ishbel Ross, *Ladies of the Press* (New York: Harper, 1936), 64.
21. These studies include Marion Marzolf, *Up from the Footnote: A History of Women Journalists* (New York: Hastings, 1977); Madelon Golden Schilpp and Sharon M. Murphy, *Great Women of the Press* (Carbondale: Southern Illinois University Press, 1983); Barbara Belford, *Brilliant Bylines: A Biographical Anthology of Notable Newspaperwomen in America* (New York: Columbia University Press, 1986); Kay Mills, *A Place in the News: From the Women's Pages to the Front Page* (New York: Dodd, Mead, 1988). More recently, books have considered a particular reporter or story sequence, as in Matthew Goodman, *Eighty Days: Nellie Bly and Elizabeth Bisland's History-Making Race around the World* (New York: Ballantine, 2013). While Winifred Black secures a page or two in encyclopedic histories, and she was the subject of a master's thesis by Ashley A. Kayes, there has been no book-length study of her work.
22. Frank Luther Mott, *American Journalism: A History of Newspapers in the United*

States through 250 Years, 1690 to 1940 (New York: Macmillan, 1962), 539.
23. Carolyn Kitch, "Women in Journalism," in *American Journalism: History, Principles, Practices*, ed. W. David Sloan and Lisa Mullikin Parcell (Jefferson, NC: McFarland, 2002), 90–91.
24. Jessica Enoch and Jordynn Jack, "Remembering Sappho: New Perspectives on Teaching (and Writing) Women's Rhetorical History," *College English* 73, no. 5 (May 2011): 518.
25. Gerda Lerner, *Why History Matters: Life and Thought* (New York: Oxford University Press, 1998), 204.
26. Michael Robertson, *Stephen Crane, Journalism and the Making of Modern American Literature* (New York: Columbia University Press, 1997), 57–58.
27. Tom Wolfe, "The New Journalism," in *The New Journalism, with an Anthology*, ed. Tom Wolfe and E.W. Johnson (New York: Harper & Row, 1973), 31–32.
28. "Winifred Black Writes About the Unafraid Girls," *San Antonio Evening News*, May 9, 1919, 6.
29. Martha Winifred Sweet Black Bonfils wrote as Annie Laurie at the *San Francisco Examiner* and in her advice columns but otherwise as Winifred Black. We will use the name Winifred Black throughout this study of her work.

## Chapter 1

1. Sweet Family, Record 6 of the Population Schedule for York (town), DuPage (county), Lombard (post office), Illinois, *US Census, 1870*, prepared by the Bureau of the Census (Washington, D.C., 1870–71), 30.
2. Michael Hendrick Fitch, *Echoes of the Civil War as I Hear Them* (New York: Fenno, 1905), 71–72; John H. Eicher and David J. Eicher, *Civil War High Commands* (Stanford: Stanford University Press, 2001), 520; George Levy, *To Die in Chicago: Confederate Prisoners at Camp Douglas 1862–1865* (Gretna, LA: Pelican, 1994), 17.
3. Levy, *To Die in Chicago*, 175.
4. Levy, *To Die in Chicago*, 264.
5. "The Chicago Conspiracy," *New York Times*, November 15, 1864, 8.
6. "Another Chicago Alleged Conspirator Pardoned," *Cincinnati Enquirer*, August 11, 1865, 2; William Bross, "Biographical Sketch of the Late Gen. B.J. Sweet: History of Camp Douglas" (paper, Chicago Historical Society, June 1878).
7. "The Chicago Conspiracy," *New York Times*, November 15, 1864, 8.
8. "Military Commission," *Cincinnati Enquirer*, April 11, 1865, 2.
9. "Letter from Cairo," *Times-Picayune* (New Orleans), April 2, 1865, 3.
10. Alan T. Nolan, *The Iron Brigade* (New York: Macmillan, 1961).

## Chapter 2

1. "A Woman Killed on the Railroad," *Lebanon Daily News* (Lebanon, Pennsylvania), August 15, 1878, 1.
2. "Jeffrey Black," *Burial Registers for Military Posts, Camps, and Stations, 1768–1921*, National Archives and Records Administration, Washington, D.C., M2014, Roll 1, 123.
3. Winifred Black, "Rambles through my Memories," Part II, *Good Housekeeping*, February 1936, 36.
4. "Honor Their Dead," *Chicago Sunday Tribune*, May 26, 1895, 34.
5. E.B. Tuttle, *The History of Camp Douglas, including Official Report of Gen. B.J. Sweet; with Anecdotes of the Rebel Prisoners* (Chicago: J.R. Walsh, 1865).
6. "Honor Their Dead," 34.
7. "Chicago's Pension Agent," *Courier-Journal* (Louisville, Kentucky), March 20, 1874, 1.
8. "Varieties," *Dallas Daily Herald*, March 25, 1874, 1.
9. John McDonald, *Secrets of the Great Whiskey Ring* (Chicago: Belford, Clarke, 1880.)
10. Ava Lawrence, "David Blakely: A Life in Music, Politics, Publishing, and Printing," *Journal of the Music and Entertainment Industry Educators Association* 8, no. 1 (2008), www.meiea.org/Journals; Timothy Rives, "Grant, Babcock, and the Whiskey Ring," *Prologue* 32, no. 3 (2000), http://www.archives.gov/publications/ prologue /2000/fall /whiskey-ring-1.html.
11. "Miss Ada Sweet's Resignation," *New York Times*, September 10, 1885, 1.
12. "Marshal Campbell," *Courier-Journal* (Louisville, Kentucky), May 11, 1876, 1.
13. "Miss Sweet's Threatener," *Inter Ocean* (Chicago), July 4, 1881, 12.
14. Sweet Family, Record 29 of the Popu-

lation Schedule for York Township, DuPage (county), Illinois, *US Census, 1880*, prepared by the Bureau of the Census (Washington, D.C., 1880–81), 17.
15. "Pension Agent," *Chicago Daily Tribune*, July 18, 1881, 4; E.R.P. Shurly, "The Conspiracy at Camp Douglas," *Chicago Daily Tribune*, February 4, 1882, 16.
16. "At Present," *Indiana Weekly Progress* (Indiana, Pennsylvania), April 23, 1885, 2.
17. Winifred Black, "Rambles," Part II, 37.
18. "At Present."
19. "Miss Ada Sweet's Resignation."
20. "Topics of the Day," *Critic* (Washington, District of Columbia), September 14, 1885, 3.
21. "Making Things Hot," *Inter Ocean* (Chicago), February 28, 1886, 16.
22. "Child of His Brain," *Chicago Daily Tribune*, November 7, 1892, 1.
23. Winifred Black, "Rambles," Part II, 36.
24. Winifred Black, "Without Long Skirts," *San Francisco Examiner*, May 29, 1892, 16.

## Chapter 3

1. Winifred Black, "Rambles through My Memories," Part IV, *Good Housekeeping* (April 1936), 226.
2. Winifred Black, "Rambles," Part IV, 228.
3. Winifred Black, "Rambles through my Memories," Part I, *Good Housekeeping* (January 1936), 153.
4. Susan R. Gannon and Ruth Anne Thompson, *Mary Mapes Dodge* (Boston: Twayne, 1992).
5. Winifred Black, "Rambles," Part I, 151.
6. Tracy Davis, *Actresses as Working Women: Their Social Identity in Victorian Culture* (London: Routledge, 1991), 3.
7. Tracy Davis, *Actresses as Working Women: Their Social Identity in Victorian Culture* (London: Routledge, 1991), 3–32; Winifred Black, "Rambles through my Memories," Part II, *Good Housekeeping* (February 1936), 37.
8. Winifred Black (as Columbine), "Playing One Night Stands," *Topeka State Journal*, February 2, 1889, 6.
9. "Zozo at the St. Charles," *Times Picayune* (New Orleans), October 22, 1888, 3.
10. Winifred Black, "Rambles," Part I, 154.
11. Winifred Black, "Rambles," Part I, 154.
12. Winifred Black, "Rambles through my Memories," Part II, *Good Housekeeping* (February 1936), 37.
13. Winifred Black (as Columbine), "Confessions of an Actress," *Chicago Daily Tribune*, February 10, 1889, 27; Winifred Black (as Columbine), "Playing One Night Stands"; Winifred Black (as Columbine), "Stage Superstitions," *Marion Star* (Marion, Ohio), January 19, 1889, 3.
14. Alice Fahs, *Out on Assignment: Newspaper Women and the Making of Modern Public Space* (Chapel Hill: University of North Carolina University Press, 2011), 24–25.
15. Winifred Black "Rambles," Part I, 155.
16. Winifred Black (as Annie Laurie), "Sign the Fine Arts Petition," *San Francisco Examiner*, December 3, 1915, 18.
17. Winifred Black, "Rambles," Part I, 155.

## Chapter 4

1. "Occupations," in *Special Census Report on Occupations of the Population of the United States at the Eleventh Census: 1890* (Washington, D.C.: GPO, 1896), 11.
2. "Annie Laurie's Experience," *San Francisco Examiner*, July 13, 1890, 13.
3. Winifred Black, "Rambles through my Memories," Part II, *Good Housekeeping* (February 1936), 37.
4. Haryot Holt Cahoon, "Women in Gutter Journalism," *Arena* 17 (December 1896–June 1897): 568; Joe Saltzman, "Sob Sisters: The Image of the Female Journalist in Popular Culture," USC Annenberg, ijpc.org/page/sobsmaster.htm.
5. Cahoon, "Women in Gutter Journalism," 572–73.
6. Edwin L. Shuman, *Practical Journalism: A Complete Manual of the Best Newspaper Methods* (New York: Appleton, 1903), 148–49.
7. Charles Olin, *Journalism* (Philadelphia: Penn, 1906), 50–51.
8. Patricia Bradley, *Women and the Press: The Struggle for Equality* (Evanston, IL: Northwestern University Press, 2005), 127.
9. Jean Marie Lutes, *Front-Page Girls: Women Journalists in American Culture and Fiction, 1880–1930* (Ithaca: Cornell University Press, 2007), 7.
10. Mary Twombly, "Women in Journalism," *Writer* 3 (August 1889): 171.
11. Lindsy Van Gelder, "Women's Pages:

You Can't Make News Out of a Silk Purse," *MS* (November 1974): 112.

12. Ishbel Ross, *Ladies of the Press* (New York: Harper, 1936), 14.

13. W. Paul Rodman, *Mining Frontiers of the Far West, 1848–1880* (Albuquerque: University of New Mexico, 1980), 63.

14. David Nasaw, *The Chief: The Life of William Randolph Hearst* (Boston: Houghton Mifflin, 2000), 32.

15. Nasaw, *The Chief: The Life of William Randolph Hearst*, 77–78.

16. Madelon Golden Schilpp and Sharon M. Murphy, *Great Women of the Press* (Carbondale: Southern Illinois University Press, 1983), 149.

17. Winifred Black, "Rambles," Part II, 211.

18. Stanley Wertheim, "Chamberlain, Samuel S.," in *A Stephen Crane Encyclopedia* (Westport, CT: Greenwood, 1997), 51.

19. Winifred Black, "Rambles," Part II, 212.

20. Wertheim, "Chamberlain, Samuel S.," 51.

21. Ishbel Ross, *Ladies of the Press*, 61–62; John Jakes, "Winifred Black: Sob Sisters Can Cry," *Great Women Reporters* (New York: Putnam's, 1969), 69–70.

22. Winifred Black (writing anonymously), "Miss Bisland's Story," *San Francisco Examiner*, November 20, 1889, 1.

23. Faye B. Zuckerman, "Winifred Black," in *American Newspaper Journalists, 1901–1925*, vol. 25, *Dictionary of Literary Biography*, ed. Perry J. Ashley (Detroit: Gale Group, 1984), 12.

24. Albert Plympton Southwick, *Short Studies in Literature* (New York: Hinds, Noble, and Eldredge, 1898), 175.

25. Francis L. Lederer, II, "Nora Marks—Reinvestigated," Northern Illinois University Digital Library, dig.lib.niu.edu/ISHS/ishs-1980spring/ishs-1980spring61.pdf.

26. Eleanor Stackhouse Atkinson (as Nora Marks), "All Jolted Alike," *Chicago Daily Tribune*, December 13, 1889, 1–2.

27. Ada C. Sweet, "How Miss Sweet Found Annie," *Chicago Daily Tribune*, December 13, 1889, 2.

28. Winifred Black (as Annie Laurie), "Annie Laurie's Story," *San Francisco Examiner*, January 19, 1890, 11.

29. Ross, *Ladies of the Press*, 60–61.

30. Maurine H. Beasley and Sheila J. Gibbons, *Taking Their Place: A Documentary History of Women and Journalism* (State College, PA: Strata, 2003), 70.

31. Maureen O'Connor, "Bigger Eyes, Fuller Lips, Broader Minds?" *New York* (July 28–August 10, 2014): 24.

32. Lutes, *Front-Page Girls*, 2.

## Chapter 5

1. Brooke Kroeger, *Nellie Bly: Daredevil, Reporter, Feminist* (New York: Times Books, 1994), 319–32; Jean Marie Lutes, *Front-Page Girls: Women Journalists in American Culture and Fiction, 1880–1930* (Ithaca: Cornell University Press, 2007), 33–34; John Keats, "Meg Merrilies," *The Poems of John Keats* (New York: Dodd, Mead, 1905), 261–62.

2. John Jakes, "Winifred Black: Sob Sisters Can Cry," *Great Women Reporters* (New York: Putnam's, 1969), 71.

3. Winifred Black, "Rambles through my Memories," Part II, *Good Housekeeping*, February 1936, 213.

4. Ishbel Ross, *Ladies of the Press* (New York: Harper, 1936), 24.

5. Edward T. James, Janet Wilson James, and Paul S. Boyer, *Notable American Women, 1607–1950: A Biographical Dictionary*, vol. 1 (Cambridge: Harvard University Press, 1971), 155.

6. Jakes, "Winifred Black: Sob Sisters Can Cry," 73.

7. Winifred Black, "Rambles," Part II, 211.

8. Winifred Black (as Annie Laurie), "'Annie Laurie's' Appeal," *San Francisco Examiner*, November 25, 1894, 17; Grace Wetzel, "Winifred Black's Teacherly Ethos: The Role of Journalism in Late-Nineteenth-Century Rhetorical Education," *Rhetoric Society Quarterly* 44, no. 1 (2014): 68–93.

9. Susan Speaker, "'The Struggle of Mankind against Its Deadliest Foe': Themes of Counter-Subversion in Anti-Narcotic Campaigns, 1920–1940," *Journal of Social History* 34, no. 3 (2001): 591–610; David T. Courtwright, *Dark Paradise: A History of Opiate Addiction in America* (Boston: Harvard University Press, 2009), 177.

10. Winifred Black (as Annie Laurie), "Boys and Girls Page," *San Francisco Examiner*, October 13, 1895, 20.

11. Kenneth Whyte, *The Uncrowned King: The Sensational Rise of William Randolph Hearst* (Berkeley: Counterpoint, 2009), 463.

12. David Nasaw, *The Chief: The Life of William Randolph Hearst* (Boston: Houghton Mifflin, 2000), 99–100.

13. Ben Procter, *William Randolph Hearst: The Early Years, 1863-1910* (New York: Oxford University Press, 1998), 117.
14. Nasaw, *The Chief*, 99-100.
15. Winifred Black, "Rambles," Part II, 218.
16. Whyte, *The Uncrowned King: The Sensational Rise of William Randolph Hearst*, 79; John Tebbel, *The Life and Good Times of William Randolph Hearst* (New York: Dutton, 1952), 113.
17. Winifred Black, "Rambles," Part II, 218.
18. Winifred Black (as Annie Laurie), "Annie Laurie in New York," *San Francisco Examiner*, November 10, 1895, 25; Winifred Black (as Annie Laurie), "House Hunting in New York," *San Francisco Examiner*, November 17, 1895, 21.
19. Winifred Black, "Rambles," Part II, 218.
20. John K. Winkler, *W.R. Hearst, an American Phenomenon* (New York: Simon & Schuster, 1928), 108.
21. Winifred Black, "A Woman among the Fighters," *New York Journal*, February 19, 1896, 7.
22. Winifred Black, "Rambles," Part II, 219.
23. Bill Hosokawa, *Thunder in the Rockies: The Incredible Denver Post* (New York: Morrow, 1976), 121; "Charles A. Bonfils Services Saturday," *Denver Post*, August 26, 1955, 2.
24. Madelon Golden Schilpp and Sharon M. Murphy, *Great Women of the Press* (Carbondale: Southern Illinois University Press, 1983), 153-54.
25. Jakes, "Winifred Black: Sob Sisters Can Cry," 71.
26. Max Binheim, *U.S. Women of the West, 1928* (Los Angeles: Publishers, 1928), 39.
27. Hosokawa, *Thunder in the Rockies*, 31.
28. Robert L. Perkin, *The First Hundred Years: An Informal History of Denver and the Rocky Mountain News* (New York: Doubleday, 1959), 404.
29. Perkin, *The First Hundred Years*, 401-04.
30. Hosokawa, *Thunder in the Rockies*, 24.
31. Hosokawa, *Thunder in the Rockies*, 121; "Charles A. Bonfils Services Saturday," 2.
32. "The Woman," *Kansas City Post*, March 14, 1910, 7.
33. Lindsy Van Gelder, "Women's Pages: You Can't Make News Out of a Silk Purse," *MS* (November 1974), 112.
34. John K. Winkler, *W.R. Hearst, an American Phenomenon*, 80-81; Edith May Marken, "Women in American Journalism before 1900" (master's thesis, University of Missouri, 1932), 94.
35. David Gudelunas, *Confidential to America: Newspaper Advice Columns and Sexual Education* (New Brunswick: Transaction, 2008), 55-74.
36. Winifred Black (as Annie Laurie), "Arise, Me Lads, and Take Salute, You Who Gave Blood to Aid Boy," *San Francisco Examiner*, March 3, 1926, 8; Winifred Black (as Annie Laurie), "Old Song Stirs Tender Memories," *San Francisco Examiner*, March 8, 1926, 6; Winifred Black (as Annie Laurie), "Is 'Puppy Love' Just Like the Toothache?" *San Francisco Examiner*, January 13, 1926, 9.
37. Winifred Black, "Other Side of World Your Backyard Today," *Lincoln Evening Journal*, December 28, 1932, 6.
38. Winifred Black, "To Have the Enthusiasm," *Evening News* (Harrisburg, Pennsylvania), October 9, 1934, 21.
39. "Annie Laurie," *Time*, October 28, 1935, 48-50.
40. Winifred Black Bonfils (Annie Laurie). Funeral Record and Death Certificate, State of California, May 25, 1936.
41. Winifred Black, "Rambles through My Memories," Part V, *Good Housekeeping* (May 1936), 258.
42. "Jeffrey Black," *World War I Selective Service System Draft Registration Cards, 1917-1918*, National Archives and Records Administration, Washington, D.C., M1509, Form 1, No. 2032, Registration Card 24.
43. "Only Son of 'Annie Laurie' Dies in Surf," *San Francisco Examiner*, June 20, 1926, 3.
44. "C.A. Bonfils Services," *Kansas City Star*, August 26, 1955, 49; Winifred Black, "Rambles through My Memories," Part IV, *Good Housekeeping* (April 1936), 230.
45. Barker Family, Population Schedule for Los Angeles, California, Illinois, *Fifteenth Census of the United States: 1930*, prepared by the Bureau of the Census (Washington, D.C., 1930-31), 160; Winifred Bonfils Barker, Death Certificate, California Death Index, 1940-1997, prepared by the Department of Health Services, (Sacramento, 1998).

## Chapter 6

1. Marion Marzolf, *Up from the Footnote: A History of Women Journalists* (New York:

Hastings, 1977), 206; Kay Mills, *A Place in the News: From the Women's Pages to the Front Page* (New York: Dodd, Mead, 1988), 15–35.

2. "The Empress of the Dailies," *San Francisco Examiner*, December 23, 1894, 17.

3. "The Power of the Press," *San Francisco Examiner*, December 2, 1894, 17.

4. "She Can Get the News," *San Francisco Examiner*, February 3, 1895, 13.

5. "Women Need Newspapers," *Post-Standard* (Syracuse), May 30, 1910, 5.

6. Judith Butler, *Bodies That Matter: On the Discursive Limits of Sex* (New York: Routledge, 1993); Ishbel Ross, *Ladies of the Press* (New York: Harper, 1936), 67.

7. Winifred Black, "Winifred Black Writes About Miss 'Flutter Budget,'" *Springfield Missouri Republican*, August 1, 1917, 4.

8. "Annie Laurie's Experience," *San Francisco Examiner*, July 13, 1890, 13.

9. Rebecca Abrams, "The Bylining and the Sidelining," *Guardian*, May 11, 1994, 11; Linda Steiner, "Critiquing Journalism: A Twenty-First-Century Feminist Perspective," in *Women, Men, and News: Divided and Disconnected in the News Media Landscape*, ed. Paula Poindexter, Sharon Meraz, and Amy Schmitz Weiss (Hillsdale, NJ: Erlbaum, 2007), 280–87; Deborah Chambers, Linda Steiner, and Carole Fleming, *Women and Journalism* (New York: Routledge, 2004), 26.

10. Winifred Black, "Winifred Black Bonfils Speaks to Press Club," *Springfield Missouri Republican*, October 19, 1912, 10.

11. Winifred Black, "Rambles," Part II, 214.

12. Winifred Black (as Annie Laurie), "As Women Never Know Them," *San Francisco Examiner*, June 5, 1892, 13.

13. "Almost Hopeless Darkness," *San Francisco Examiner*, April 16, 1893, 13.

14. Paula Uruburu, *American Eve: Evelyn Nesbit, Stanford White, the Birth of the "It" Girl, and the Crime of the Century* (New York: Penguin), 2008.

15. Barbara Belford, *Brilliant Bylines: A Biographical Anthology of Notable Newspaperwomen in America* (New York: Columbia University Press, 1986), 106–07.

16. Irvin S. Cobb, *Exit Laughing* (Indianapolis: Bobbs-Merrill, 1941), 230–34.

17. Jean Marie Lutes, *Front-Page Girls: Women Journalists in American Culture and Fiction, 1880–1930* (Ithaca: Cornell University Press, 2007), 66.

18. "Gleason's Actions Are Damaging to Defense," *San Francisco Examiner*, January 31, 1907, 2.

19. Winifred Black (as Annie Laurie), "Thaw Relieved at Choice of Jury," *San Francisco Examiner*, February 2, 1907, 2.

20. "Thaw's Incoherent Lines Tell of Deep Affection for His Wife," *San Francisco Examiner*, February 9, 1907, 3.

21. "Gleason's Actions Are Damaging to Defense," 2.

22. Winifred Black, "Prisoner in Tears during Wife's Ordeal," *New York American*. February 8, 1907, 1.

23. "Winifred Black, 73, Journalist, Dead," *New York Times*, May 26, 1936, 26.

24. "Beloved Writer Devoted Career to Worthy Causes," *San Francisco Examiner*, May 26, 1936, 8.

25. Mary Margaret McBride, *A Long Way from Missouri* (New York: Putnam's, 1959), 73–74.

26. Agness Underwood, *Newspaperwoman* (New York: Harper, 1949), 151; Howard Good, *Girl Reporter: Gender, Journalism, and the Movies* (Lanham, MD: Scarecrow, 1998), 50.

27. "'Annie Laurie' on Murdermania," *San Francisco Examiner*, April 1, 1894, 20.

28. Winifred Black, "The Illogical Sex," *El Paso Herald*, February 17, 1912, 22.

29. "Winifred Black Writes About 'Only a Woman,'" *Fort Wayne Journal-Gazette*, November 12, 1918, 9.

30. Winifred Black, "No Double Standard of Justice," *San Francisco Examiner*, April 5, 1915, 18.

31. Winifred Black, "Working or Dreaming: Girl Is Fortunate Who Can Do Both," *El Paso Herald*, April 15, 1912, 11.

32. Winifred Black, "Winifred Black Writes About a Would-Be Journalist," *San Antonio Evening News*, April 29, 1919, 6.

33. Winifred Black, "Winifred Black Writes About Proving Yourself 'Advanced,'" *San Bernardino County Sun*, April 19, 1923, 15.

34. Winifred Black, "Winifred Black Writes About Heart-Patterns of Life," *Springfield Missouri Republican*, May 5, 1917, 4.

35. Winifred Black, "Do You Let the World Go in One Eye and Out the Other? Writing Impressions on Shifting Sands." *Lincoln Evening Journal*, May 27, 1927, 7.

36. Winifred Black (as Annie Laurie), "The Children's Page," *San Francisco Examiner*, June 16, 1895, 17.

37. Winifred Black, "The Soul Saver," *Springfield Missouri Republican*, October 22, 1915, 6.
38. Winifred Black, "Is New Tragedy Fruit of Ancient Wrong?" *San Francisco Examiner*, July 18, 1919, 3.
39. Winifred Black, "Winifred Black Writes About a New 'Heroine,'" *Springfield Missouri Republican*, June 14, 1922, 6.
40. Winifred Black, "Winifred Black Writes About a Woman with a Present," *Springfield Missouri Republican*, March 23, 1922, 8.
41. Winifred Black, "The 'Successful' Husband," *Springfield Missouri Republican*, June 24, 1915, 6.
42. Winifred Black, "Winifred Black Cheers Us by Saying Life Is Not a Tragedy," *Coshocton Tribune* (Coshocton, Ohio), December 19, 1923, 4.

## Chapter 7

1. Winifred Black (as Annie Laurie), "Preparing for Work," *San Francisco Examiner*, March 23, 1890, 14; Winifred Black (as Annie Laurie), "Among the Lepers," *San Francisco Examiner*, April 13, 1890, 13.
2. Winifred Black (as Annie Laurie), "My Visit to Miss Harraden," *San Francisco Examiner*, November 18, 1894, 17; John Sutherland, *Lives of the Novelists: A History of Fiction in 294 Lives* (New Haven: Yale University Press, 2012), 48–49.
3. Winifred Black (as Annie Laurie), "Corpse-laden Waters Lit by Funeral Pyres," *San Francisco Examiner*, September 15, 1900, 1.
4. Winifred Black, "Rambles through My Memories," Part V, *Good Housekeeping* (May 1936), 36.
5. Winifred Black (as Annie Laurie), "Three Million Dollars," *San Francisco Examiner*, November 13, 1892, 15.
6. Winifred Black, "Mother's Pets Unable to Deny Urge to Slay?" *San Antonio Evening News*, July 17, 1919, 7.
7. Winifred Black, "The Joy of Children," *El Paso Herald*, July 1, 1913, 11; Winifred Black (as Annie Laurie), "Advice to Girls," *Fort Wayne Journal-Gazette*, October 14, 1918, 6.
8. Winifred Black, "The Greatest Woman," *Fort Wayne Sentinel*, January 2, 1912, 4.
9. Winifred Black, "A Defense of Kissing," *Washington Post*, May 10, 1911, 6.
10. Winifred Black, "The Madness of Love," *Springfield Missouri Republican*, August 12, 1917, 14.
11. Winifred Black, "Gone—Where?" in *Roses and Rain* (San Francisco: Winifred Black, 1920), 55.
12. Winifred Black, "A Case of Mother-in-Law," *Springfield Leader* (Springfield, Missouri), July 29, 1910, 6.
13. Winifred Black, "How to Treat an In-Law," *El Paso Herald*, January 15, 1913, 5.
14. Winifred Black, "Telling a Friend the Truth," *El Paso Herald*, July 19, 1912, 13.
15. Winifred Black, "Why the Tango Is Moral," *Indianapolis Star*, February 11, 1914, 9.
16. Winifred Black (as Annie Laurie), "Forgive Others More Than Yourself," *San Francisco Examiner*, January 9, 1915, 18.
17. Winifred Black (as Annie Laurie), "Preparing for Work."
18. Winifred Black, "The Case of Mrs. John Smith of London: A Simple Story of the Suffrage Question in England," *Cosmopolitan*, August 1910, 390.

## Chapter 8

1. Kathryn Harrison, *The Kiss: A Memoir* (New York: Random House, 1998), 3.
2. Winifred Black, "Imperfection Is Crown of the All-Too-Perfect," *Springfield Missouri Republican*, August 1, 1915, 16.
3. Winifred Black, "Selling Youth for a Share in Riches," *Brownsville Herald*, May 29, 1930, 16.
4. Winifred Black (as Annie Laurie), "The Fourteen Black Sheep," *San Francisco Examiner*, April 8, 1894, 19.
5. Winifred Black, "Child and Charity Trust," *Good Housekeeping*, June 1912, 741.
6. Winifred Black (as Annie Laurie), "'Street of Living Dead' Harbors Dope Sellers in Heart of San Francisco," *San Francisco Examiner*, October 11, 1921, 1.
7. Winifred Black, "How He Cheated the Waves," *San Francisco Examiner*, August 12, 1894, 13.
8. Winifred Black, "The Case of Mrs. John Smith of London: A Simple Story of the Suffrage Question in England," 381.
9. Jean Marie Lutes, *Front-Page Girls: Women Journalists in American Culture and Fiction, 1880–1930* (Ithaca: Cornell University Press, 2007), 16–22.
10. Winifred Black, "Small Families or

Large?" *Springfield Missouri Republican*, August 6, 1916, 14.

11. Harvey W. Wiley, "The Housewife and the Eight-Hour Day," *Good Housekeeping*, January 1917, 50–51.

12. Winifred Black, "Selfishness: Chief Cause of Divorce," *Indianapolis Star*, February 24, 1917, 7.

13. Winifred Black, "Grow Up, Girls! The Professor Is Getting Impatient," *Journal News* (Hamilton, Ohio), June 29, 1928, 34.

14. Winifred Black, "Winifred Black Writes About a College Complaint," *Iowa City Press-Citizen*, July 21, 1923, 2.

15. Winifred Black, "A School of Courtship," *El Paso Herald*, April 18, 1912, 11.

16. Ian Robert Dowbiggin, *Keeping America Sane: Psychiatry and Eugenics in the United States and Canada, 1880–1940* (Ithaca: Cornell University Press, 1997), 126.

17. Winifred Black, "Some 'Unfit' Better for Humanity Than the 'Fit' Declares Writer," *Washington Post*, July 19, 1913, 4.

18. Winifred Black, "Winifred Black Writes About Man's 'Interest' in Women," *Springfield Missouri Republican*, January 30, 1917, 4.

19. Winifred Black, "Why Men Who Play Don't Have Hysterics," *San Bernardino County Sun*, July 25, 1925, 6.

20. Joan Didion, "On Going Home," in *Slouching Towards Bethlehem* (New York: Macmillan, 1968), 166.

21. Winifred Black, "Gold of the Burning Desert," *Cosmopolitan*, September 1905, 521.

22. Winifred Black (as Annie Laurie), "He That Ruleth a City," *San Francisco Examiner*, March 15, 1891, 13.

23. Winifred Black (as Annie Laurie), "What Prompts Man to Become a Slayer?" *San Francisco Examiner*, July 17, 1919, 6.

24. Winifred Black, *Dope: The Story of the Living Dead* (New York: Star, 1928), 10–11.

25. Winifred Black, "Winifred Black Writes About Pictures and Realities," *Springfield Missouri Republican*, February 3, 1917, 4.

26. Winifred Black, "Silly Teenage Girl Will Change," *Springfield Missouri Republican*, January 2, 1916, 12.

27. Winifred Black, "The 'Graceful Gazelle' on Dieting," *Springfield Missouri Republican*, October 7, 1915, 6.

28. Winifred Black (as Annie Laurie), "'Street of Living Dead.'"

29. Barbara Belford, *Brilliant Bylines: A Biographical Anthology of Notable Newspaperwomen in America* (New York: Columbia University Press, 1986), 100.

30. Winifred Black, "Horrors of the Storm," *Lawrence Daily Journal*, October 5, 1900, 2.

31. Winifred Black (as Annie Laurie), "Annie Laurie Tells of the Spectral City," *San Francisco Examiner*, April 22, 1906, 10.

32. Winifred Black (as Annie Laurie), "The Bear with a Scarlet Cross," *San Francisco Examiner*, December 9 1894, 17.

33. Winifred Black, "Pankhurst Is Free and Happy Now in the US," *Chronicle-Telegram* (Elyria, Ohio), October 21, 1913, 1.

34. Ishbel Ross, *Ladies of the Press* (New York: Harper, 1936), 62.

35. "Annie Laurie's Story," *San Francisco Examiner*, January 19, 1890, 11.

36. Winifred Black (as Annie Laurie), "The Women of the A.R.U.," *San Francisco Examiner*, July 22, 1894, 15; Charles Kingsley, "The Three Fishers," in *Masterpieces from Charles Kingsley* (London: Woodward, 1893), 108.

37. Winifred Black (as Annie Laurie), "San Francisco's Shame," *San Francisco Examiner*, August 17, 1890, 11.

38. Thomas Gray, *An Elegy Written in a Country Churchyard* (Philadelphia: Lippincott, 1883), 19.

39. Winifred Black, "That Naughty Cover," *Iola Register* (Iola, Kansas), June 23, 1910, 4.

40. Winifred Black (as Annie Laurie), "Paying the Price," *San Francisco Examiner*, March 3, 1910, 22.

41. Winifred Black (as Annie Laurie), "Homes Not Wrecked by Women Voting," *San Francisco Examiner*, April 26, 1915, 18.

42. Winifred Black, "Love and Marriage," *Oshkosh Daily Northwestern*, June 22, 1901, 9.

43. Winifred Black (as Annie Laurie), "Is Divorce an Evil: What the Women Say," *San Francisco Examiner*, June 26, 1892, 17.

44. Winifred Black (as Annie Laurie), "Do They Want to Vote?" *San Francisco Examiner*, November 2, 1890, 14.

45. Winifred Black, "Winifred Black Writes About Man's 'Interest' in Women."

46. Winifred Black, "Matrimony and Business," *Indianapolis Star*, November 5, 1916, 58.

47. Winifred Black, "Can Cave-Woman Be Coming into Style?" *Kokomo Tribune* (Kokomo, Indiana), June 17, 1930, 8.

48. Winifred Black (as Annie Laurie), "Advice to Girls," *Indianapolis Star*, March 30, 1914, 7.

49. Winifred Black, "When Clothes Com-

plicate a Camp Party," *Springfield Missouri Republican*, August 2, 1925, 13.

50. Winifred Black (as Annie Laurie), "Advice to Girls," *Springfield Missouri Republican*, October 10, 1915, 14.

51. Winifred Black, "Winifred Black Writes About 'Luck' and 'Hardship,'" *Iowa City Press-Citizen*, January 26, 1923, 11.

52. Winifred Black, "Winifred Black Writes About Fixing the Responsibility," *Bridgeport Telegram* (Bridgeport, Connecticut), January 15, 1921, 23.

## Chapter 9

1. Winifred Black, "Winifred Black Writes About Barefoot Time," *Springfield Missouri Republican*, March 18, 1921, 6.

2. Winifred Black, "Golf for Women," *Washington Post*, February 26, 1910, 6.

3. Winifred Black, "Telling a Friend the Truth," *El Paso Herald*, July 19, 1912, 13.

4. Winifred Black, "Winifred Black Writes About Have Women Changed?" *Springfield Missouri Republican*, December 9, 1921, 6.

5. Winifred Black, "Girls' Shocking Dress," *El Paso Herald*, May 28, 1913, 17.

6. Winifred Black, "Safeguarding Our Girls," *Indianapolis Star*, May 14, 1916, 56; Peter Engelman, *A History of the Birth Control Movement in America* (Santa Barbara: ABC-CLIO, 2011), 75–140.

7. Winifred Black, "San Mateo Women Dim Aladdin's Lamp," *San Francisco Examiner*, July 14, 1919, 5.

8. Winifred Black, "The Life Worth Living," *El Paso Herald*, February 2, 1912, 13.

9. Winifred Black, "The New Fashioned Girl," *Springfield Missouri Republican*, December 19, 1915, 2.

10. Winifred Black, "Winifred Black Writes About 'The New Girl,'" *Springfield Missouri Republican*, December 9, 1916, 2.

11. Winifred Black, "Winifred Black Writes About a Pretty Naughty Girl," *Winnipeg Tribune*, January 23, 1920, 4.

12. Winifred Black, "Winifred Black Says that Women Are Not Angels," *Evening News* (Harrisburg, Pennsylvania), July 2, 1919, 18.

13. Winifred Black, "Winifred Black Writes About Dances and Dancers," *Springfield Missouri Republican*, May 19, 1921, 6.

14. Winifred Black, "Winifred Black Writes About Babies, Hearts and Hopes," *Iowa City Press-Citizen*, May 18, 1923, 3.

15. Winifred Black, "Winifred Black Writes About Modern Parents' Worries," *Coshocton Tribune* (Coshocton, Ohio), September 26, 1923, 4.

16. Kate Mulvey and Melissa Richards, *Decades of Beauty* (New York: Checkmark Books, 1998), 16.

17. Winifred Black, "Winifred Black Writes About a Better Understanding," *Manitowoc Herald-Times* (Manitowoc, Wisconsin), September 18, 1922, 11.

18. Winifred Black, "A Lesson in Fortitude by a Modern Mother," *Kokomo Tribune* (Kokomo, Indiana), March 12, 1931, 10.

## Chapter 10

1. Judith Butler, *Gender Trouble: Feminism and the Subversion of Identity* (New York: Routledge, 1990).

2. Winifred Black, "Jealousy Not Feminine Foible," *Post-Standard* (Syracuse), March 16, 1910, 8.

3. Winifred Black, "As Women Never Know Them," *San Francisco Examiner*, June 5, 1892, 13.

4. June Culp Zeitner and Lincoln Borglum, *Borglum's Unfinished Dream: Mount Rushmore* (Aberdeen, SD: North Plains, 1976), 99–100.

5. Winifred Black, "Who Carries the World, Old Atlas or His Wife?" *Indianapolis Star*, April 19, 1915, 7.

6. Winifred Black (as Annie Laurie), "Advice to Girls," *The Indianapolis Star*, January 26, 1914, 7.

7. Winifred Black, "Too Good for a Girl's Work," *Indianapolis Star*, February 18, 1914, 13.

8. Winifred Black, "Winifred Black Writes About a Woman in Business," *Springfield Missouri Republican*, November 2, 1919, 16.

9. Winifred Black, "Do Women Love Children More Than Men Do?" *Springfield Missouri Republican*, June 19, 1915, 4.

10. Winifred Black, "Winifred Black Writes About 'Just Like a Woman,'" *Springfield Missouri Republican*, May 28, 1922, 16.

11. Winifred Black, "A Lesson in Fortitude by a Modern Mother," *Kokomo Tribune* (Kokomo, Indiana), March 12, 1931, 10.

12. Winifred Black, "Do Women Love Children More Than Men Do?" *Springfield Missouri Republican*, June 19, 1915, 4.

13. Winifred Black, "Is There a Double

Standard?" *Springfield Missouri Republican*, November 30, 1915, 6.

14. Andrew Scull, *Hysteria: The Disturbing History* (New York: Oxford University Press, 2011), 84–104; Mary Roach, *Bonk: The Curious Coupling of Science and Sex* (New York: Norton, 2009), 214.

15. Winifred Black, "Golf for Women," *Washington Post*, February 26, 1910, 6.

16. Winifred Black, "Winifred Black Writes About a Husband's Strange Trick," *San Bernardino County Sun*, July 18, 1922, 4.

17. Winifred Black, "Winifred Black Writes About Nagging Men," *San Antonio Evening News*, September 9, 1919, 6.

18. Winifred Black, "Hanging on to Youth," *Springfield Missouri Republican*, May 2, 1916, 6.

19. Winifred Black (as Annie Laurie), "Advice to Girls," *Indianapolis Star*, March 3, 1914, 9.

20. Winifred Black, "Winifred Black Writes About Dollars and Marriage," *Springfield Missouri Republican*, July 5, 1919, 4.

21. Winifred Black, "Why Should Men Talk 'Up' or 'Down' to Women?" *Springfield Missouri Republican*, October 5, 1915, 6.

22. Winifred Black, "Woman Wants Brains, Not Beauty, Praised," *San Francisco Examiner*, October 26, 1915, 20.

23. Winifred Black, "Tumult and Shouting and Cheers and Tears in Great Convention Demonstration," *Times Herald* (Olean, New York), July 1, 1920, 8.

24. Winifred Black, "Winifred Black Writes About Masculine Vanity," *Springfield Missouri Republican*, January 27, 1917, 4.

25. Winifred Black, "Winifred Black Writes About Man's 'Interest' in Women," *Springfield Missouri Republican*, January 30, 1917, 4.

## Chapter 11

1. Winifred Black, "Winifred Black Writes About Prejudice the Wrecker," *Washington Post*, October 17, 1921, 11.

2. Winifred Black, "Spring-Cleaning for Our Minds—Why Not?" *Amarillo Globe-Times*, April 3, 1929, 20.

3. Winifred Black, "Winifred Black Writes About 'Just Like a Woman,'" *Springfield Missouri Republican*, May 28, 1922, 16.

4. Lillian Faderman, *Odd Girls and Twilight Lovers: A History of Lesbian Life in Twentieth-Century America* (New York: Columbia University Press, 1991), 63.

5. Winifred Black, "Winifred Black Writes About 'Just Like a Woman.'"

6. Dorothy Dix, "Mirandy on New Year Resolutions," *San Francisco Examiner*, January 7, 1906, 44.

7. Winifred Black, "The Real Kentuckian," *Lebanon Daily News* (Lebanon, Pennsylvania), February 19, 1900, 1; Philip Dray, *At the Hands of Persons Unknown: The Lynching of Black America* (New York: Random House, 2007), 487.

8. Winifred Black, "Homicide—Legal and Otherwise," *Scranton Republican*, December 13, 1900, 4; Jennifer Eastman Attebery, *Up in the Rocky Mountains: Writing the Swedish Immigrant Experience* (Minneapolis: University of Minnesota Press, 2007), 127.

9. Winifred Black (as Annie Laurie), "The Rich and the Poor—Really, Who Are They?" *San Francisco Examiner*, April 3, 1915, 18.

10. Winifred Black, "A Woman and a Savage," *San Francisco Examiner*, June 19, 1892, 13.

11. Winifred Black, "Gold of the Burning Desert," *Cosmopolitan*, September 1905, 520–21.

12. Julia Garbus, "Service-Learning, 1902," *College English* 64 (2002): 547–65; Katherine H. Adams and Michael L. Keene, *Alice Paul and the American Suffrage Campaign* (Urbana: University of Illinois Press, 2007), 6.

13. Winifred Black (as Annie Laurie), "The Rich and the Poor—Really, Who Are They?"

14. Winifred Black, "Winifred Black Tells Us About Girls Who Defy Conventions," *Coshocton Tribune* (Coshocton, Ohio), November 14, 1923, 7.

15. Winifred Black, "The Painted Woman," *El Paso Herald*, July 11, 1912, 3.

16. Winifred Black, "Maudlin Sympathy," *El Paso Herald*, January 9, 1911, 4.

17. Katie N. Johnson, *Sisters in Sin: Brothel Drama in America, 1900–1920* (New York: Cambridge University Press, 2006), 117–18.

18. Winifred Black (as Annie Laurie), "The Rich and the Poor—Really, Who Are They?"

19. Winifred Black, "'Horrible' Examples Harmful," *Indianapolis Star*, February 9, 1914, 7; Kendall R. Phillips, *Controversial Cinema: The Films that Outraged America* (Santa Barbara: ABC-CLIO, 2008), 23–24.

20. Winifred Black, "Ignorance or Innocence—Which Prevails Socially?" *Indianapolis Star*, May 2, 1914, 9.

21. Winifred Black, "Selfishness Prompts Despair," *El Paso Herald*, October 16, 1913, 4.

## Chapter 12

1. Winifred Black, "Winifred Black Writes About Roses and Daughters," *Lincoln Evening Journal*, March 24, 1923, 5.
2. Winifred Black, "Winifred Black Writes About a Daughter's Problem," *Logansport Pharos-Tribune* (Logansport, Indiana), January 5, 1923, 8.
3. Winifred Black, "A Discouraged Girl," *Lincoln Evening Journal*, December 26, 1922, 5.
4. "Winifred Black, "Winifred Black Writes About Two Wall-Flower Girls," *Fort Wayne Journal-Gazette*, February 1, 1919, 9.
5. Winifred Black, "A Discouraged Girl."
6. Winifred Black, "Are We Really Independent?" *Indianapolis Star*, February 15, 1914, 34.
7. Winifred Black, "Winifred Black Writes About Why Girls Leave Home," *Evening News* (Harrisburg, Pennsylvania), May 15, 1917, 10; David Mayer, "*Why Girls Leave Home*: Victorian and Edwardian 'Bad-Girl' Melodrama Parodied in Early Film," *Theatre Journal* 58, no. 4 (2006): 575–93.
8. Winifred Black, "What Threatens the Girl Art Student?" *Indianapolis Star*, March 11, 1914, 7.
9. Winifred Black, "Winifred Black Writes About Daughters Who Won't Marry," *Fort Wayne Journal-Gazette*, May 18, 1919, 20.

## Chapter 13

1. Winifred Black, "Rambles through My Memories," Part V, *Good Housekeeping*, May 1936, 258.
2. *Historical Statistics of the United States, Colonial Times to 1970*, vol. 1 (Washington, D.C.: U.S. Department of the Commerce, 1975), 132.
3. *Historical Statistics of the United States, Colonial Times to 1957* (Washington, D.C.: U.S. Department of the Commerce, 1960), 74.
4. Winifred Black, "Who Are the World's Greatest Women?" *Indianapolis Star*, May 15, 1914, 15.
5. Winifred Black, "If She Minds Her Business," *San Francisco Examiner*, September 16, 1894, 19.

6. Winifred Black, "Some Advice to Women," *San Francisco Examiner*, July 20, 1908, 14.
7. Winifred Black, "Winifred Black Writes About the Wages of Women," *Springfield Missouri Republican*, September 13, 1917, 4.
8. Winifred Black, "Yes, Women Take Men's Jobs Despite All Social Theories," *Amarillo Globe-Times*, January 3, 1928, 8.
9. Winifred Black, "The Army of Women in Business," *Evening News* (Harrisburg, Pennsylvania), November 1, 1934, 25.
10. *Historical Statistics of the United States, Colonial Times to 1970*, vol. 1, 132.
11. Alice Kessler-Harris. *Out to Work: A History of America's Wage-earning Women in the United States* (New York: Oxford University Press, 1982), 148.
12. "Women to Be Given Preference in Clerical Position Appointments in Navy Hereafter" in *Official U.S. Bulletin*, vol. 1 (Washington, D.C.: United States Committee on Public Information, 1917), 7.
13. Paula E. Calvin and Deborah A. Deacon, *American Women Artists in Wartime, 1776–2010* (Jefferson, NC: McFarland, 2011), 75–76.
14. Winifred Black, "Winifred Black Writes About the Wages of Women."
15. Patricia Anne Carter, *"Everybody's Paid but the Teacher": The Teaching Profession and the Women's Movement* (New York: Teachers College Press, 2002), PN4874.H31 C2.97–106.
16. Winifred Black, "Married Woman Should be Allowed to Keep Her Place if She Can Teach," *El Paso Herald*, November 20, 1929, 5.
17. Winifred Black, "Unkissed Stenographers," *Washington Post*, March 15, 1907, 12.
18. Winifred Black, "The Hungry Stenographer," *El Paso Herald*, February 6, 1912, 8.
19. Winifred Black, "Foolish Pride," *Post-Standard* (Syracuse), May 3, 1910, 12.
20. Winifred Black, "Some Advice to Women."
21. Winifred Black, "Matrimony and Business," *Indianapolis Star*, November 5, 1916, 58.
22. Winifred Black, "Winifred Black Writes About 'Smile and Look Pretty,'" *San Bernardino County Sun*, April 28, 1922, 6.
23. Winifred Black, "The Army of Women in Business."
24. Valerie A. Ramey, "Time Spent in Home Production in the Twentieth-Century

United States: New Estimates from Old Data," *Journal of Economic History* 69, no. 1 (March 2009): 13.

25. Winifred Black, "The Business Girl," *Springfield Missouri Republican*, December 27, 1916, 4.

26. Winifred Black, "Loaf Like a Man," *Journal News* (Hamilton, Ohio), February 22, 1930, 41.

27. Winifred Black, "Why the Business Woman Should Act Like the Business Man," *Springfield Missouri Republican*, August 16, 1916, 4.

28. Winifred Black, "Gold of the Burning Desert," *Cosmopolitan*, September 1905, 522.

29. Winifred Black (as Annie Laurie), "One of the Chorus," *San Francisco Examiner*, December 22, 1889, 11.

30. Winifred Black, "Revising the Marriage Service," *Indianapolis Star*, November 27, 1916, 7.

31. *Historical Statistics of the United States, Colonial Times to 1957*, 72; *Statistical Abstract of the United States: The National Data Book 2003* (Washington, U.S. Census Bureau, 2003), 52.

32. Winifred Black, "A Man Who Wants a Wife but Needs a Housekeeper," *San Francisco Examiner*, April 15, 1906, Editorial Section, 3.

33. Winifred Black, "The Poor, Tired Shopgirl, " *El Paso Herald*, December 21, 1911, 8.

34. Winifred Black, "Revising the Marriage Service."

35. Winifred Black, "Wife Desertion a Felony," *El Paso Herald*, February 10, 1912, 6.

36. Winifred Black, "Grandma Goes to Work: Winifred Black's Topic Today," *Amarillo Globe-Times*, March 4, 1930, 13.

## Chapter 14

1. Charlotte Perkins Gilman, "Why These Clothes?" *Independent* 58 (March 2, 1905): 467–68.

2. Rob Schorman, *Selling Style: Clothing and Social Change at the Turn of the Century* (Philadelphia: University of Pennsylvania Press, 2003), 51, 122.

3. Christine Bayles Kortsch, *Dress Culture in Late Victorian Women's Fiction: Literacy, Textiles, and Activism* (Burlington, VT: Ashgate, 2013), 69–71.

4. Irene Castle, *Castles in the Air* (Garden City, NY: Doubleday, 1958), 115.

5. Schorman, *Selling Style: Clothing and Social Change at the Turn of the Century*, 144.

6. Corban Goble, "Newspaper Technology," in *History of the Mass Media in the United States: An Encyclopedia*, ed. Margaret A. Blanchard (New York: Routledge, 2013), 457–63.

7. Stephen Gundle, "The Hollywood Star System" in *Glamour: A History* (New York: Oxford University Press, 2008), 172–98.

8. Victoria Sherrow, *Encyclopedia of Hair: A Cultural History* (Westport, CT: Greenwood, 2006), 3–66.

9. Kate Mulvey and Melissa Richards, *Decades of Beauty* (New York: Checkmark, 1998), 20–39, 69–73.

10. Winifred Black, "Valueless and Poisonous," *San Francisco Examiner*, January 25, 1891, 14.

11. Nancy Tomes, *The Gospel of Germs: Men, Women, and the Microbe in American Life* (Boston: Harvard University Press, 1999), 157.

12. Winifred Black, "An Erratic View of Trailing Skirt," *Atlanta Constitution*, July 15, 1900, 15.

13. Winifred Black, "The Matter of Dress," *Post-Standard* (Syracuse), April 21, 1910, 12.

14. Winifred Black, "Pride Goeth before the Fall: Love of Dress, not Poverty, Fatal Lure of Girls," *The Iola Register* (Iola, Kansas), March 25, 1910, 4.

15. Winifred Black, "Beauty Craze," *Delaware County Daily Times* (Chester, Indiana), November 8, 1911, 8.

16. Winifred Black, "Winifred Black Writes About Pictures and Realities," *Springfield Missouri Republican*, February 3, 1917, 4.

17. Winifred Black, "Vanity of Woman," *Washington Post*, June 5, 1910, 7.

18. Winifred Black, "Winifred Black Writes About Twenty-Five 'Perfect' Men," *Fort Wayne Journal-Gazette*, December 26, 1919, 19.

19. Winifred Black, "Winifred Black Writes About Homeliness and Marriage," *Bridgeport Telegram* (Bridgeport, Connecticut), September 17, 1920, 25.

20. Winifred Black, "Winifred Black Writes About the Abused Buyer," *Springfield Missouri Republican*, June 14, 1917, 4.

21. Winifred Black, "When Clothes Complicate a Camp Party," *Springfield Missouri Republican*, August 2, 1925, 13.

22. Winifred Black, "Yes, 'Tis Sad, They All Look the Same," *San Francisco Examiner*, March 13, 1924, 10.

23. Winifred Black, "Winifred Black Says that Bobbed Hair Will Stay," *Coshocton Tribune* (Coshocton, Ohio), November 10, 1923, 4.

24. Winifred Black, "Winifred Black Doubts that Corsets Will Return," *Coshocton Tribune* (Coshocton, Ohio), April 15, 1925, 7.

25. Elizabeth Crisp Crawford, *Tobacco Goes to College: Cigarette Advertising in Student Media, 1920–1980* (Jefferson, NC: McFarland, 2014), 11–13.

26. Winifred Black, "Winifred Black Writes About Changing Fashions," *Springfield Missouri Republican*, October 5, 1919, 14.

27. Winifred Black, "Stylish Stouts Still the Vogue in England," *Amarillo Globe-Times*, September 4, 1930, 10.

28. Winifred Black (as Annie Laurie), "Stylish Stout," *San Francisco Examiner*, May 7, 1936, 11.

29. Winifred Black, "The Golden Slippers, Winifred Black's Story Today," *Brownsville Herald*, March 20, 1920, 4.

30. Winifred Black, "Woman's Vain Fight," *Springfield Leader* (Springfield, Missouri), October 18, 1910, 8.

31. Winifred Black, "Stage Struck at Forty," *El Paso Herald*, August 15, 1912, 9.

32. Winifred Black, "Do You See Life as It Is, or Through Your Emotions?" *Springfield Missouri Republican*, June 18, 1915, 6.

33. Winifred Black, "Shall It Be Always the Summer Season?" *Springfield Missouri Republican*, July 20, 1915, 6.

34. Winifred Black, "The Chill That Pretense Causes," *Springfield Missouri Republican*, February 8, 1916, 4.

35. Winifred Black, "Winifred Black Writes About Once-Upon-a-Time Beauties," *Springfield Missouri Republican*, April 26, 1917, 4.

36. "History of Plastic Surgery," The Sloane Clinic, www.sloaneclinic.com/en-sg/theplastic/; Kathy Davis, *Dubious Equalities and Embodied Differences: Cultural Studies on Cosmetic Surgery* (Lanham, MD: Rowman and Littlefield, 2003), 19–35.

37. Winifred Black, "Winifred Black Writes About Holding onto Youth," *Springfield Missouri Republican*, May 27, 1922, 6.

38. Winifred Black, "Duse Engagement Recalls 'Age of Giants,'" *San Francisco Examiner*, February 13, 1924, 6.

39. Winifred Black, "To Grow Old Gracefully—Ah, There's an Art," *Journal News* (Hamilton, Ohio), September 19, 1931, 29.

40. Leola Allard, "Oh! These Women!" *Tyrone Daily Herald* (Tyrone, Pennsylvania), May 18, 1931, 4.

## Chapter 15

1. "Love at Forty," *Springfield Missouri Republican*, September 6, 1917, 4.

2. *Historical Statistics of the United States, Colonial Times to 1957* (Washington, D.C.: U.S. Department of the Commerce, 1960), 15.

3. Winifred Black, "Revising the Marriage Service," *Indianapolis Star*, November 27, 1916, 7.

4. Winifred Black, "Winifred Black Writes About Have Women Changed?" *Springfield Missouri Republican*, December 9, 1921, 6.

5. Winifred Black (as Annie Laurie), "Advice to Girls," *Logansport Pharos-Tribune* (Logansport, Indiana), June 2, 1924, 6.

6. Winifred Black (as Annie Laurie), "Advice to Girls," *Springfield Missouri Republican* (Springfield, Missouri), July 6, 1919, 10.

7. Winifred Black (as Annie Laurie), "Are the Picture Brides Such a Gamble?" *San Francisco Examiner*, January 14, 1915, 18.

8. Winifred Black, "Marrying without Love," *El Paso Herald*, July 14, 1911, 6.

9. Winifred Black (as Annie Laurie), "Advice to Girls," *Springfield Missouri Republican*, March 23, 1917, 4.

10. Winifred Black (as Annie Laurie), "Advice to Girls," *The Evening News* (Harrisburg, Pennsylvania), February 24, 1919, 12.

11. Winifred Black (as Annie Laurie), "Evil 'Romances' Invariably End Alike," *San Francisco Examiner*, February 26, 1915, 20.

12. Winifred Black, "A Runaway Wife," *Springfield Leader*, October 1, 1910, 4.

13. Winifred Black (as Annie Laurie), "Advice to Girls," *Indianapolis Star*, April 9, 1914, 17.

14. Winifred Black (as Annie Laurie), "Advice to Girls," *Springfield Missouri Republican*, January 27, 1917, 4.

15. Winifred Black, "Jealousy," *Daily Republican* (Monongahela, Pennsylvania), July 7, 1910, 2.

16. Winifred Black, "Winifred Black Writes About for Better or Worse," *Springfield Missouri Republican*, April 15, 1921, 6.

17. Winifred Black, "Buried, though Alive," *Bridgeport Telegram* (Bridgeport, Connecticut), February 19, 1921, 4.

18. Winifred Black, "She Who Is Too Good

to Work," *Indianapolis Star*, February 14, 1914, 15.

19. Winifred Black, "Do Real Men Love These Dumbbells?" *Courier-Express* (Dubois, Pennsylvania), July 26, 1927, 4.

20. Winifred Black, "The Jailer-Husband Is Due for a Shock—Unless He Gives His Wife Some Leeway," *Kokomo Tribune* (Kokomo, Indiana), August 9, 1930, 8.

21. Winifred Black, "An American Abroad Boasts of Corruption," *Iowa City Press-Citizen*, December 6, 1926, 10.

22. Winifred Black, "Advice to a Neglected Wife," *Springfield Leader* (Springfield, Missouri), October 5, 1910, 6.

23. Winifred Black, "Foolish Bridey-Brides, How They Start Husbands on the Wrong Road," *El Paso Herald*, November 5, 1912, 4.

24. Winifred Black, "Winifred Black Writes About a Desperate Girl," *Springfield Missouri Republican*, December 11, 1919, 6.

25. Winifred Black, "Making Over a Skinflint," *El Paso Herald*, December 9, 1912, 4.

26. Winifred Black, "The Stenographer's Side," *Washington Post* (Washington, District of Columbia), January 20, 1912, 9.

27. Winifred Black (as Annie Laurie), "Advice to Girls," *Springfield Missouri Republican*, April 28, 1917, 4.

28. Winifred Black, "A Case of Mother-in-Law," *Springfield Leader* (Springfield, Missouri), July 29, 1910, 6.

29. Winifred Black, "A 10,000,000 Widow," *El Paso Herald*, December 5, 1911, 6.

30. Reva B. Siegel, "'The Rule of Love': Wife Beating as Prerogative and Privacy," Yale Faculty Scholarship Series, Paper 1092, 1996, http://digitalcommons.law.yale.edu/fss_papers/1092.

31. "Threw Wife Out of Window/She Puts in a Good Word for 'Mike' When Patrolmen Finds Her on the Sidewalk," *New York Tribune*, August 29, 1908, 1.

32. "Woman, Gagged, in Burning Room," *New York Tribune*, October 17, 1916, 4.

33. "Bloodstain Causes Fatal Shock," *New York Tribune*, May 23, 1908, 2.

34. "Two Slain Over Woman," *New York Tribune*, May 15, 1908, 4.

35. Winifred Black, "Divorce—A Knell to Faith," *Springfield Missouri Republican*, November 21, 1915, 15.

36. Winifred Black (as Annie Laurie), "Is Divorce an Evil: What the Women Say," *San Francisco Examiner*, June 26, 1892, 17.

37. Winifred Black, "When Wives Are Beaten," *Topeka Daily Capital*, January 8, 1906, 8.

38. Winifred Black, "Wife Desertion a Felony," *El Paso Herald*, February 10, 1912, 6.

39. Winifred Black, "Bad Husbands," *Nebraska State Journal* (Lincoln), August 23, 1909, 6.

40. Winifred Black, "Social Sets of Other Cities," *Washington Post*, May 25, 1910, 7.

41. Winifred Black, "Winifred Black Writes About Why Women Rebel," *Winnipeg Tribune*, September 15, 1920, 7.

42. Winifred Black, "Divorce and Second Marriage," *Bridgeport Telegram* (Bridgeport, Connecticut), September 8, 1920, 5.

43. Winifred Black, "Husband Nagging Has Gone Out of Fashion," *Springfield Missouri Republican*, July 18, 1915, 6.

44. Winifred Black, "A Human Door-Mat and Tragedy!" *Altoona Tribune*, November 19, 1921, 10.

45. Winifred Black, "Winifred Black Writes About an Interesting Widow," *San Bernardino County Sun*, December 1, 1922, 6.

46. Gerda Gallop-Goodman, *Crimes Against Women* (New York: Facts on File, 2002), 38–39.

47. Winifred Black, "Queer Laws for Women," *El Paso Herald*, August 20, 1913, 6.

48. Donald G. Nieman, *Black Southerners and the Law, 1865–1900* (New York: Taylor & Francis, 1994), 42–43.

49. Winifred Black, "Queer Laws for Women."

50. Winifred Black, "Peculiar Laws of North Carolina," *Las Cruces Sun-News*, October 30, 1914, 3.

51. Winifred Black (as Annie Laurie), "Women with Vote Face Big Problems," *San Francisco Examiner*, June 6, 1919, 4.

52. Winifred Black, "A Strange Letter," *Sheboygan Press Telegram*, November 16, 1922, 14.

53. Winifred Black, "The Case of Mrs. John Smith of London: A Simple Story of the Suffrage Question in England," *Cosmopolitan*, August 1910, 381–90.

54. *Historical Statistics of the United States, Colonial Times to 1957*, 15.

55. Winifred Black, "When Shall a Woman Leave her Husband," *Indianapolis Star*, May 25, 1914, 7.

56. Winifred Black, "What Should a Wife Do?" *El Paso Herald*, September 12, 1912, 4.

57. Winifred Black, "Love and Marriage,"

*Oshkosh Daily Northwestern*, June 22, 1901, 9.
58. Winifred Black, "One of Nature's Successes," *Indianapolis Star*, January 26, 1914, 7.
59. Winifred Black, "Winifred Black Writes About Bobbed Hair and Divorce," *Sheboygan Press Telegram*, June 2, 1922, 12.
60. Winifred Black, "Do We Expect Too Much from Marriage?" *Iowa City Press-Citizen*, September 22, 1925, 9.
61. Winifred Black, "Figures of Divorce Reveal Weaknesses," *Daily Free Press* (Carbondale, Illinois), October 25, 1927, 7.
62. Winifred Black, "Should Women Take Alimony?" *Indianapolis Star*, July 3, 1915, 9.
63. Winifred Black, "Telling a Friend the Truth," *El Paso Herald*, July 19, 1912, 13.
64. Winifred Black, "Divorce and Second Marriage."

## Chapter 16

1. Winifred Black, "The New Jersey Vote against Suffrage," *New York Times*, October 21, 1915, 10.
2. "Hunting Big Game: The Misses Herberts' Exciting Exploits in Africa," *New York Tribune*, August 6, 1908, 4.
3. "Suffragettes at Outing," *New York Tribune*, June 20, 1910, 5.
4. "Oratory Flows Freely," *New York Tribune*, September 9, 1910, 8.
5. "Women Will Parade," *New York Tribune*, February 3, 1908, 5.
6. Winifred Black (as Annie Laurie), "Annie Laurie in Politics," *San Francisco Examiner*, October 16, 1892, 13-14.
7. Winifred Black (as Annie Laurie), "Politics as They Seem," *San Francisco Examiner*, August 24, 1890, 13.
8. Winifred Black (as Annie Laurie), "Two Views of the Woman's Congress: As 'Annie Laurie' Saw It," *San Francisco Examiner*, May 26, 1895, 13.
9. Winifred Black, "American Husbands," *Springfield Leader* (Springfield, Missouri), July 23, 1910, 4.
10. Winifred Black, "Winifred Black Bonfils Speaks to Press Club," *Springfield Missouri Republican*, October 19, 1912, 10.
11. Winifred Black (as Annie Laurie), "Do They Want to Vote?" *San Francisco Examiner*, November 2, 1890, 14.
12. Winifred Black, "Why 'Women for Women' Is Bad Cry for Suffrage," *Indianapolis Star*, January 25, 1915, 7.
13. Winifred Black (as Annie Laurie), "Homes Not Wrecked by Women Voting," *San Francisco Examiner*, April 26, 1915, 18.
14. Winifred Black, "The Little Feminist," *Indianapolis Star*, February 7, 1914, 15.
15. Winifred Black, "Taking a Motor Ride with a Stranger," *Kane Republican* (Kane, Pennsylvania), March 16, 1927, 6.
16. Winifred Black, "Wife Desertion a Felony."
17. George Madden Martin, "American Women and Public Affairs," *Atlantic Monthly*, February 1924, 169-78.
18. "How Woman Suffrage Works," *New York Times*, March 8, 1924, 10.
19. Charles Edward Russell, "Is Woman Suffrage a Failure?" *The Century*, March 1924, 725-26.
20. "Woman Suffrage Declared a Failure," *Literary Digest*, April 12, 1924, 12.
21. Winifred Black, "Why 'Women for Women' Is Bad Cry for Suffrage," *Indianapolis Star*, January 25, 1915, 7.
22. Winifred Black (as Annie Laurie), "Women with Vote Face Big Problems," *San Francisco Examiner*, June 6, 1919, 4.
23. Winifred Black, "The Case of Mrs. John Smith of London: A Simple Story of the Suffrage Question in England," 389.
24. Winifred Black, "Women Have Won All They Demanded in Dem. Platform," *Times Herald* (Olean, New York), July 3, 1920, 9.
25. Winifred Black, "What's the Next Step for Women Suffragists—If Any," *Journal News* (Hamilton, Ohio), April 24, 1928, 8.
26. Winifred Black, "Votes for Women! In Hidebound China—Centuries of Prejudice Overthrown," *Amarillo Globe-Times*, February 16, 1931, 11.
27. Winifred Black, "Winifred Black Writes About Have Women Changed?" *Springfield Missouri Republican*, December 9, 1921, 6.

# *Bibliography*

Abrams, Rebecca. "The Bylining and the Sidelining." *Guardian*, May 11, 1994, 11.
Abramson, Phyllis Leslie. *Sob Sister Journalism*. Westport, CT: Greenwood, 1990.
Adams, Katherine H., and Michael L. Keene. *Alice Paul and the American Suffrage Campaign*. Urbana: University of Illinois Press, 2007.
Allard, Leola. "Oh! These Women!" *Tyrone Daily Herald* (Tyrone, Pennsylvania), May 18, 1931, 4.
Amott, Teresa L., and Julie A Matthaei. *Race, Gender, and Work: A Multicultural Economic History of Women in the United States*. Montreal: Black Rose, 1991.
"Annie Laurie." *Time*, October 28, 1935, 48–50.
"'Annie Laurie,' Beloved Writer, Taken by Death." *Times Picayune* (New Orleans), May 26, 1936, 1.
"Annie Laurie in Politics." *San Francisco Examiner*, October 16, 1892, 13–14.
"Annie Laurie Lies in State at City Hall." *San Francisco Examiner*, May 27, 1936, 5.
"Annie Laurie, Noted Writer, Dies in Calif." *Evening Star and Bradford Daily Record* (Bradford, Pennsylvania), May 26, 1936, 1.
"Annie Laurie Pall Bearers." *San Francisco Examiner*, May 28, 1936, 7.
"Annie Laurie Says We Are on Right Track." *The Springfield Missouri Republican*, January 26, 1922, 10.
"Another Chicago Alleged Conspirator Pardoned." *Cincinnati Enquirer*, August 11, 1865, 2.
Atkinson, Eleanor Stackhouse (as Nora Marks). "All Jolted Alike." *Chicago Daily Tribune*, December 13, 1889, 1–2.
"At Present." *Indiana Weekly Progress* (Indiana, Pennsylvania) , April 23, 1885, 2.
Attebery, Jennifer Eastman. *Up in the Rocky Mountains: Writing the Swedish Immigrant Experience*. Minneapolis: University of Minnesota Press, 2007.
Banner, Lois W. *American Beauty*. New York: Knopf, 1983.
Beasley, Maurine H., and Sheila J. Gibbons. *Taking Their Place: A Documentary History of Women and Journalism*. State College, PA: Strata, 2003.
Belford, Barbara. *Brilliant Bylines: A Biographical Anthology of Notable Newspaperwomen in America*. New York: Columbia University Press, 1986.
"Beloved Writer Devoted Career to Worthy Causes." *San Francisco Examiner*, May 26, 1936, 8.
Binheim, Max. *U.S. Women of the West, 1928*. Los Angeles: Publishers, 1928.

**Black, Winifred: Her bibliographic entries all appear here, arranged by whether her writing appeared without a by-line or as written by Columbine, by Annie Laurie, or by Winifred Black.**

## Written by Winifred Black without Byline

_____. "Miss Bisland's Story." *San Francisco Examiner*, November 20, 1889, 1.

## Written by Winifred Black as Columbine

_____. "Confessions of an Actress." *Chicago Daily Tribune*, February 10, 1889, 27.
_____. "Playing One Night Stands." *Topeka State Journal*, February 2, 1889, 6.
_____. "Stage Superstitions." *Marion Star* (Marion, Ohio), January 19, 1889, 3.

## Written by Winifred Black as Annie Laurie

_____. "Advice to Girls." *Indianapolis Star*, January 26, 1914, 7.
_____. "Advice to Girls." *Indianapolis Star*, March 3, 1914, 9.
_____. "Advice to Girls." *Indianapolis Star*, March 30, 1914, 7.
_____. "Advice to Girls." *Indianapolis Star*, April 9, 1914, 17.
_____. "Advice to Girls." *Springfield Missouri Republican*, January 27, 1917, 4.
_____. "Advice to Girls." *Springfield Missouri Republican*, March 23, 1917, 4.
_____. "Advice to Girls." *Springfield Missouri Republican*, April 28, 1917, 4.
_____. "Advice to Girls." *Springfield Missouri Republican*, August 1, 1917, 4.
_____. "Advice to Girls." *Fort Wayne Journal-Gazette*, October 14, 1918, 6.
_____. "Advice to Girls." *Fort Wayne Journal-Gazette*, December 19, 1918, 9.
_____. "Advice to Girls." *The Evening News* (Harrisburg, Pennsylvania), February 24, 1919, 12.
_____. "Advice to Girls." *Springfield Missouri Republican*, July 6, 1919, 10.
_____. "Advice to Girls." *Washington Post*, November 6, 1920, 9.
_____. "Advice to Girls." *Sheboygan Press Telegram*, October 6, 1923, 11.
_____. "Advice to Girls." *Logansport Pharos-Tribune* (Logansport, Indiana), June 2, 1924, 6.
_____. "Almost Hopeless Darkness." *San Francisco Examiner*, April 16, 1893, 13.
_____. "Among the Lepers." *San Francisco Examiner*, April 13, 1890, 13.
_____. "Annie Laurie in New York." *San Francisco Examiner*, November 10, 1895, 25.
_____. "'Annie Laurie' on Murdermania." *San Francisco Examiner*, April 1, 1894, 20.
_____. "Annie Laurie Tells of the Spectral City." *San Francisco Examiner*, April 22, 1906, 10.
_____. "'Annie Laurie's' Appeal." *San Francisco Examiner*, November 25, 1894, 17.
_____. "Annie Laurie's Experience." *San Francisco Examiner*, July 13, 1890, 13.
_____. "Annie Laurie's Story." *San Francisco Examiner*, January 19, 1890, 11.
_____. "Are the Picture Brides Such a Gamble?" *San Francisco Examiner*, January 14, 1915, 18.
_____. "Arise, Me Lads, and Take Salute, You Who Gave Blood to Aid Boy." *San Francisco Examiner*, March 3, 1926, 8.
_____. "As Women Never Know Them." *San Francisco Examiner*, June 5, 1892, 13.
_____. "The Bear with a Scarlet Cross." *San Francisco Examiner*, December 9, 1894, 17.
_____. "Boys and Girls Page." *San Francisco Examiner*, October 13, 1895, 20.
_____. "The Children's Page." *San Francisco Examiner*, June 16, 1895, 17.
_____. "Do They Want to Vote?" *San Francisco Examiner*, November 2, 1890, 14.
_____. "Duse Engagement Recalls 'Age of Giants.'" *San Francisco Examiner*, February 13, 1924, 6.

———. "The Empress of the Dailies." *San Francisco Examiner*, December 23, 1894, 17.
———. "Evil 'Romances' Invariably End Alike." *San Francisco Examiner*, February 26, 1915, 20.
———. "Forgive Others More Than Yourself." *San Francisco Examiner*, January 9, 1915, 18.
———. "The Fourteen Black Sheep." *San Francisco Examiner*, April 8, 1894, 19.
———. "Gleason's Actions Are Damaging to Defense." *San Francisco Examiner*, January 31, 1907, 2.
———. "Gone—Where?" In *Roses and Rain*, 52–55. San Francisco: Winifred Black, 1920.
———. "He That Ruleth a City." *San Francisco Examiner*, March 15, 1891, 13.
———. "Homes Not Wrecked by Women Voting." *San Francisco Examiner*, April 26, 1915, 18.
———. "House Hunting in New York." *San Francisco Examiner*, November 17, 1895, 21.
———. "How He Cheated the Waves." *San Francisco Examiner*, August 12, 1894, 13.
———. "If She Minds Her Business." *San Francisco Examiner*, September 16, 1894, 19.
———. "Is Divorce an Evil: What the Women Say." *San Francisco Examiner*, June 26, 1892, 17.
———. "Is New Tragedy Fruit of Ancient Wrong?" *San Francisco Examiner*, July 18, 1919, 3.
———. "Is 'Puppy Love' Just Like the Toothache?" *San Francisco Examiner*, January 13, 1926, 9.
———. "Ladies, or Women." *San Francisco Examiner*, March 8, 1910, 20.
———. "A Man Who Wants a Wife but Needs a Housekeeper." *San Francisco Examiner*, April 15, 1906, Editorial Section, 3.
———. "My Visit to Miss Harraden." *San Francisco Examiner*, November 18, 1894, 17.
———. "No Double Standard of Justice." *San Francisco Examiner*, April 5, 1915, 18.
———. "Old Song Stirs Tender Memories." *San Francisco Examiner*, March 8, 1926, 6.
———. "One of the Chorus." *San Francisco Examiner*, December 22, 1889, 11.
———. "Paying the Price." *San Francisco Examiner*, March 3, 1910, 22.
———. "Politics as They Seem." *San Francisco Examiner*, August 24, 1890, 13.
———. "The Power of the Press." *San Francisco Examiner*, December 2, 1894, 17.
———. "Preparing for Work." *San Francisco Examiner*, March 23, 1890, 14.
———. "The Rich and the Poor—Really, Who Are They?" *San Francisco Examiner*, April 3, 1915, 18.
———. *Roses and Rain*. San Francisco: Winifred Black, 1920.
———. "San Francisco's Shame." *San Francisco Examiner*, August 17, 1890, 11.
———. "San Mateo Women Dim Aladdin's Lamp." *San Francisco Examiner*, July 14, 1919, 5.
———. "She Can Get the News." *San Francisco Examiner*, February 3, 1895, 13.
———. "Sign the Fine Arts Petition." *San Francisco Examiner*, December 3, 1915, 18.
———. "Some Advice to Women." *San Francisco Examiner*, July 20, 1908, 14.
———. "'Street of Living Dead' Harbors Dope Sellers in Heart of San Francisco." *San Francisco Examiner*, October 11, 1921, 1.
———. "Stylish Stout." *San Francisco Examiner*, May 7, 1936, 11.
———. "Thaw Relieved at Choice of Jury." *San Francisco Examiner*, February 2, 1907, 2.
———. "Thaw's Incoherent Lines Tell of Deep Affection for His Wife." *San Francisco Examiner*, February 9, 1907, 3.
———. "Three Million Dollars." *San Francisco Examiner*, November 13, 1892, 15.
———. "Two Views of the Woman's Congress: As 'Annie Laurie' Saw It." *San Francisco Examiner*, May 26, 1895, 13.

———. "Valueless and Poisonous." *San Francisco Examiner*, January 25, 1891, 14.
———. "Without Long Skirts." *San Francisco Examiner*, May 29, 1892, 16.
———. "A Woman and a Savage." *San Francisco Examiner*, June 19, 1892, 13.
———. "Woman Wants Brains, Not Beauty, Praised." *San Francisco Examiner*, October 26, 1915, 20.
———. "The Women of the A.R.U." *San Francisco Examiner*, July 22, 1894, 15.
———. "Women with Vote Face Big Problems." *San Francisco Examiner*, June 6, 1919, 4.
———. "Yes, 'Tis Sad, They All Look the Same." *San Francisco Examiner*, March 13, 1924, 10.

## Written as Winifred Black

———. "Advice to a Neglected Wife." *Springfield Leader* (Springfield, Missouri), October 5, 1910, 6.
———. "An American Abroad Boasts of Corruption." *Iowa City Press-Citizen*, December 6, 1926, 10.
———. "American Husbands." *Springfield Leader* (Springfield, Missouri), July 23, 1910, 4.
———. "Are We Really Independent?" *Indianapolis Star*, February 15, 1914, 34.
———. "The Army of Women in Business." *Evening News* (Harrisburg, PA), November 1, 1934, 25.
———. "Bad Husbands." *Nebraska State Journal* (Lincoln), August 23, 1909, 6.
———. "The Beauty Craze." *Delaware County Daily Times* (Chester, Indiana), November 8, 1911, 8.
———. "Bloodstain Causes Fatal Shock." *New York Tribune*, May 23, 1908, 2.
———. "Buried, though Alive." *Bridgeport Telegram* (Bridgeport, Connecticut), February 19, 1921, 4.
———. "The Business Girl. " *Springfield Missouri Republican*, December 27, 1916, 4.
———. "Can Cave-Woman Be Coming into Style?" *Kokomo Tribune* (Kokomo, Indiana), June 17, 1930, 8.
———. "A Case of Mother-in-Law." *Springfield Leader* (Springfield, Missouri), July 29, 1910, 6.
———. "The Case of Mrs. John Smith of London: A Simple Story of the Suffrage Question in England." *Cosmopolitan*, August 1910, 381–90.
———. "Child and Charity Trust." *Good Housekeeping*, June 1912, 740–49.
———. "The Chill That Pretense Causes." *Springfield Missouri Republican*, February 8, 1916, 4.
———. "A Defense of Kissing." *Washington Post*, May 10, 1911, 6.
———. "A Discouraged Girl." *Lincoln Evening Journal*, December 26, 1922, 5.
———. "Divorce—A Knell to Faith." *Springfield Missouri Republican*, November 21, 1915: 15.
———. "Divorce and Second Marriage." *Bridgeport Telegram* (Bridgeport, Connecticut), September 8, 1920, 5.
———. "Do Real Men Love These Dumbbells?" *Courier-Express* (Dubois, Pennsylvania), July 26, 1927, 4.
———. "Do We Expect Too Much from Marriage?" *Iowa City Press-Citizen*, September 22, 1925, 9.
———. "Do Women Love Children More than Men Do?" *Springfield Missouri Republican*, June 19, 1915, 4.

———. "Do You Let the World Go in One Eye and Out the Other?: Writing Impressions on Shifting Sands." *Lincoln Evening Journal*, May 27, 1927, 7.
———. "Do You See Life as It Is, or Through Your Emotions?" *Springfield Missouri Republican*, June 18, 1915, 6.
———. *Dope: The Story of the Living Dead*. New York: Star, 1928.
———. "An Erratic View of Trailing Skirt." *Atlanta Constitution*, July 15, 1900, 15.
———. "Figures of Divorce Reveal Weaknesses." *Daily Free Press* (Carbondale, Illinois), October 25, 1927, 7.
———. "Foolish Bridey-Brides, How They Start Husbands on the Wrong Road." *El Paso Herald*, November 5, 1912, 4.
———. "Foolish Pride." *Post-Standard* (Syracuse), May 3, 1910, 12.
———. "Girls' Shocking Dress." *El Paso Herald*, May 28, 1913, 17.
———. "The Golden Slippers, Winifred Black's Story Today." *Brownsville Herald*, March 20, 1930, 4.
———. "Gold of the Burning Desert." *Cosmopolitan*, September 1905, 519–26.
———. "Golf for Women." *Washington Post*, February 26, 1910, 6.
———. "The 'Graceful Gazelle' on Dieting." *Springfield Missouri Republican*, October 7, 1915, 6.
———. "Grandma Goes to Work: Winifred Black's Topic Today." *Amarillo Globe-Times*, March 4, 1930, 13.
———. "The Greatest Woman." *Fort Wayne Sentinel*, January 2, 1912, 4.
———. "Grow Up, Girls! The Professor Is Getting Impatient." *Journal News* (Hamilton, Ohio), June 29, 1928, 34.
———. "Hanging on to Youth." *Springfield Missouri Republican*, May 2, 1916, 6.
———. "Homicide—Legal and Otherwise." *Scranton Republican*, December 13, 1900, 4.
———. "'Horrible' Examples Harmful." *Indianapolis Star*, February 9, 1914, 7.
———. "Horrors of the Storm," *Lawrence Daily Journal*, October 5, 1900, 2.
———. "How to Treat an In-Law." *El Paso Herald*, January 15, 1913. 5.
———. "A Human Door-Mat and Tragedy!" *Altoona Tribune*, November 19, 1929, 10.
———. "The Hungry Stenographer." *El Paso Herald*, February 6, 1912, 8.
———. "Husband Nagging Has Gone out of Fashion." *Springfield Missouri Republican*, July 18, 1915, 6.
———. "Ignorance or Innocence—Which Prevails Socially?" *Indianapolis Star*, May 2, 1914, 9.
———. "The Illogical Sex." *El Paso Herald*, February 17, 1912, 22.
———. "Imperfection Is Crown of the All-Too-Perfect." *Springfield Missouri Republican*, August 1, 1915, 16.
———. "Is There a Double Standard?" *Springfield Missouri Republican*, November 30, 1915, 6.
———. "The Jailer-Husband Is Due for a Shock—Unless He Gives His Wife Some Leeway." *Kokomo Tribune* (Kokomo, Indiana), August 9, 1930, 8.
———. "Jealousy." *Daily Republican* (Monongahela, Pennsylvania), July 7, 1910, 2.
———. "Jealousy Not Feminine Foible." *Post-Standard* (Syracuse), March 16, 1910, 8.
———. "The Joy of Children." *El Paso Herald*, July 1, 1913, 11.
———. "A Lesson in Fortitude by a Modern Mother." *Kokomo Tribune* (Kokomo, Indiana), March 12, 1931, 10.
———. *The Life and Personality of Phoebe Apperson Hearst*. San Francisco: J.H. Nash, 1928.
———. "The Life Worth Living." *El Paso Herald*, February 2, 1912, 13.

_____. *The Little Boy Who Lived on the Hill: A Story for Wee Bits of Tykes*. San Francisco: Doxey, 1895.
_____. "The Little Feminist." *Indianapolis Star*, February 7, 1914, 15.
_____. "Loaf Like a Man." *Journal News* (Hamilton, Ohio), February 22, 1930, 41.
_____. "Love and Marriage." *Oshkosh Daily Northwestern*, June 22, 1901, 9.
_____. "Love at Forty." *Springfield Missouri Republican*, September 6, 1917, 4.
_____. "The Madness of Love." *Springfield Missouri Republican*, August 12, 1917, 14.
_____. "Making Over a Skinflint." *El Paso Herald*, December 9, 1912, 4.
_____. "Married Woman Should be Allowed to Keep Her Place if She Can Teach." *El Paso Herald*, November 20, 1929, 5.
_____. "Marrying without Love." *El Paso Herald*, July 14, 1911, 6.
_____. "Marshal Campbell." *Courier-Journal* (Louisville, Kentucky), May 11, 1876, 1.
_____. "Matrimony and Business." *Indianapolis Star*, November 5, 1916, 58.
_____. "The Matter of Dress." Post-Standard (Syracuse), April 21, 1910, 1-2.
_____. "Maudlin Sympathy." *El Paso Herald*, January 9, 1911, 4.
_____. "Mother's Pets Unable to Deny Urge to Slay?" *San Antonio Evening News*, July 17, 1919, 7.
_____. "The New Fashioned Girl." *Springfield Missouri Republican*, December 19, 1915, 2.
_____. "One of Nature's Successes." *Indianapolis Star*, January 26, 1914, 7.
_____. "Other Side of World Your Backyard Today." *Lincoln Evening Journal*, December 28, 1932, 6.
_____. "The Painted Woman." *El Paso Herald*, July 11, 1912, 3.
_____. "Pankhurst Is Free and Happy Now in the U.S." *The Chronicle-Telegram* (Elyria, Ohio), October 21, 1913, 1.
_____. "Peculiar Laws of North Carolina." *Las Cruces Sun-News*, October 30, 1914, 3.
_____. "The Poor, Tired Shopgirl. " *El Paso Herald*, December 21, 1911, 8.
_____. "Pride Goeth before the Fall. Love of Dress, Not Poverty, Fatal Lure of Girls." *The Iola Register* (Iola, Kansas), March 25, 1910, 4.
_____. "Prisoner in Tears during Wife's Ordeal." *New York American*, February 8, 1907, 1.
_____. "Queer Laws for Women." *El Paso Herald*, August 20, 1913. 6.
_____. "Rambles through My Memories." Part I. *Good Housekeeping*, January 1936, 18–21+.
_____. "Rambles through My Memories." Part II. *Good Housekeeping*, February 1936, 36–37+.
_____. "Rambles through My Memories." Part III. *Good Housekeeping*, March 1936, 44–45+.
_____. "Rambles through My Memories." Part IV. *Good Housekeeping*, April 1936, 84–85+.
_____. "Rambles through My Memories." Part V. *Good Housekeeping*, May 1936, 36–37+.
_____. "The Real Kentuckian." *Lebanon Daily News* (Lebanon, Pennsylvania), February 19, 1900, 1.
_____. "Revising the Marriage Service." *Indianapolis Star*, November 27, 1916, 7.
_____. "Rose from Its Ashes." *Emporia Gazette* (Emporia, Kansas), September 19, 1911, 1.
_____. "A Runaway Wife." *Springfield Leader*, October 1, 1910, 4.
_____. "Safeguarding Our Girls." *Indianapolis Star*, May 14, 1916, 56.
_____. "A School of Courtship." *El Paso Herald*, April 18, 1912, 11.
_____. "Selfishness: Chief Cause of Divorce." *Indianapolis Star*, February 24, 1917, 7.
_____. "Selfishness Prompts Despair," *El Paso Herald*, October 16, 1913, 4.

# Bibliography 197

_____. "Selling Youth for a Share in Riches." *Brownsville Herald*, May 29, 1930, 16.
_____. "Shall It Be Always the Summer Season?" *Springfield Missouri Republican*, July 20, 1915, 6.
_____. "She Who Is Too Good to Work." *Indianapolis Star*, February 14, 1914, 15.
_____. "Should Women Take Alimony?" *Indianapolis Star*, July 3, 1915, 9.
_____. "Silly Teenage Girl Will Change." *Springfield Missouri Republican*, January 2, 1916, 12.
_____. "Small Families or Large?" *Springfield Missouri Republican*, August 6, 1916, 14.
_____. "Social Sets of Other Cities." *Washington Post*, May 25, 1910, 7.
_____. "Some 'Unfit' Better for Humanity Than the 'Fit' Declares Writer." *Washington Post*, July 19, 1913, 4 .
_____. "The Soul Saver." *Springfield Missouri Republican*, October 22, 1915, 6.
_____. "Spring-Cleaning for Our Minds—Why Not?" *Amarillo Globe-Times*, April 3, 1929, 20.
_____. "Stage Struck at Forty." *El Paso Herald*, August 15, 1912, 9.
_____. "The Stenographer's Side." *Washington Post*, January 20, 1912, 9.
_____. "A Strange Letter." *Sheboygan Press Telegram*, November 16, 1922, 14.
_____. "Stylish Stouts Still the Vogue in England." *Amarillo Globe-Times*, September 4, 1930, 10.
_____. "The 'Successful' Husband." *Springfield Missouri Republican*, June 24, 1915, 6.
_____. "Taking a Motor Ride with a Stranger." *The Kane Republican* (Kane, Pennsylvania), March 16, 1927, 6.
_____. "Telling a Friend the Truth." *El Paso Herald*, July 19, 1912, 13.
_____. "A 10,000,000 Widow." *El Paso Herald*, December 5, 1911, 6.
_____. "That Naughty Cover." *Iola Register* (Iola, Kansas), June 23, 1910, 4.
_____. "To Grow Old Gracefully—Ah, There's an Art." *Journal News* (Hamilton, Ohio), September 19, 1931, 29.
_____. "To Have the Enthusiasm." *Evening News* (Harrisburg, Pennsylvania), October 9, 1934, 21.
_____. "Too Good for a Girl's Work." *Indianapolis Star*, February 18, 1914, 13.
_____. "Tumult and Shouting and Cheers and Tears in Great Convention Demonstration." *Times Herald* (Olean, New York), July 1, 1920, 8.
_____. "Unkissed Stenographers." *Washington Post*, March 15, 1907, 12.
_____. "Vanity of Woman." *Washington Post*, June 5, 1910, 7.
_____. "Votes for Women! In Hidebound China—Centuries of Prejudice Overthrown." *Amarillo Globe-Times*, February 16, 1931, 11.
_____. "What Prompts Man to Become a Slayer?" *San Francisco Examiner*, July 17, 1919, 6.
_____. "What Should a Wife Do?" *El Paso Herald*, September 12, 1912, 4.
_____. "What's the Next Step for Women Suffragists—If Any." *Journal News* (Hamilton, Ohio), April 24, 1928, 8.
_____. "What Threatens the Girl Art Student." *Indianapolis Star*, March 11, 1914, 7.
_____. "When Clothes Complicate a Camp Party." *Springfield Missouri Republican*, August 2, 1925, 13.
_____. "When Shall a Woman Leave her Husband." *Indianapolis Star*, May 25, 1914, 7.
_____. "When Wives Are Beaten." *Topeka Daily Capital*, January 8, 1906, 8.
_____. "Who Are the World's Greatest Women?" *Indianapolis Star*, May 15, 1914, 15.
_____. "Who Carries the World, Old Atlas or His Wife?" *Indianapolis Star*, April 19, 1915, 7.
_____. "Why Men Who Play Don't Have Hysterics." *San Bernardino County Sun*, July 25, 1925, 6.

———. "Why Should Men Talk 'Up' or 'Down' to Women?" *Springfield Missouri Republican*, October 5, 1915, 6.
———. "Why the Business Woman Should Act Like the Business Man." *Springfield Missouri Republican*, August 16, 1916, 4.
———. "Why the Tango Is Moral." *Indianapolis Star*, February 11, 1914, 9.
———. "Why 'Women for Women' Is Bad Cry for Suffrage." *Indianapolis Star*, January 25, 1915, 7.
———. "Wife Desertion a Felony." *El Paso Herald*, February 10, 1912, 6.
———. "Winifred Black Cheers Us by Saying Life Is Not a Tragedy." *Coshocton Tribune* (Coshocton, Ohio), December 19, 1923, 4.
———. "Winifred Black Doubts That Corsets Will Return." *Coshocton Tribune* (Coshocton, Ohio), April 15, 1925, 7.
———. "Winifred Black Says That Bobbed Hair Will Stay." *Coshocton Tribune* (Coshocton, Ohio), November 10, 1923, 4.
———. "Winifred Black Says That Women Are Not Angels." *Evening News* (Harrisburg, Pennsylvania), July 2, 1919, 18.
———. "Winifred Black Tells Us About Girls Who Defy Conventions." *Coshocton Tribune* (Coshocton, Ohio), November 14, 1923, 7.
———. "Winifred Black Today Discusses Clara Ann Perkin's Will." *Springfield Missouri Republican*, June 2, 1925, 7.
———. "Winifred Black Writes About a Better Understanding." *Manitowoc Herald-Times* (Manitowoc, Wisconsin), September 18, 1922, 11.
———. "Winifred Black Writes About a College Complaint." *Iowa City Press-Citizen*, July 21, 1923, 2.
———. "Winifred Black Writes About a Daughter's Problem." *Logansport Pharos-Tribune* (Logansport, Indiana), January 5, 1923, 8.
———. "Winifred Black Writes About a Desperate Girl." *Springfield Missouri Republican*, December 11, 1919, 6.
———. "Winifred Black Writes About a Husband's Strange Trick." *San Bernardino County Sun*, July 18, 1922, 4.
———. "Winifred Black Writes About a New 'Heroine.'" *Springfield Missouri Republican*, June 14, 1922, 6.
———. "Winifred Black Writes About an Interesting Widow." *San Bernardino County Sun*, December 1, 1922, 6.
———. "Winifred Black Writes About a Pretty Naughty Girl." *Winnipeg Tribune*, January 23, 1920, 4.
———. "Winifred Black Writes About a Woman in Business." *Springfield Missouri Republican*, November 2, 1919, 16.
———. "Winifred Black Writes About a Woman with a Present." *Springfield Missouri Republican*, March 23, 1922, 8.
———. "Winifred Black Writes About a Would-Be Journalist." *San Antonio Evening News*, April 29, 1919, 6.
———. "Winifred Black Writes About Babies, Hearts and Hopes." *Iowa City Press-Citizen*, May 18, 1923, 3.
———. "Winifred Black Writes About Barefoot Time." *Springfield Missouri Republican*, March 18, 1921, 6.
———. "Winifred Black Writes About Bobbed Hair and Divorce." *Sheboygan Press Telegram*, June 2, 1922, 12.
———. "Winifred Black Writes About Changing Fashions." *Springfield Missouri Republican*, October 5, 1919, 14.

———. "Winifred Black Writes About Dances and Dancers." *Springfield Missouri Republican*, May 19, 1921, 6.
———. "Winifred Black Writes About Daughters Who Won't Marry." *Fort Wayne Journal-Gazette*, May 18, 1919, 20.
———. "Winifred Black Writes About Dollars and Marriage." *Springfield Missouri Republican*, July 5, 1919, 4.
———. "Winifred Black Writes About Fixing the Responsibility." *Bridgeport Telegram* (Bridgeport, Connecticut), January 15, 1921, 23.
———. "Winifred Black Writes About for Better or Worse." *Springfield Missouri Republican*, April 15, 1921, 6.
———. "Winifred Black Writes About Have Women Changed?" *Springfield Missouri Republican*, December 9, 1921, 6.
———. "Winifred Black Writes About Heart-Patterns of Life." *Springfield Missouri Republican*, May 5, 1917, 4.
———. "Winifred Black Writes About Holding onto Youth." *Springfield Missouri Republican*, May 27, 1922, 6.
———. "Winifred Black Writes About Homeliness and Marriage." *Bridgeport Telegram* (Bridgeport, Connecticut), September 17, 1920, 25.
———. "Winifred Black Writes About 'Just Like a Woman.'" *Springfield Missouri Republican*, May 28, 1922, 16.
———. "Winifred Black Writes About 'Luck' and 'Hardship.'" *Springfield Missouri Republican*, January 26, 1923, 7.
———. "Winifred Black Writes About Man's 'Interest' in Women." *Springfield Missouri Republican*, January 30, 1917, 4.
———. "Winifred Black Writes About Masculine Vanity." *Springfield Missouri Republican*, January 27, 1917, 4.
———. "Winifred Black Writes About Miss 'Flutter Budget.'" *Springfield Missouri Republican*, August 1, 1917, 4.
———. "Winifred Black Writes About Modern Parents' Worries." *Coshocton Tribune* (Coshocton, Ohio), September 26, 1923, 4.
———. "Winifred Black Writes About Nagging Men." *San Antonio Evening News* September 9, 1919, 6.
———. "Winifred Black Writes About Once-Upon-a-Time Beauties." *Springfield Missouri Republican*, April 26, 1917, 4.
———. "Winifred Black Writes About 'Only a Woman.'" *Fort Wayne Journal-Gazette*, November 12, 1918, 9.
———. "Winifred Black Writes About Pictures and Realities." *Springfield Missouri Republican*, February 3, 1917, 4.
———. "Winifred Black Writes About Prejudice the Wrecker." *Washington Post*, October 17, 1921, 11.
———. "Winifred Black Writes About Proving Yourself 'Advanced.'" *San Bernardino County Sun*, April 19, 1923, 15.
———. "Winifred Black Writes About Roses and Daughters." *Lincoln Evening Journal*, March 24, 1923, 5.
———. "Winifred Black Writes About 'Smile and Look Pretty.'" *San Bernardino County Sun*, April 28, 1922, 6.
———. "Winifred Black Writes About the Abused Buyer." *Springfield Missouri Republican*, June 14, 1917, 4.
———. "Winifred Black Writes About 'The New Girl.'" *Springfield Missouri Republican*, December 9, 1916, 2.

_____. "Winifred Black Writes About the Unafraid Girls." *San Antonio Evening News* May 9, 1919, 6.

_____. "Winifred Black Writes About the Wages of Women." *Springfield Missouri Republican*, September 13, 1917, 4.

_____. "Winifred Black Writes About Twenty-Five 'Perfect' Men." *Fort Wayne Journal-Gazette*, December 26, 1919, 19.

_____. "Winifred Black Writes About Two Wall-Flower Girls." *Fort Wayne Journal-Gazette*, February 1, 1919, 9.

_____. "Winifred Black Writes About Why Girls Leave Home." *Evening News* (Harrisburg, Pennsylvania), May 15, 1917, 10.

_____. "Winifred Black Writes About Why Some Women Rebel." *Winnipeg Tribune*, September 15, 1920, 7.

_____. "The Woman." *Lincoln Daily News*, March 14, 1910, 7.

_____. "A Woman among the Fighters." *Kansas City Star*, February 19, 1896, 7.

_____. "Woman's Vain Fight." *Springfield Leader* (Springfield, Missouri), October 18, 1910, 8.

_____. "Women Have Won All They Demanded in Dem. Platform." *Times Herald* (Olean, New York), July 3, 1920, 9.

_____. "Women Need Newspapers." *Post-Standard* (Syracuse), May 30, 1910, 5.

_____. "Working or Dreaming: Girl Is Fortunate Who Can Do Both." *El Paso Herald*, 15 April 1912, 11.

_____. "Yes, Women Take Men's Jobs Despite All Social Theories." *Amarillo Globe-Times*, January 3, 1928, 8.

Bradley, Patricia. *Women and the Press: The Struggle for Equality*. Evanston, IL: Northwestern University Press, 2005.

Bross, William. "Biographical Sketch of the Late Gen. B.J. Sweet: History of Camp Douglas." Paper presented at the Chicago Historical Society, Chicago, June 1878.

Butler, Judith. *Bodies That Matter: On the Discursive Limits of Sex*. New York: Routledge, 1993.

_____. *Gender Trouble: Feminism and the Subversion of Identity*. New York: Routledge, 1990.

"C.A. Bonfils Services." *Kansas City Star*, August 26, 1955, 49.

Cahoon, Haryot Holt. "Women in Gutter Journalism." *Arena* 17 (December 1896–June 1897): 568–74.

Calvin, Paula E., and Deborah A. Deacon. *American Women Artists in Wartime, 1776–2010*. Jefferson, NC: McFarland, 2011.

Capote, Truman. *In Cold Blood*. New York: Random House, 1966.

Carter, Patricia Anne. *"Everybody's Paid But the Teacher": The Teaching Profession and the Women's Movement*. New York: Teachers College Press, 2002. PN4874 .H31 C2.

Castle, Irene. *Castles in the Air*. Garden City, NY: Doubleday, 1958.

Chambers, Deborah, Linda Steiner, and Carole Fleming. *Women and Journalism*. New York: Routledge, 2004.

"Charles A. Bonfils Services Saturday." *Denver Post*, August 26, 1955, 2.

"The Chicago Conspiracy." *New York Times*, November 15, 1864, 8.

"Chicago's Pension Agent." *Courier-Journal* (Louisville, Kentucky), March 20, 1874, 1.

"Child of His Brain." *Chicago Daily Tribune*, November 7, 1892, 1.

"A City's Disgrace." *San Francisco Examiner*, January 19, 1890, 11.

"City's Grief Expressed by Supervisors." *San Francisco Examiner*, May 27, 1936, 6.

"City's Official Tributes Given for Annie Laurie." *San Francisco Examiner*, May 26, 1936, 8.

Cobb, Irvin S. *Exit Laughing*. New York: Bobbs-Merrill, 1941.
"The Colonel's Little Doctor." *Washington Post*, October 8, 1905, 84.
Conover, Ted. *Newjack: Guarding Sing Sing*. New York: Random House, 2001.
Courtwright, David T. *Dark Paradise: A History of Opiate Addiction in America*. Boston: Harvard University Press, 2009.
Crawford, Elizabeth Crisp. *Tobacco Goes to College: Cigarette Advertising in Student Media, 1920–1980*. Jefferson, NC: McFarland, 2014.
Davis, Kathy. *Dubious Equalities and Embodied Differences: Cultural Studies on Cosmetic Surgery*. Lanham, MD: Rowman & Littlefield, 2003.
Davis, Tracy. *Actresses as Working Women: Their Social Identity in Victorian Culture*. London: Routledge, 1991.
Didion, Joan. "On Going Home." In *Slouching Towards Bethlehem*, 164–70. New York: Macmillan, 1968.
Dillard, Annie. *For the Time Being*. New York: Knopf, 1999.
Dix, Dorothy. "Mirandy on New Year Resolutions." *San Francisco Examiner*, January 7, 1906, 44.
Dowbiggin, Ian Robert. *Keeping America Sane: Psychiatry and Eugenics in the United States and Canada, 1880–1940*. Ithaca: Cornell University Press, 1997.
Dray, Philip. *At the Hands of Persons Unknown: The Lynching of Black America*. New York: Random House, 2007.
Eggers, Dave. *Zeitoun*. San Francisco: McSweeney's, 2009.
Ehrenreich, Barbara. *Nickel and Dimed: On (Not) Getting By in America*. New York: Metropolitan, 2001.
Eicher, John H., and David J. Eicher. *Civil War High Commands*. Stanford: Stanford University Press, 2001.
Ellison, Ralph. *Shadow and Act*. 1953. New York: Vintage, 1995.
Engelman, Peter. *A History of the Birth Control Movement in America*. Santa Barbara: ABC-CLIO, 2011.
Enoch, Jessica, and Jordynn Jack. "Remembering Sappho: New Perspectives on Teaching (and Writing) Women's Rhetorical History." *College English* 73, no. 5 (May 2011): 518–37.
Ephron, Nora. *Crazy Salad: Some Things About Women*. New York: Modern Library, 1975.
Faderman, Lillian. *Odd Girls and Twilight Lovers: A History of Lesbian Life in Twentieth-Century America*. New York: Columbia University Press, 1991.
Fahs, Alice. *Out on Assignment: Newspaper Women and the Making of Modern Public Space*. Chapel Hill: University of North Carolina University Press, 2011.
Fitch, Michael Hendrick. *Echoes of the Civil War as I Hear Them*. New York: Fenno, 1905.
Gallop-Goodman, Gerda. *Crimes against Women*. New York: Facts on File, 2002.
Gannon, Susan R., and Ruth Anne Thompson. *Mary Mapes Dodge*. Boston: Twayne, 1992.
Garbus, Julia. "Service-Learning, 1902." *College English* 64, no. 5 (2002): 547–65.
Gilbert, Sandra M., and Susan Gubar. *The Madwoman in the Attic: The Woman Writer and the Nineteenth Century Literary Imagination*. New Haven: Yale University Press, 1979.
Gilman, Charlotte Perkins. "Why These Clothes?" *Independent* 58 (March 2, 1905): 466–69.
Gladwell, Malcolm. *David and Goliath: Underdogs, Misfits, and the Art of Battling Giants*. New York: Little, Brown, 2013.

Goble, Corban. "Newspaper Technology." In *History of the Mass Media in the United States: An Encyclopedia*, edited Margaret A. Blanchard, 457–65. New York: Routledge, 2013.
Good, Howard. *Girl Reporter: Gender, Journalism, and the Movies*. Lanham, MD: Scarecrow, 1998.
Goodman, Matthew. *Eighty Days: Nellie Bly and Elizabeth Bisland's History-Making Race around the World*. New York: Ballantine, 2013.
"Good Old Laura Jean." *Hutchinson News* (Hutchinson, Kansas), November 17, 1910, 4.
Gray, Thomas. *An Elegy Written in a Country Churchyard*. Philadelphia: Lippincott, 1883.
Greenwald, Maurine Weiner. *Women, War, and Work: The Impact of World War I on Women Workers in the United States*. Ithaca: Cornell University Press, 1990.
Gudelunas, David. *Confidential to America: Newspaper Advice Columns and Sexual Education*. New Brunswick: Transaction, 2008.
Gundle, Stephen. *Glamour: A History*. New York: Oxford University Press, 2008.
Harrison, Kathryn. *The Kiss: A Memoir*. New York: Random House, 1998.
*Historical Statistics of the United States, Colonial Times to 1957*. Washington: U.S. Department of the Commerce, 1960.
*Historical Statistics of the United States, Colonial Times to 1970*. Vol. 1. Washington: U.S. Department of the Commerce, 1975.
"History of Plastic Surgery." The Sloane Clinic. www.sloaneclinic.com/en-sg/theplastic/.
"Honor Their Dead." *Chicago Sunday Tribune*, May 26, 1895, 33–34.
Hosokawa, Bill. *Thunder in the Rockies: The Incredible Denver Post*. New York: Morrow, 1976.
"How Woman Suffrage Works." *New York Times*, March 8, 1924, 10.
"Hunting Big Game: The Misses Herberts' Exciting Exploits in Africa." *New York Tribune*, August 6, 1908, 4.
Jakes, John. "Winifred Black: Sob Sisters Can Cry." In *Great Women Reporters*, 57–73. New York: Putnam's, 1969.
James, Edward T., Janet Wilson James, and Paul S. Boyer. *Notable American Women, 1607–1950: A Biographical Dictionary*. Vol. 1. Cambridge: Harvard University Press, 1971.
Johnson, Katie N. *Sisters in Sin: Brothel Drama in America, 1900–1920*. New York: Cambridge University Press, 2006.
Kayes, Ashley A. "Winifred Black: More Than a Sob Sister." Master's thesis, George Mason University, 2006.
Keats, John. "Meg Merrilies." In *The Poems of John Keats*, 261–62. New York: Dodd, Mead, 1905.
Kessler-Harris, Alice. *Out to Work: A History of America's Wage-earning Women in the United States*. New York: Oxford University Press, 1982.
Kidder, Tracy. *House*. Boston: Houghton Mifflin, 1985.
Kingsley, Charles. "The Three Fishers." In *Masterpieces from Charles Kingsley*, 108. London: Woodward, 1893.
Kitch, Carolyn. "Women in Journalism." In *American Journalism: History, Principles, Practices*, 87–96, edited by W. David Sloan and Lisa Mullikin Parcell. Jefferson, NC: McFarland, 2002.
Kleinberg, S.J. *Women in the United States, 1830–1945*. New Brunswick: Rutgers University Press, 1999.
Kortsch, Christine Bayles. *Dress Culture in Late Victorian Women's Fiction: Literacy, Textiles, and Activism*. Burlington, VT: Ashgate, 2013.

Krakauer, Jon. *Into Thin Air*. New York: Anchor, 1997.
Kroeger, Brooke. *Nellie Bly: Daredevil, Reporter, Feminist*. New York: Times Books, 1994.
Lawrence, Ava. "David Blakely: A Life in Music, Politics, Publishing, and Printing." *Journal of the Music and Entertainment Industry Educators Association* 8, no. 1 (2008). http://www.meiea.org/Journal/html_ver/Vol08_No01/Lawrence-2008-MEIEA-Journal-Vol-8-No-1-p75.htm.
"Leaders Mourn Annie Laurie." *San Francisco Examiner*, May 26, 1936, 10.
Lederer, Francis L, II. "Nora Marks—Reinvestigated." Northern Illinois University Digital Library. dig.lib.niu.edu/ISHS/ishs-1980spring/ishs-1980spring61.pdf.
Lerner, Gerda. *Why History Matters: Life and Thought*. Cambridge: Oxford University Press, 1998.
"Letter from Cairo." *Times-Picayune* (New Orleans), April 2, 1865, 3.
Levy, George. *To Die in Chicago: Confederate Prisoners at Camp Douglas 1862–1865*. Gretna, LA: Pelican, 1994.
Lutes, Jean Marie. *Front-Page Girls: Women Journalists in American Culture and Fiction, 1880–1930*. Ithaca: Cornell University Press, 2007.
"Making Things Hot." *Inter Ocean* (Chicago), February 28, 1886, 16.
Marken, Edith May. "Women in American Journalism before 1900." Master's thesis, University of Missouri, 1932.
Martin, George Madden. "American Women and Public Affairs." *Atlantic Monthly*, February 1924, 169–78.
Marzolf, Marion. *Up from the Footnote: A History of Women Journalists*. New York: Hastings, 1977.
Mayer, David. "*Why Girls Leave Home*: Victorian and Edwardian "Bad-Girl" Melodrama Parodied in Early Film." *Theatre Journal* 58, no. 4 (2006): 575–93.
McBride, Mary Margaret. *A Long Way from Missouri*. New York: Putnam's, 1959.
McDonald, John. *Secrets of the Great Whiskey Ring*. Chicago: Belford, Clarke, 1880.
McGehee, Florence W. "Fie upon Winnie." *Woodland Daily Democrat* (Woodland, California), August 25, 1934, 8.
———. "Orchids and Onions." *Woodland Daily Democrat* (Woodland, California), August 29, 1933, 6.
McPhee, John. *Coming into the Country*. New York: Farrar, Straus and Giroux, 1977.
Micale, Mark S. *Approaching Hysteria: Disease and Its Interpretations*. Princeton: Princeton University Press, 1995.
"Military Commission." *Cincinnati Enquirer*, April 11, 1865, 2.
Mills, Kay. *A Place in the News: From the Women's Pages to the Front Page*. New York: Dodd, Mead, 1988.
"Miss Ada Sweet's Resignation." *New York Times*, September 10, 1885, 1.
"Miss Sweet's Threatener." *Inter Ocean* (Chicago), July 4, 1881, 12.
"Most Widely Known Woman of American Journalistic Work Will Write for This Paper." *Coshocton Tribune* (Coshocton, Ohio), March 30, 1922, 9.
Mott, Frank Luther. *American Journalism: A History of Newspapers in the United States through 250 Years, 1690 to 1940*. New York: Macmillan, 1962.
Mulvey, Kate, and Melissa Richards. *Decades of Beauty*. New York: Checkmark Books, 1998.
Nasaw, David. *The Chief: The Life of William Randolph Hearst*. Boston: Houghton Mifflin, 2000.
"The New Jersey Vote against Suffrage." *New York Times*, October 21, 1915, 10.
Nieman, Donald G. *Black Southerners and the Law, 1865–1900*. New York: Taylor & Francis, 1994.

Nolan, Alan T. *The Iron Brigade*. New York: Macmillan, 1961.
O'Brien, Willis. "All S.F. Mourns for Annie Laurie." *San Francisco Examiner*, 27 May 1936, 1+.
"Occupations." In *Special Census Report on Occupations of the Population of the United States at the Eleventh Census: 1890*, 11. Washington, D.C.: GPO, 1896.
O'Connor, Maureen. "Bigger Eyes, Fuller Lips, Broader Minds?" *New York*, July 28–August 10, 2014, 22–27+.
Olin, Charles H. *Journalism*. Philadelphia: Penn, 1906.
"Only Son of 'Annie Laurie' Dies in Surf." *San Francisco Examiner*, June 20, 1926, 3.
"Oratory Flows Freely." *New York Tribune*, September 9, 1910, 8.
Orlean, Susan. "The American Man, Age Ten." *Esquire*, December 1992, 115–27.
Parsons, Louella. "The Passing of Winifred Black." *Fresno Bee*, May 27, 1936, 10.
"Pension Agent." *Chicago Daily Tribune*, July 18, 1881, 4.
Perkin, Robert L. *The First Hundred Years: An Informal History of Denver and the Rocky Mountain News*. New York: Doubleday, 1959.
Phillips, Kendall R. *Controversial Cinema: The Films that Outraged America*. Santa Barbara: ABC-CLIO, 2008.
Procter, Ben. *William Randolph Hearst: The Early Years, 1863–1910*. New York: Oxford University Press, 1998.
Ramey, Valerie A. "Time Spent in Home Production in the Twentieth-Century United States: New Estimates from Old Data." *Journal of Economic History* 69, no. 1 (2009): 1–47.
"The Real Annie Laurie." *San Francisco Examiner*, December 18, 1892, 13.
"Right Off the Jump: 40 Big Reasons." *San Bernandino County Sun*, August 28, 1921, 3.
Rives, Timothy. "Grant, Babcock, and the Whiskey Ring." *Prologue* 32, no. 3 (2000). http://www.archives.gov/publications/prologue/2000/fall/whiskey-ring-1.html.
Roach, Mary. *Bonk: The Curious Coupling of Science and Sex*. New York: Norton, 2009.
Robertson, Michael. *Stephen Crane, Journalism and the Making of Modern American Literature*. New York: Columbia University Press, 1997.
Rodman, W. Paul. *Mining Frontiers of the Far West, 1848–1880*. Albuquerque: University of New Mexico, 1980.
Ross, Ishbel. *Ladies of the Press*. New York: Harper, 1936.
Russell, Charles Edward. "Is Woman Suffrage a Failure?" *The Century*, March 1924, 724–30.
Saltzman, Joe. "Sob Sisters: The Image of the Female Journalist in Popular Culture. The Image of the Journalist in Popular Culture." USC Annenberg. ijpc.org/page/sobsmaster.htm.
Scharf, Lois. *Decades of Discontent: The Women's Movement, 1920–1940*. Westport, CT: Greenwood, 1983.
Schilpp, Madelon Golden, and Sharon M. Murphy. *Great Women of the Press*. Carbondale: Southern Illinois University Press, 1983.
Schorman, Rob. *Selling Style: Clothing and Social Change at the Turn of the Century*. Philadelphia: University of Pennsylvania Press, 2003.
Scull, Andrew. *Hysteria: The Disturbing History*. New York: Oxford University Press, 2011.
Sherrow, Victoria. *Encyclopedia of Hair: A Cultural History*. Westport, CT: Greenwood, 2006.
Shuman, Edwin L. *Practical Journalism: A Complete Manual of the Best Newspaper Methods*. New York: Appleton, 1903.

Shurly, E.R.P. "The Conspiracy at Camp Douglas." *Chicago Daily Tribune*, February 4, 1882, 16.
Siegel, Reva B. "'The Rule of Love': Wife Beating as Prerogative and Privacy." Yale Faculty Scholarship Series, Paper 1092, 1996. http://digitalcommons.law.yale.edu /fss_papers/ 1092.
Southwick, Albert Plympton. *Short Studies in Literature*. New York: Hinds, Noble, and Eldredge, 1898.
Speaker, Susan. "'The Struggle of Mankind against Its Deadliest Foe': Themes of Counter-Subversion in Anti-Narcotic Campaigns, 1920–1940." *Journal of Social History* 34, no. 3 (2001): 591–610.
*Statistical Abstract of the United States: The National Data Book 2003*. Washington, D.C.: U.S. Census Bureau, 2003.
Steiner, Linda. "Critiquing Journalism: A Twenty-First-Century Feminist Perspective." In *Women, Men, and News: Divided and Disconnected in the News Media Landscape*, 280–87, edited by Paula Poindexter, Sharon Meraz, and Amy Schmitz Weiss. Hillsdale, NJ: Erlbaum, 2007.
"Suffragettes at Outing." *New York Tribune*, June 20, 1910, 5.
Sutherland, John. *Lives of the Novelists: A History of Fiction in 294 Lives*. New Haven: Yale University Press, 2012.
Sweet, Ada C. "How Miss Sweet Found Annie." *Chicago Daily Tribune*, December 13, 1889, 2.
Tebbel, John. *The Life and Good Times of William Randolph Hearst*. New York: Dutton, 1952.
"Threw Wife Out of Window/She Puts in a Good Word for 'Mike' When Patrolmen Finds Her on the Sidewalk." *New York Tribune*, August 29, 1908, 1.
Tomes, Nancy. *The Gospel of Germs: Men, Women, and the Microbe in American Life*. Boston: Harvard University Press, 1999.
"Topics of the Day." *Critic* (Washington, D.C.), September 14, 1885, 3.
"Tribute Is Paid to Writer." *San Francisco Examiner*, May 27, 1936, 6.
Tuttle, the Rev. E.B. *The History of Camp Douglas, Including Official Report of Gen. B.J. Sweet; with Anecdotes of the Rebel Prisoners*. Chicago: J.R. Walsh, 1865.
Twombly, Mary. "Women in Journalism." *Writer* 3 (August 1889): 169–72.
"Two Slain Over Woman." *New York Tribune*, May 15, 1908, 4.
Underwood, Agness. *Newspaperwoman*. New York: Harper, 1949.
Uruburu, Paula. *American Eve: Evelyn Nesbit, Stanford White, the Birth of the "It" Girl, and the Crime of the Century*. New York: Penguin, 2008.
Van Gelder, Lindsy. "Women's Pages: You Can't Make News Out of a Silk Purse." *MS*, November 1974, 112–16.
"Varieties." *The Dallas Daily Herald*, March 25, 1874, 1.
Wertheim, Stanley. "Chamberlain, Samuel S." In *A Stephen Crane Encyclopedia*, 51. Westport, CT: Greenwood, 1997.
Westbrook, Perry D. *Mary Wilkins Freeman*. Boston: Twayne, 1988.
Wetzel, Grace. "Winifred Black's Teacherly Ethos: The Role of Journalism in Late-Nineteenth-Century Rhetorical Education." *Rhetoric Society Quarterly* 44, no. 1 (2014): 68–93.
Whyte, Kenneth. *The Uncrowned King: The Sensational Rise of William Randolph Hearst*. Berkeley: Counterpoint, 2009.
Wiley, Harvey W. "The Housewife and the Eight-Hour Day." *Good Housekeeping* January 1917, 50–51.
"Winifred Black." *Emporia Weekly Gazette* (Emporia, Kansas), May 19, 1910, 1.

"Winifred Black, 73, Journalist, Dead." *New York Times*, May 26, 1936, 26.
"Winifred Black Bonfils Speaks to Press Club." *Springfield Missouri Republican*, October 19, 1912, 10.
Winkler, John K. *W.R. Hearst, an American Phenomenon*. New York: Simon & Schuster, 1928.
Wolfe, Tom. "The New Journalism." In *The New Journalism*, 1–52, edited by Tom Wolfe and E.W. Johnson. New York: Harper & Row, 1973.
Wollstonecraft, Mary. *A Vindication of the Rights of Woman: With Strictures on Political and Moral Subjects*. Boston: Peter Edes, 1792.
"Woman, Gagged, in Burning Room." *New York Tribune*, October 17, 1916, 4.
"A Woman Killed on the Railroad." *Lebanon Daily News* (Lebanon, Pennsylvania), August 15, 1878, 1.
"Woman Suffrage Declared a Failure." *Literary Digest*, April 12, 1924, 12–13.
"Women to Be Given Preference in Cleric al Position Appointments in Navy Hereafter." In *Official Bulletin*, Vol. 1, 7. Washington, D.C.: Committee on Public Information, 1917.
"Women Will Parade." *New York Tribune*, February 3, 1908, 5.
Zeitner, June Culp, and Lincoln Borglum. *Borglum's Unfinished Dream: Mount Rushmore*. Aberdeen, SD: North Plains, 1976.
"Zozo at the St. Charles." *Times-Picayune* (New Orleans), October 22, 1888, 3.
Zuckerman, Faye B. "Winifred Black." In *Dictionary of Literary Biography* 25, 12–19, edited by Perry J. Ashley. Detroit: Gale Group, 1984.

# Index

Abrams, Rebecca 54
acting 23, 24, 26, 32, 43
action 65, 80–86
activists 111, 166, 171
adultery 147–150
advice column 40, 47–49, 60, 68, 89, 101, 145–148, 159, 174
agency 26, 96, 99, 108, 114, 139, 152
aging 88, 140–143
"Annie Laurie" 35
Atkinson, Eleanor Stackhouse 36
autobiography 20, 29, 48, 52, 58, 121, 173

beauty 132, 135–139
Bisland, Elizabeth 34
Blakely, David 14–16
Bly, Nellie 31–34, 37, 39, 76, 114
Bonfils, Charles Alden (Charley) 44, 69, 144
Bonfils, Frederick 40, 44–46, 49

Cahoon, Haryot Holt 30
camp, prison 9–11, 14
Chamberlain, Sam 33
children, page for 41–42, 52
Chubbuck, Emily 22, 61
crisis, health 37

dating 143–146, 174
descriptions, longer 82
dialogue 56, 66, 84–85, 109, 131, 153, 173, 196
diets 139–140
direct address 89–90, 137, 167, 173
discourse, gendered 105–106
discovery, as necessary to nonfiction 65–66
disguise 55–56
divorce 154, 159–161
Dodge, Mary Mapes 22
domestic violence 89, 144, 152–158
Douglas, William 35

Egbert Comedy Company 24
end of career 48–49
entrepreneurs 7, 9, 29, 44, 49
equal rights 97, 122, 166, 172
exaggeration 87, 166

fiction, versus nonfiction 9, 35, 41, 61–64
Field, Eugene 17
figure, cultural 3

Gay, Eva 31
gender 74, 88–89, 99–106
Gibson Girls 136–139
Grenfel, George St. Leger 11
Guiteau, Charles 16

hairstyles 134
halftone photoengraving 133
harassment, sexual 125–126
Harrison, Pres. Benjamin 20–21, 73
Hearst, William Randolph 29, 31–33, 35–37, 39–40, 42
hurricane, in Galveston 46, 67, 82–83
hysteria 57, 103, 144

independence 24, 117–121, 136, 147, 161

law, martial 11
Lerner, Gerda 6
"literary lions" 22
Lutes, Jean Marie 31, 38, 57

marriage 58, 94–95, 106, 119, 130, 144
modesty, and reserve 61, 93–94
muckrakers 5

name change (to Winifred Black) 43
native Americans 110–112
Nelson, Nell 31, 114
New Journalism 6, 68, 72
the new normal 92–96, 174

the Other  107–108, 112, 116

page, for women  40, 47, 50–52, 54, 58, 61, 64, 65, 120, 124, 125, 143
Pension Agent  9, 11, 13, 15, 18
persona: complex 73; undercover 4–5, 55, 60, 65, 68, 73, 174
prostitution  112–118
Pulitzer, Joseph  32

questions  90, 96, 109, 150, 156, 170
quotations  57, 85–86, 196

race  108–110, 117, 163
Republican Party convention  23
reputation  4–5, 30, 79
Roosevelt, Eleanor  171

settling  146
sexual harassment  125–126
shirtwaists  132–133, 136
Shuman, Edwin L.  30
*Sob Sister Journalism*  57–58
"sob sisters"  56–80
Steiner, Linda  54
stunt girl  5, 29, 37–38, 65, 76, 114
suffrage  162–164, 166
Sweet, Ada  9, 13–19, 36–37, 49; influence on Winifred 18–19
Sweet, Benjamin Jeffrey  9–13, 26–27, 36

Tammen, Harry Heye  40, 44–45
Taylor, William  21
techniques, nonfiction  6, 39–40, 64–65, 73, 88, 90
Thaw, Harry, trial  46, 56–59

values, cultural  73
vanity  104, 123, 142
voting  87, 164, 169–170

Whiskey Ring  15
who, what, when, where  33–35, 40, 64, 73, 90, 173
widowhood  152
women: as readers 52–54; working 59, 79, 86, 128–130
work  29–30, 122–124
writer, as character  68, 73
writers, community of  21–23, 28
writing  4–8, 22, 61; nonfiction 7, 9; as subject 60–63

yellow journalism  5, 9, 31, 44, 74

*Zozo, the Magic Queen*  25

www.ingramcontent.com/pod-product-compliance
Lightning Source LLC
Chambersburg PA
CBHW032056300426
44116CB00007B/771